Jocelyn McWhirter is Assistant Professor of
Religious Studies at Albion College, Michigan.

Many interpreters of the Fourth Gospel detect allusions to biblical texts about marriage, but none offers a comprehensive analysis of these proposed allusions or a convincing explanation for their presence. Building on the work of Richard Hays and Donald Juel, Jocelyn McWhirter argues that John alludes to biblical texts about marriage in order to develop a metaphor for Jesus and how he relates to his followers. These texts seem to have been interpreted as messianic prophecies, and applied by John to events in Jesus' life and death. McWhirter shows how verbal parallels link John's evoked marriage texts to Psalm 45 about God's anointed king. Messianic interpretation of these texts allows John to use them in portraying Jesus as a bridegroom-Messiah and depicting Jesus' relationship with his followers in terms of marriage.

JOCELYN MCWHIRTER is an Assistant Professor of Religious Studies at Albion College in Albion, Michigan. This is her first book.

SOCIETY FOR NEW TESTAMENT STUDIES

MONOGRAPH SERIES

Recent titles in the series

120. Belly and Body in the Pauline Epistles
     KARL OLAV SANDNES
     0 521 81535 5

121. The First Christian Historian
     DANIEL MARGUERAT
     0 521 81650 5

122. An Aramaic Approach to Q
     MAURICE CASEY
     0 521 81723 4

123. Isaiah's Christ in Matthew's Gospel
     RICHARD BEATON
     0 521 81888 5

124. God and History in the Book of Revelation
     MICHAEL GILBERSTON
     0 521 82466 4

125. Jesus' Defeat of Death
     PETER G. BOLT
     0 521 83036 2

126. From Hope to Despair in Thessalonica
     COLIN R. NICHOLL
     0 521 83142 3

127. Matthew's Trilogy of Parables
     WESLEY G. OLMSTEAD
     0 521 83154 7

128. The People of God in the Apocalypse
     STEPHEN PATTEMORE
     0 521 83698 0

129. The Exorcism Stories in Luke–Acts
     TODD KLUTZ
     0 521 83804 5

130. Jews, Gentiles and Ethnic Reconciliation
     TET-LIM N. YEE
     0 521 83831 2

131. Ancient Rhetoric and Paul's Apology
     FREDRICK J. LONG
     0 521 84233 6

132. Reconstructing Honor in Roman Philippi
     JOSEPH H. HELLERMAN
     0 521 84909 8

The Bridegroom Messiah and the People of God

Marriage in the Fourth Gospel

JOCELYN McWHIRTER

Albion College

CAMBRIDGE
UNIVERSITY PRESS

CAMBRIDGE UNIVERSITY PRESS
Cambridge, New York, Melbourne, Madrid, Cape Town, Singapore, São Paulo

CAMBRIDGE UNIVERSITY PRESS
The Edinburgh Building, Cambridge CB2 2RU, UK

Published in the United States of America by Cambridge University Press, New York

www.cambridge.org
Information on this title: www.cambridge.org/9780521864251

First published 2006

Printed in the United Kingdom at the University Press, Cambridge

A catalogue record for this publication is available from the British Library

ISBN-13 978 0 521 86425 1 hardback
ISBN-10 0 521 86425 9 hardback

For Jamie and Teddy
τέκνα θεοῦ
and in memory of Donald Juel
μακάριοι οἱ μὴ ἰδόντες καὶ πιστεύσαντες

CONTENTS

ix

ACKNOWLEDGMENTS

This monograph is a revision of my doctoral dissertation, submitted to Princeton Theological Seminary in 2001. It has been thoroughly updated to reflect developments in scholarship since then.

Many others have played an instrumental role in its production. I owe thanks first to my teachers. Rod Whitacre at Trinity Episcopal School for Ministry got me interested in the Fourth Gospel. My dissertation director, the late Donald Juel, introduced me to the concept of messianic exegesis, patiently reviewed most of this document's many versions, and consistently steered me in the right direction. Beverly Gaventa added helpful comments to an early attempt. Committee members James Charlesworth and Ross Wagner carefully read the final drafts and offered crucial insights.

Additional thanks are due to several of my colleagues. My friend Elisabeth Johnson offered a thoughtful response to the first draft of Chapter 3. John Miller shared information about the *Testament of Judah*. Alan Iser, my colleague at Saint Joseph's University, answered my questions about Jewish exegetical traditions and contemporary praxis. I must also acknowledge my fellow residents Charlene Moss, Michael Daise, Bill Campbell, Lidija Novakovic, and Raquel St. Clair, whose contributions to my intellectual development and emotional stability cannot be measured.

My friends and family members have been a constant source of support and encouragement since this project began. I am especially grateful to my children Jamie and Teddy, who put up with me as I made the final revisions.

ABBREVIATIONS

1Q28b	*Rule of the Blessings*
2 Bar	*2 Baruch*
4 Kgdms	4 Kingdoms
4QCant[a–c]	*4QCanticles[a–c]*
4QComm-Cant	*Commentary on Canticles*
4QFlor	*Florilegium*
4QpIsa[a]	*Isaiah Pesher[a]*
6QCant	*6QCanticles*
11QPs[a]	*Psalms Scroll[a]*
AB	Anchor Bible
'Abot R. Nat.	*'Abot R. Nathan*
ACW	Ancient Christian Writers
AnBib	Analecta biblica
Ant.	*Jewish Antiquities* (Josephus)
AOAT	Alter Orient und Altes Testament
Bar	Baruch
BDAG	Bauer, W., F. W. Danker, W. F. Arndt, and F. W. Gingrich. *Greek–English Lexicon of the New Testament and Other Early Christian Literature* 3rd edn. Chicago, 1999
BDF	Blass, F., A. Debrunner, and R. W. Funk. *A Greek Grammar of the New Testament and Other Early Christian Literature* Chicago, 1961
BETL	Bibliotheca ephemeridum theologicarum lovaniensium
BFCT	Beiträge zur Förderung christlicher Theologie
BGBE	Beiträge zur Geschichte der biblischen Exegese
BHS	*Biblia Hebraica Stuttgartensia*. Edited by Karl Ellinger and Wilhelm Rudolph. Stuttgart, 1983

Bib	*Biblica*
BJRL	*Bulletin of the John Rylands University Library of Manchester*
BJS	Brown Judaic Studies
BNTC	Black's New Testament Commentaries
BSac	*Bibliotheca sacra*
BTB	*Biblical Theology Bulletin*
BVC	Bible et vie chrétienne
BZ	*Biblische Zeitschrift*
BZNW	Beihefte zur Zeitschrift für die neutestamentliche Wissenschaft
CB	*Cultura biblica*
CBET	Contributions to Biblical Exegesis and Theology
CBQ	*Catholic Biblical Quarterly*
CGTSC	Cambridge Greek Testament for Schools and Colleges
Comm. Cant.	*Commentarius in Canticum* (Origen)
ConBNT	Coniectanea biblica: New Testament Series
CRINT	Compendia rerum iudaicarum ad Novum Testamentum
Dial.	*Dialogue with Trypho* (Justin)
DRev	*Downside Review*
Ebib	*Etudes bibliques*
EgT	*Eglise et Théologie*
EvJ	*Evangelical Journal*
EvT	*Evangelische Theologie*
FC	Fathers of the Church
GCS	Die griechische christliche Schriftsteller der ersten drei Jahrhunderte
HBT	*Horizons in Biblical Theology*
HeyJ	*Heythrop Journal*
HNT	Handbuch zum Neuen Testament
Hom. Cant.	*Homiliae in Canticum* (Origen)
Hom. Gen.	*Homiliae in Genesim* (Origen)
HTS	Harvard Theological Studies
HUCM	Monographs of the Hebrew Union College
ICC	International Critical Commentary
Int	*Interpretation*
ITQ	*Irish Theological Quarterly*
JBL	*Journal of Biblical Literature*
JSNT	*Journal for the Study of the New Testament*

JSNTSup	Journal for the Study of the New Testament: Supplement Series
JSOT	*Journal for the Study of the Old Testament*
JTS	*Journal of Theological Studies*
LXX	Septuagint
MT	Masoretic Text
m. Yad.	*Mishnah Yadayim*
NA[27]	*Novum Testamentum Graece*, Nestle-Aland, 27th edn.
NCB	New Century Bible
NeoT	*Neotestamentica*
NICNT	New International Commentary on the New Testament
NIV	New International Version
NovT	Novum Testamentum
NovTSup	Novum Testamentum Supplements
NPNF[1]	*Nicene and Post-Nicene Fathers*, Series 1
NRSV	New Revised Standard Version
NT	New Testament
NTS	*New Testament Studies*
Odes Sol.	*Odes of Solomon*
OTP	*Old Testament Pseudepigrapha*. Edited by J. H. Charlesworth. 2 vols. New York, 1983
PL	Patrologia latina. Edited by J.-P. Migne. 217 vols. Paris, 1844–64
Pss. Sol.	*Psalms of Solomon*
PTMS	Pittsburgh Theological Monograph Series
RB	*Revue biblique*
RSR	*Recherches de science religieuse*
RSV	Revised Standard Version
RThom	*Revue Thomiste*
RUO	*Revue de l'université d'Ottawa*
SBLDS	Society of Biblical Literature Dissertation Series
SBLSymS	Society of Biblical Literature Symposium Series
ScrHier	Scripta hierosolymitana
SJLA	Studies in Judaism in Late Antiquity
SJT	*Scottish Journal of Theology*
SNT	Studien zum Neuen Testament
SNTSMS	Society for New Testament Studies Monograph Series
SP	Sacra pagina
ST	*Studia Theologica*
StABH	Studies in American Biblical Hermeneutics

TBT	*The Bible Today*
TDNT	*Theological Dictionary of the New Testament.* Edited by G. Kittel and G. Friedrich. Translated by G. W. Bromiley. 10 vols. Grand Rapids, 1964–76
ThTo	*Theology Today*
T. Jud.	*Testament of Judah*
T. Lev.	*Testament of Levi*
TNTC	Tyndale New Testament Commentaries
Tract. Ev. Jo.	*In Evangelium Johannis tractatus*
TS	*Theological Studies*
TSAJ	Texte und Studien zum antiken Judentum
t. Sanh.	*Tosefta Sanhedrin*
VTSup	Vetus Testamentum Supplements
WUNT	Wissenschaftliche Untersuchungen zum Neuen Testament
ZAW	*Zeitschrift für die alttestamentliche Wissenschaft*
ZNW	*Zeitschrift für die neutestamentliche Wissenschaft und die Kunde der älteren Kirche*

1

ALLUSIONS TO BIBLICAL TEXTS ABOUT MARRIAGE

"You see that everywhere the mysteries are in agreement," writes Origen of Alexandria (ca. 185–ca. 253). "You see the patterns of the New and Old Testament to be harmonious."[1] Origen's belief in the theological unity of the Bible leads him to recognize all kinds of parallels between passages in the New Testament and portions of Israel's Scriptures. Among these are similarities between two of John's stories and certain biblical texts that involve marriage. In his *Commentary on John*, for example, he compares the Samaritan woman of John 4:4–42 with Rebekah in Gen. 24:1–67. Just as Rebekah meets Abraham's servant at a well, so the Samaritan woman meets Jesus at a well. Origen notes one important difference: whereas Rebekah gives Abraham's servant a drink from her water jar and does not leave it behind (Gen. 24:18), the Samaritan woman accepts the water of eternal life from Jesus and forsakes her own jar – that is, her former opinions (John 4:28).[2] In his *Genesis Homily*, Origen goes on to extend the connection to two other biblical scenes: the stories of Jacob and Rachel in Gen. 29:1–20 and of Moses and Zipporah in Exod. 2:15–22. He then propounds the unified theological message of the Old and New Testament accounts: "There, one comes to the wells and the waters that brides may be found; and the church is united to Christ in the bath of water."[3]

Origen also perceives a connection between John's story of the anointing at Bethany and the Song of Songs. He interprets Song 1:12, "While the king was on his couch, my nard gave forth its fragrance," in light of John 12:3, "Mary took a pound of costly perfume made of pure

---

[1] Origen, *Hom. Gen.* 10.5, in *Homilies on Genesis and Exodus* (trans. Ronald E. Heine; FC 71; Washington, D.C.: The Catholic University of America Press, 1982), 167.

[2] Origen, *Commentarii in evangelium Joannis* 13.175–78, in *Commentary on the Gospel According to John: Books 13–32* (trans. Ronald E. Heine; FC 89; Washington, D.C.: The Catholic University of America Press, 1993), 105–6.

[3] Origen, *Hom. Gen.* 10.5.

nard, anointed Jesus' feet, and wiped them with her hair. The house was filled with the fragrance of the perfume."[4] Origen contends that the spiritual meaning of the bride's nard giving forth its odor is found in John's anointing story. As Mary (the soul) anoints Jesus, the nard absorbs Jesus' fragrance (his teaching and the Holy Spirit). That fragrance is then transferred back to Mary (the soul) by means of her hair, and eventually fills the house (the soul, the church, or the world).[5]

Origen is not the only ancient interpreter to observe similarities between stories in John's Gospel and biblical texts about marriage. His contemporary Hippolytus (who was Bishop of Rome from 222 to 235) notices parallels between Song 3:1–4 and John's tomb scene. Song of Songs 3:1–4 describes the nocturnal search of a woman for her beloved. Hippolytus specifically quotes John 20:16–17 to support his interpretation of Song 3:1–4 as a prophecy about the women in the four Gospels who go to the tomb on Easter morning.[6] John 20:16–17 shows how the women look for Jesus by night, how they encounter watchmen (the angels), and how they finally find Jesus and hold him – just like the woman in the Song of Songs.[7]

Most twenty-first-century exegetes would find several aspects of these third-century interpretations untenable. Allegorical readings of the New Testament have been widely discredited since the rise of rationalism in the eighteenth century. Origen would be hard-pressed today to persuade most historical and literary critics that John's anointing story is really about the soul receiving Jesus' teaching and then transmitting it to the world. He would find it even more difficult to persuade most feminist interpreters that the Samaritan woman and Mary of Bethany are symbolic brides who represent believers in relationship to Jesus. Eighteenth-century rationalism has also called into question

---

[4] Unless otherwise noted, all biblical quotations in English are taken from the NRSV.

[5] Origen, *Comm. Cant.* 2.9, in *The Song of Songs: Commentary and Homilies* (trans. R. P. Lawson; ACW 26; Westminster, Md.: Newman, 1957), 160–61. See also his *Hom. Cant. 2* 2 (in ACW 26, 285–86). Nobody knows whether Origen recognized any other connections between the Song of Songs and the Fourth Gospel, since the greater part of his commentaries on both books has been lost.

[6] Since Hippolytus harmonizes the four Gospel accounts, he ignores the discrepancy between John and the Synoptics about the actual number of women who came to the tomb. He does not consider that in John Mary Magdalene comes alone whereas according to the Synoptics she has company.

[7] Hippolytus, Εἰς τὸ ᾆσμα, Frag. 15, in *Exegetische und Homiletische Schriften* (ed. and trans. G. Nathanael Bonwetsch and Hans Achelis; GCS, Hippolytus I, Part I; Leipzig: Hinrichs, 1897), 350–52. This commentary on the Song of Songs, attributed to Hippolytus, has been preserved in Slavonic, Syriac, and Armenian fragments. The text appears to be ancient, if not authentic (see Bonwetsch and Achelis, *Exegetische Schriften*, xx–xxi).

the notion that the Old and New Testaments present one unified theological message. Not many contemporary scholars would agree that biblical stories about a man and a woman meeting at a well have anything to do with baptism, or that Song 1:12 should be interpreted in light of John 12:3. Indeed, only a few would understand the Song of Songs as anything but erotic poetry that found its way into the canon because it was attributed to Solomon, interpreted allegorically, and championed by R. Akibah.[8]

Recent developments, however, have opened the way for a renewed appreciation of ancient interpretations. Within the last few decades, some exegetes have challenged many of the presuppositions of eighteenth-century rationalism, as well as of nineteenth- and twentieth-century historical criticism. Chief among these is the assumption that the Bible is subject to objective interpretation through analysis of historical and literary evidence, along with the related assumption that only modern critics who perform such analyses deserve a hearing. It has been persuasively argued that objective interpretation is impossible.[9] In light of this realization, the academy now welcomes contributions from reader-response critics, post-modern exegetes, and many whose political agendas render their readings overtly subjective. As A. K. M. Adam observes, "If . . . there are not transcendent criteria for interpretation, but only local customs and guild rules, the reluctance modern New Testament theologians express about admitting the possible legitimacy of other appropriations of the New Testament is an expression of cultural imperialism and intellectual xenophobia."[10]

This suggests that the readings of so-called pre-critical interpreters should not be dismissed out of hand. In this monograph, I will argue that Origen and Hippolytus were on the right track in several respects. For one, they were not hearing things when they detected echoes of well betrothal stories and the Song of Songs in the Fourth Gospel. I will make the case that John indeed alludes to four biblical texts about marriage. One involves similarities between Jesus' encounter with the Samaritan woman in John 4:4–42 and the story about Jacob and Rachel in Gen. 29:1–20. Two others evoke the Song of Songs. Mary of Bethany perfumes the reclining Jesus in a scene reminiscent of Song 1:12, and

---

[8] Marvin Pope briefly discusses the Song's canonical status in *Song of Songs* (AB 7C; Garden City: Doubleday, 1977), 18–19.

[9] See, e.g., Mary Ann Tolbert, "Defining the Problem: The Bible and Feminist Hermeneutics," *Semeia* 28 (1983): 113–26.

[10] A. K. M. Adam, *Making Sense of New Testament Theology: "Modern" Problems and Prospects* (StABH 11; Macon, Ga.: Mercer University Press, 1995), 179.

Mary Magdalene seeks and finds her missing man as does the woman in Song 3:1–4. A fourth allusion is the first to occur in the Gospel narrative. In John 3:29, John the Baptist declares, "He who has the bride is the bridegroom.[11] The friend of the bridegroom, who stands and hears him, rejoices greatly at the bridegroom's voice (τὴν φωνὴν τοῦ νυμφίου)."[12] This saying recalls Jer. 33:10–11: "In . . . the towns of Judah and the streets of Jerusalem . . . there shall once more be heard the voice of mirth and the voice of gladness, the voice of the bridegroom (φωνὴ νυμφίου) and the voice of the bride."[13]

Origen was also right to attribute some figurative meaning to John's well and anointing stories. In my interpretation of the four allusions, I will show how they develop a marriage metaphor, introduced in the Cana wedding scene (John 2:1–11), that describes Jesus as the Messiah and depicts his relationship with the believing community. I will stress that all Christians should be able to accept and appreciate this metaphor since John does not use it to reinforce oppressive gender roles.

Finally, Origen's and Hippolytus' belief in the theological unity of the Scriptures is relevant because it closely resembles that of the Fourth Evangelist. I will argue that the Gospel's implied author considered Jer. 33:10–11, Gen. 29:1–20, and the Song of Songs appropriate for illustrating the life, death, and resurrection of Jesus because of their messianic significance. According to the conventions of first-century exegesis – conventions based on a belief in the theological unity of Scripture – they can be interpreted as messianic prophecies in light of Ps. 45, which celebrates the wedding of God's anointed king.

A tumult of reverberations

I am certainly not the first post-Enlightenment critic to hear echoes of biblical texts about marriage in the Fourth Gospel. In fact, early traditions of interpreting John 4:4–42 and 20:1–18 in light of well betrothal narratives and the Song of Songs have been perpetuated through the Enlightenment and into the present. Both The Venerable Bede (673–735) and St. John of the Cross (1542–91) link John's tomb

---

[11] The appellation "John the Baptist" never appears in the Fourth Gospel. I use it here to distinguish John the Baptist from John the Evangelist.

[12] The Greek text of the Fourth Gospel is taken from NA[27]. I discuss significant variants in the footnotes.

[13] The passage reckoned as Jer. 33:1–13 in Hebrew and English Bibles appears at Jer. 40:1–13 in the LXX.

story with Song 3:1–4.[14] This exegetical tradition has found its way into the Roman Catholic lectionary: Song 3:1–5 is read on the Feast of St. Mary Magdalene (July 22). A similar tradition has been preserved in the work of at least one nineteenth-century Protestant scholar. In his magnum opus, *The Life of Jesus Critically Examined*, David Friedrich Strauss explores the connection between John 4 and the Genesis well stories.[15]

In the wake of these traditions, several twentieth-century exegetes have proposed allusions to Gen. 29:1–20, Song 1:12; 3:1–4, and Jer. 33:10–11. They have also detected references to a whole host of other texts, most of which have something to do with marriage. For example, Michel Cambe hears several echoes in John 3:29. He affirms that John the Baptist's bridegroom saying may allude to Jer. 33:10–11.[16] He also agrees with John H. Bernard and Walter Bauer, who note the similarity between John's phrase "the bridegroom's voice (τὴν φωνὴν τοῦ νυμφίου)" and "the voice of the bridegroom (φωνὴ νυμφίου)" mentioned in Jer. 7:32–34, 16:9, and 25:10.[17] These prophecies describe how "the voice of the bridegroom," along with "the voice of the bride" and the sound of mirth and gladness, will eventually cease in Jerusalem. In addition, Cambe notes that others have detected echoes of the Song of Songs in John 3:29. André Feuillet makes the case for allusions to Song 2:8–14 and 5:2–6, passages that describe the bride's eager response to her beloved's voice.[18] Even more convincing for

---

[14] The Venerable Bede, *In Cantica Canticorum Allegorica Expositio*, in PL 91:1120; St. John of the Cross, *Dark Night of the Soul* 2.13.6, in *Dark Night of the Soul* (trans. and ed. E. Allison Peers; 3 vols; 3rd rev. edn.; New York: Doubleday, 1990), 140–42.

[15] David Friedrich Strauss, *The Life of Jesus Critically Examined* (ed. Peter C. Hodgson; trans. George Eliot; Philadelphia: Fortress, 1972), 308.

[16] Michel Cambe, "L'influence du Cantique des Cantiques sur le Nouveau Testament," *RThom* 62 (1962): 14. See also Jacques Winandy, "Le Cantique des Cantiques et le Nouveau Testament," *RB* 71 (1964): 168–69; François-Marie Braun, *Jean le théologien 2: Les grandes traditions d'Israël et l'accord des écritures selon le quatrième évangile* (*Ebib*; Paris: Gabalda, 1964), 197 and *Jean le théologien 3.1: Sa théologie: Le mystère de Jésus-Christ* (*Ebib*; Paris: Gabalda, 1966), 101; Martin Hengel, "The Interpretation of the Wine Miracle at Cana: John 2:1–11," trans. Gerhard Schmidt, in *The Glory of Christ in the New Testament* (ed. L. D. Hurst and N. T. Wright; Oxford: Clarendon, 1987), 101–2; Mirjam Zimmermann and Ruben Zimmermann, "Der Freund des Bräutigams (Joh 3,29): Deflorations- oder Christuszeuge?" *ZNW* 90 (1999): 126–27.

[17] John H. Bernard, *A Critical and Exegetical Commentary on the Gospel According to St. John* (ed. A. H. McNeile; ICC; Edinburgh: T&T Clark, 1928), I:131; Walter Bauer, *Das Johannes-Evangelium* (3rd edn.; HNT 6; Tübingen: Mohr Siebeck, 1933), 63.

[18] André Feuillet, "Le symbolisme de la colombe dans les récits évangéliques du Baptême," *RSR* 46 (1958): 540; "Le Cantique des cantiques et l'Apocalypse," *RSR* 49 (1961): 334, n. 8; "La recherche du Christ dans la nouvelle alliance d'après la christophanie de Jo 20,11–18: Comparaison avec Cant. 3,1–4 et l'épisode des pèlerins

Cambe is P. Joüon's belief that John 3:29 alludes to Song 8:13: "O you who dwell in the gardens, my companions are listening for your voice; let me hear it."[19]

Allusions to marriage texts are also discerned in the well scene of John 4:4–42. Jerome H. Neyrey and Calum M. Carmichael contend with me that this scene alludes to the Jacob and Rachel story in Gen. 29:1–20.[20] Others hear different echoes. Scholars such as François-Marie Braun and Marie-Émile Boismard point out several verbal similarities between John 4:4–42 and the scene with Abraham's servant and Rebekah in Gen. 24:1–67, while E. C. Hoskyns and Gerhard Friedrich recognize an allusion to the encounter between Moses and Zipporah (Exod. 2:15–22) as told by Josephus (*Ant.* 2.257).[21] Aileen Guilding suggests that John refers to Exod. 2:15–22 along with one of the Genesis stories; for Annie Jaubert, the relevant passages are Exod. 2:15–22 and Gen. 29:1–20.[22]

---

d'Emmaüs," in *L'homme devant Dieu* (Théologie 56–58; Paris: Aubier, 1963), I:106; *Le Mystère de l'amour divin dans la théologie johannique* (*Ebib*; Paris: Gabalda, 1972), 231; and *Jesus and His Mother: The Role of the Virgin Mary in Salvation History and the Place of Woman in the Church* (trans. L. Maluf; Still River, Mass.: St. Bede's, 1974), 12; Cambe, "Influence du Cantique," 13.

[19] P. Joüon, *Le Cantique des cantiques* (Paris: Beauchesne, 1909), 331–32; Cambe, "Influence du Cantique," 15. See also Braun, *Jean le théologien 2*, 198 and *Jean le théologien 3.1*, 93, 101–2; Feuillet, "Symbolisme de la colombe," 540; "Cantique et l'Apocalypse," 334 n. 8; "Recherche du Christ," 106; *Mystère de l'amour divin*, 231; and *Jesus and His Mother*, 12. For a critique of this position, see Winandy, "Cantique et le NT," 167, 172.

[20] Jerome H. Neyrey, "Jacob Traditions and the Interpretation of John 4:10–26," *CBQ* 41 (1979): 425–26; Calum M. Carmichael, "Marriage and the Samaritan Woman," *NTS* 26 (1980): 332–37.

[21] Braun, *Jean le théologien 3.1*, 93–95; Marie-Émile Boismard, "Aenon près de Salem: Jean III.23," *RB* 80 (1973): 225; Marie-Émile Boismard and Arnaud Lamouille, *L'Évangile de Jean* (Synopse des quatre évangiles en français III; Paris: Cerf, 1979), 136; E. C. Hoskyns, *The Fourth Gospel* (ed. Francis Noel Davey; London: Faber & Faber, 1940), 263; Gerhard Friedrich, *Wer ist Jesus? Die Verkündigung des vierten Evangelisten, dargestellt an Joh 4,4–42* (Stuttgart: Calwer, 1967), 25. In agreement with Braun and Boismard are Philippe Dagonet (*Selon Saint Jean: Une femme de Samarie* [Paris: Cerf, 1979], 47–53) and Marc Girard ("Jésus en Samarie [Jean 4, 1–42]: Analyse des structures stylistiques et du procès de symbolisation," *EgT* 17 [1986]: 302–3).

[22] Aileen Guilding, *The Fourth Gospel and Jewish Worship: A Study of the Relation of St. John's Gospel to the Ancient Jewish Lectionary System* (Oxford: Oxford University Press, 1960), 231; Annie Jaubert, "La symbolique du puits de Jacob: Jean 4,12," in *L'homme devant Dieu*, I:63–73; *Approches de l'Évangile de Jean* (Paris: Seuil, 1976), 58–63; and "La symbolique des femmes dans les traditions religieuses: Une reconsidération de l'Évangile de Jean," *RUO* 50 (1980): 118–19. Normand R. Bonneau builds on Guilding's work ("The Woman at the Well, John 4 and Genesis 24," *TBT* 67 [1973]: 1252–59), as does Eugene D. Stockton ("The Fourth Gospel and the Woman," in *Essays in Faith and Culture* [ed. Neil Brown; Faith and Culture 3; Catholic Institute of Sydney, 1979], 142). Birger Olsson develops Jaubert's thesis (*Structure and Meaning in the Fourth*

These critics were joined by many more following the publication of Robert Alter's *The Art of Biblical Narrative* in 1981. One of the many contributions to literary criticism of the Bible put forward by Alter in that volume is his hypothesis concerning conventional type-scenes. To illustrate their function, he presents a detailed analysis of the so-called "betrothal type-scene" in which a man on a journey meets a maiden at a well, water is drawn and shared, and a marriage is arranged.[23]

As a professor of Hebrew and Comparative Literature, Alter never extends his observations to include the story of Jesus and the Samaritan woman. New Testament scholars, however, have not hesitated to avail themselves of his insights in interpreting this passage. After all, John 4:4–42 follows the standard format of a "betrothal type-scene": Jesus journeys to Samaria, meets a woman at a well, and engages her in a conversation about water. Among the many who read John 4:4–42 as a "betrothal type-scene" are P. Joseph Cahill, R. Alan Culpepper, Paul D. Duke, and Jeffrey Lloyd Staley.[24]

Gospel: A Text-Linguistic Analysis of John 2:1–11 and 4:1–42 [trans. Jean Gray; *CB* 6; Lund: Gleerup, 1974], 169–73, 256–57). For more general references to echoes of biblical well betrothal narratives in John 4, see Joseph Colson, "Les noces du Christ (Nouveau Testament)," in *Un roi fit des noces à son fils* (Bruges: Desclée de Brouwer, 1961), 134–35; John Bligh, "Jesus in Samaria," *HeyJ* 3 (1962): 332; J. N. Sanders, *A Commentary on the Gospel According to St. John* (ed. B. A. Mastin; BNTC; London: Black, 1968), 140–41, 144; James D. Purvis, "The Fourth Gospel and the Samaritans," *NovT* 17 (1975): 194; J. Duncan M. Derrett, "The Samaritan Woman's Pitcher," *DRev* 102 (1984): 252–61.

[23] Robert Alter, *The Art of Biblical Narrative* (New York: Basic Books, 1981), 51–58. Alter follows the lead of Robert C. Culley, who concludes that the similarities between the Genesis and Exodus well betrothal narratives suggest the possibility that "a traditional episode . . . has been employed in and adapted to different contexts" (*Studies in the Structure of Hebrew Narrative* [Philadelphia: Fortress, 1976], 41–43).

[24] P. Joseph Cahill, "Narrative Art in John IV," *Religious Studies Bulletin* 2 (1982): 41–48; R. Alan Culpepper, *Anatomy of the Fourth Gospel: A Study in Literary Design* (Philadelphia: Fortress, 1983), 136; Paul D. Duke, *Irony in the Fourth Gospel* (Atlanta: John Knox, 1985), 101–3; Jeffrey Lloyd Staley, *The Print's First Kiss: A Rhetorical Investigation of the Implied Reader in the Fourth Gospel* (SBLDS 82; Atlanta: Scholars Press, 1988), 98–102. For additional references to John 4:4–42 as a "betrothal type-scene," see Walter Rebell, *Gemeinde als Gegenwelt: Zur soziologischen und didaktischen Funktion des Johannesevangelium* (Frankfurt: Lang, 1987), 189; Lyle Eslinger, "The Wooing of the Woman at the Well: Jesus, the Reader, and Reader-Response Criticism," *Literature and Theology* 1/1 (1987): 167–83; repr. in *The Gospel of John as Literature* (ed. Mark W. G. Stibbe; Leiden: Brill, 1993), 165–82; Paul Trudinger, "Of Women, Wells, Waterpots and Wine! Reflections on Johannine Themes (John 2:1–11 and 4:1–42)," *St. Mark's Review* 151 (1992): 10–16; Mark W. G. Stibbe, *John* (Sheffield: JSOT Press, 1993), 68–69; Adele Reinhartz, "The Gospel of John," in *Searching the Scriptures: A Feminist Commentary* (ed. Elisabeth Schüssler Fiorenza, et al.; New York: Crossroad, 1994), II:572–73; C. Clifton Black, "Rhetorical Criticism and the New Testament," in *Hearing the New Testament: Strategies for Interpretation* (ed. Joel B. Green; Grand Rapids: Eerdmans, 1995), 270–71; Joan E. Cook, "Wells, Women, and Faith," in *Proceedings, Eastern Great Lakes and Midwest Biblical Societies* 17 (1997): 11–18; Larry Paul Jones, *The Symbol of Water in*

A few scholars also detect allusions in both the anointing scene of John 12:1–8 and the resurrection appearance of John 20:1–18. Cambe points out several parallels between the anointing scenes in John 12:3 and Song 1:12.[25] Anthony Tyrrell Hanson proposes instead that John 12:3 alludes to Hag. 2:6–9, in which the Lord promises to fill the temple with splendor.[26] Feuillet, Sandra M. Schneiders, and Hanson join Cambe in suggesting that Mary Magdalene's search in John 20:1–18 bears a strong resemblance to Song 3:1–4.[27] In addition, some of these scholars propose various other evoked texts, including a similar nocturnal search in Song 5:5–6, the description of the Shulammite maiden who turns and turns in Song 6:13 (7:1), and the scene in Song 8:13 where companions listen for the voice of one who dwells in the gardens.[28]

the Gospel of John (JSNTSup 145; Sheffield: Sheffield Academic Press, 1997), 91–96; Colleen M. Conway, *Men and Women in the Fourth Gospel: Gender and Johannine Characterization* (SBLDS 167; Atlanta: Society of Biblical Literature, 1999).

[25] Cambe, "Influence du Cantique," 15–17. See also Bauer, *Johannes-Evangelium,* 159; Jacques Winandy, *Le Cantique des Cantiques: Poème d'amour mué en écrit de sagesse* (BVC 16; Tournai, Belgium: Castermann, 1960), 60 and "Cantique et le NT," 166–67; Mary Rose D'Angelo, "(Re)Presentations of Women in the Gospels: John and Mark," in *Women and Christian Origins* (ed. Ross Shepard Kraemer and Mary Rose D'Angelo; New York: Oxford University Press, 1999), 136; Adele Reinhartz, *Befriending the Beloved Disciple: A Jewish Reading of the Gospel of John* (New York: Continuum, 2001), 108.

[26] Anthony Tyrrell Hanson, *The New Testament Interpretation of Scripture* (London: SPCK, 1980), 118–21.

[27] Cambe, "Influence du Cantique," 17–19, 25; Feuillet, "Recherche du Christ, 103–7 and *Mystère de l'amour divin,* 231; Sandra M. Schneiders, "The Johannine Resurrection Narrative: An Exegetical and Theological Study of John 20 as a Synthesis of Johannine Spirituality" (D.S.T. diss., Pontificia Universitas Gregoriana, 1975), I:394, 407–8, 413–16, 429; "John 20:11–18: The Encounter of the Easter Jesus with Mary Magdalene: A Transformative Feminist Reading," in *"What is John?" Readers and Readings of the Fourth Gospel* (ed. Fernando F. Segovia; SBLSymS 3; Atlanta: Scholars Press, 1996), I:161; and *Written That You May Believe: Encountering Jesus in the Fourth Gospel* (New York: Crossroad, 1999), 195; Anthony Tyrrell Hanson, *The Prophetic Gospel: A Study of John and the Old Testament* (Edinburgh: T&T Clark, 1991), 228–30. See also Jaubert, "Symbolique des femmes," 117; Godfrey C. Nicholson, *Death As Departure: The Johannine Descent-Ascent Schema* (SBLDS 63; Chico, Calif.: Scholars Press, 1983), 73; Carolyn M. Grassi and Joseph A. Grassi, *Mary Magdalene and the Women in Jesus' Life* (Kansas City, Mo.: Sheed & Ward, 1986), 109–10; Teresa Okure, "The Significance Today of Jesus' Commission of Mary Magdalene," *International Review of Mission* 81 (1992): 181; J. Duncan M. Derrett, "Miriam and the Resurrection (John 20:16)," *DRev* 111 (1993), 178, 181; Stibbe, *John,* 205; Jack R. Lundbom, "Mary Magdalene and Song of Songs 3:1–4," *Int* 49 (1995): 172–75; Frédéric Manns, *L'évangile de Jean à la lumière du judaïsme* (Studium Biblicum Franciscanum 33; Jerusalem: Franciscan, 1999), 415–17; D'Angelo, "(Re)Presentations of Women," 136; Reinhartz, *Befriending the Beloved Disciple,* 108.

[28] Cambe, "Influence du Cantique," 17–19, 25; Feuillet, "Recherche du Christ, 103–7 and *Mystère de l'amour divin,* 231; Schneiders, "Resurrection Narrative," I:394, 407–8, 413–16, 429; "Easter Jesus," 161; and *Written That You May Believe,* 195; Hanson, *Prophetic Gospel,* 227–30. The notation "6:13 (7:1)" reflects the fact that this verse is

The most sustained treatment to date of John's allusions to marriage texts is the work of Ann Roberts Winsor. She devotes her book, *A King Is Bound in the Tresses*, to the numerous echoes of the Song of Songs she detects in John 12:1–3 and 20:1, 11–18. Winsor contends that John's "allusions to the Song follow the intertextual practice character- istic of biblical narrative."[29] She finds this practice described by Michel Riffaterre and Ziva Ben-Porat, so she uses their theories to develop a method for identifying and interpreting allusions in John's anointing and garden scenes.[30] First, Winsor notes the presence in John's narra- tive of what Riffaterre terms "ungrammaticalities"; that is, details that seem out of place.[31] Such details signal an allusion to another text where they are more at home.[32] Next, Winsor determines the evoked text by examining its verbal and thematic similarities with the originat- ing text.[33] Once the evoked text is recognized, it changes the context of the originating text such that all elements of both texts begin to interact.[34]

Using this method, Winsor finds that thirteen words or ideas in John 12:1–3; 20:1, 11–18 correspond with about sixty verbal and thematic parallels in the Song of Songs. In John 12:1–2, for example, Jesus at table is reminiscent of the reclining king of Song 1:12.[35] The term πιστικῆς in John 12:3 may be a corruption of τῆς στακτῆς, mentioned in Song 1:13: "My beloved is to me a bag of myrrh (τῆς στακτῆς) that lies between my breasts."[36] Mary of Bethany's wiping Jesus' feet with her hair in John 12:3 calls to mind the king of Song 7:5 (6) who is held captive in his lover's tresses, along with the bathed feet of the aroused woman in Song 5:3 and the graceful feet of the queenly maiden

---

reckoned as 6:13 in English translations but as 7:1 by the MT and LXX. Similar notation elsewhere indicates similar variations of verse and chapter numbers in Song 6–7.

[29] Ann Roberts Winsor, *A King Is Bound in the Tresses: Allusions to the Song of Songs in the Fourth Gospel* (Studies in Biblical Literature 6; New York: Lang, 1999), 1.

[30] See Michel Riffaterre, *Semiotics of Poetry* (Advances in Semiotics; Bloomington: Indiana University Press, 1978; Ziva Ben-Porat, "The Poetics of Literary Allusion," *PTL: A Journal for Descriptive Poetics and Theory of Literature* 1 (1976): 105–28.

[31] Winsor, *A King Is Bound*, 8; Riffaterre, *Semiotics*, 5.

[32] Winsor, *A King Is Bound*, 8–9; Riffaterre, *Semiotics*, 164–65.

[33] Winsor, *A King Is Bound*, 10; Ben-Porat, "Poetics," 107–8.

[34] Winsor, *A King Is Bound*, 11; Ben-Porat, "Poetics," 116.

[35] Winsor, *A King Is Bound*, 22.

[36] Ibid., 23. The idea of a possible corruption originated with Paul-Louis Couchoud ("Notes de critique verbale sur St. Marc et St. Matthieu," *JTS* 34 [1933]: 128). See also Raymond E. Brown, *The Gospel According to John I–XII* (AB 29; Garden City: Double- day, 1966), 220–21.

in Song 7:1 (2).[37] The fragrant perfume of John 12:3 alludes to the bag of myrrh in Song 1:13 and the scent of Song 1:3, 4, and 12 – along with twenty-eight other references to scent in the Song of Songs.[38]

Similar parallels link the Song to John 20:1, 11–18. For instance, the tomb (μνημεῖον) in John 20:1, 11 is reminiscent of the chamber (ταμίειον) in Song 1:4; 3:4; and 8:2, while the garden (John 19:41) evokes the Song's setting (4:12, 16; 5:1; 8:13).[39] Mary Magdalene's nocturnal search (John 20:1, 15) echoes Song 3:1–4.[40] Her two enigmatic turns in John 20:14, 16 are ungrammaticalities that signal an allusion to the turning Shulammite maiden of Song 6:13 (7:1).[41] Jesus' address in John 20:16 alludes to the beloved's voice in Song 5:2, 6, while Mary's testimony in John 20:18 resembles the voice from the garden in Song 8:13.[42] Finally, Jesus' prohibition "Do not hold me" (John 20:17) marks a reference to Song 3:4.[43]

Winsor concludes that the Fourth Gospel alludes to the entire Song. "Understanding the Johannine anointing and resurrection appearance narratives requires a grasp of the [Song of Songs] as well," she writes, "for the Song is alluded to not just once or incidentally, but comprehensively."[44] She supports this argument by pointing out that the Fourth Gospel and the Song of Songs share similar tendencies and may have emerged from similar social settings. The Song stands "as a singular affirmation of women's experience and authority," and the Fourth Gospel shares the Song's understanding of gender roles.[45] Winsor theorizes that "those who composed, preserved, and handed down the songs that became the Song" were women.[46] She then suggests that John's allusions to the Song may have originated in an early stratum of the Johannine community. She postulates a group influenced largely by women who valued the Song's emphasis on human relationships and physical sensation.[47]

Making sense of the echoes

The echoes heard by Origen and Hippolytus have certainly not died away. Scholars still detect them, along with a whole tumult of reverberations that those two venerable theologians would never have imagined.

---

[37] Winsor, *A King Is Bound*, 20–22, 23–25.
[38] Ibid., 22–23, 25–27. See also Derrett, "Miriam and the Resurrection," 178.
[39] Winsor, *A King Is Bound*, 41–42.
[40] Ibid., 41–43.   [41] Ibid., 37–39.   [42] Ibid., 43–44.
[43] Ibid., 40–41.   [44] Ibid., 49.   [45] Ibid., 61–62.
[46] Ibid., 65.   [47] Ibid., 89–90.

The echoes are rarely heard in concert, however. Although many detect references to marriage texts in the Fourth Gospel, few listen for echoes in more than one or two passages. No one has yet attempted to make sense of proposed allusions to marriage texts in John 3:29, 4:4–42, 12:3, and 20:1–18 together, and it has never been suggested that John interprets the marriage texts as messianic prophecies in light of Ps. 45. Only recently has anyone published an account of the fact that more than two of these Gospel passages, not to mention the Cana wedding scene in John 2:1–11, may refer to marriage in some way.[48]

One such scholar is Gilberte Baril, who consolidates previous research into a brief yet broad summary of marriage imagery in John. She devotes five pages of her book, *The Feminine Face of the People of God*, to "The espoused community in St John."[49] Relying on the work of Boismard, Baril contends that John the Baptist's saying in John 3:29 establishes Jesus as "the bridegroom of the Messianic nuptials." As the friend of the bridegroom, John the Baptist purifies the espoused community and presents them to Jesus.[50] The wedding scene in John 2:1–11 also reminds her of "the eternal nuptial feast" celebrating the union of Jesus and his followers.[51] Baril affirms Braun's theory that John 2:1–11 and John 3:29 are linked thematically to John 4:4–42.[52] Following Jaubert, she identifies allusions to Gen. 29:1–20 and Exod. 2:15–22 in John 4:4–42.[53] She also concedes that John 20:1–18 may echo Song 3:1–4, as proposed by Cambe.[54] The Samaritan woman and Mary Magdalene, Baril concludes, represent the believing community united to Christ.[55]

---

[48] Among those who briefly sketch the connections between John 2:1–11, 3:29, and 4:4–42 are Bligh ("Jesus in Samaria," 332), Braun (*Jean le théologien 3.1*, 93), John Marsh (*Saint John* [Westminster Pelican Commentaries; Philadelphia: Westminster, 1968], 142–47, 196, 214–16), Jaubert (*Approches*, 61), Neyrey ("Jacob Traditions," 426), Carmichael ("Marriage and the Samaritan Woman," 332–33), Cahill ("Narrative Art," 45), Duke (*Irony*, 101), Staley (*Print's First Kiss*, 90, 101 n. 35), Stibbe (*John*, 61, 69), Manns (*Lumière du judaïsme*, 134–35), and Jones (*Symbol of Water*, 92). Winandy separately evaluates proposed allusions in John 3:29; 12:8; 20:1–18 ("Cantique et le NT," 166–73).

[49] Gilberte Baril, *The Feminine Face of the People of God: Biblical Symbols of the Church as Bride and Mother* (trans. Florestine Audette; Collegeville, Minn.: Liturgical Press, 1990), 92–97.

[50] Ibid., 93; cf. Marie-Émile Boismard, "L'ami de l'époux (Jo., III, 29)," in *A la rencontre de Dieu* (Paris: Mappus, 1961), 289–95.

[51] Baril, *Feminine Face*, 93.

[52] Ibid.; cf. Braun, *Jean le théologien 3.1*, 93.

[53] Baril, *Feminine Face*, 94–95; cf. Jaubert, *Approches*, 61.

[54] Baril, *Feminine Face*, 96–97; cf. Cambe, "Influence du Cantique," 17–19.

[55] Baril, *Feminine Face*, 97.

Schneiders also sketches the development of a nuptial theme in the Fourth Gospel. In her book, *Written That You May Believe*, she compiles some of her previous work on the Cana miracle, the bridegroom saying, the Samaritan story, and the resurrection narrative. She sees John 2:1–11 as the introduction of Jesus as the true Bridegroom who supplies the wine for the wedding feast. In John 3:29, Jesus is again identified as a Bridegroom whose bride is the New Israel.[56] Schneiders affirms Cahill's theory that John 4:4–42 is a "type-story."[57] The Samaritan woman represents her people, "woo[ed] . . . to full covenant fidelity in the New Israel by Jesus, the new Bridegroom."[58] Finally, Schneiders argues that John 20:1–18 echoes various scenes from the Song of Songs. Mary Magdalene searches for Jesus (John 20:1–2, 11–18) just as the Song's bride searches for her missing man (3:1–4; 5:1–8); first the Beloved Disciple, then Mary look (παρακύπτω) into the tomb (John 20:5, 11) just as the Song's beloved looks (παρακύπτω) into the bride's chamber (Song 2:9); Jesus and Mary pronounce each other's names (John 20:16) just as the Song's lovers claim one another (Song 2:16); the entire scene takes place in a garden (John 19:41) as does much of the Song (e.g. Song 4:12). Since first-century interpreters understood the Song of Songs to celebrate the covenant between God and Israel, John's Mary Magdalene symbolizes "the Johannine Community as the New Israel, spouse of the New Covenant."[59] Echoes of the Song of Songs in John 20 thus form the culmination of John's nuptial theme, illustrating the New Covenant between Jesus and believers made possible by the resurrection.[60]

Baril's and Schneiders' work is suggestive, but too cursory to be convincing. This is because each of them studies John's marriage motif as part of a larger project. Adeline Fehribach discusses the motif in more detail. She offers an extensive analysis of John's female characters in her book *The Women in the Life of the Bridegroom*. Fehribach asserts that "the implied author of the Fourth Gospel drew on the literary and cultural conventions of the day to portray the female

---

[56] Schneiders, *Written That You May Believe*, 35, 135. See also her "Resurrection Narrative," I:359 and *The Revelatory Text: Interpreting the New Testament as Sacred Scripture* (2nd edn.; Collegeville, Minn.: Liturgical Press, 1999), 187.

[57] Schneiders, *Written That You May Believe*, 135–36, 138; cf. Cahill, "Narrative Art," 41–48. See also Schneiders, "Resurrection Narrative," I:360 and *Revelatory Text*, 187.

[58] Schneiders, *Written That You May Believe*, 141.

[59] Schneiders, "Resurrection Narrative," I:338. See also her "Easter Jesus," 161 and *Written That You May Believe*, 35.

[60] Schneiders, *Written That You May Believe*, 35, 195–99. See also her "Resurrection Narrative," I:338, 394–439 and "Easter Jesus," 161.

characters in such a way as to have them support the characterization of Jesus as the messianic bridegroom."[61] The "literary conventions of the day" include character types, type-scenes, and techniques of characterization.[62] These can be found first of all in the Hebrew Bible, "one of the most important literary resources for understanding the Fourth Gospel" and the source for several allusions.[63] Important background literature also includes Hellenistic-Jewish writings such as the books of Judith and Susanna, as well as popular Greco-Roman novels like Xenophon's *An Ephesian Tale* and Chariton's *Chaereas and Callirhoe*. Fehribach also refers to cultural conventions, like the operation of honor and shame in gender relations and the social status of first-century women, as reconstructed by modern scholars.[64] She argues that John uses these literary and cultural conventions to portray Jesus as the messianic bridegroom. The mother of Jesus acts as the "mother of an important son" and Martha of Bethany functions as the messianic bridegroom's sister-in-law. The Samaritan woman, Mary of Bethany, and Mary Magdalene are all depicted as his betrothed or bride.[65]

In support of her argument about the Samaritan woman, Mary of Bethany, and Mary Magdalene, Fehribach mentions allusions to biblical texts about marriage. She shows how the allusions indicate the literary and exegetical conventions that John uses to portray female characters. According to Fehribach, John 4:4–42 alludes to the "betrothal type-scene" convention.[66] Jesus' symbolic betrothal to the Samaritan woman is foreshadowed by John 2:1–11 and 3:29.[67] An allusion to Song 1:12 in John 12:3 likens Mary of Bethany to the Song's bride, conventionally understood as the people of God.[68] An allusion to Song 3:1–4 in John 20:1–18 allows Mary Magdalene to assume the conventional role of the woman in search of her dead lover's body.[69] John's female characters become paradigms of faith because they represent the believing community, as do characters like Judith and Susanna.[70] Apart from their representative function, however, they are marginalized. They suffer the fate of all women in the patriarchal society that produced the Fourth Gospel.[71] Fehribach laments the fact that her historical-literary analysis offers so little hope to her feminist readers. She

[61] Adeline Fehribach, *The Women in the Life of the Bridegroom: A Feminist Historical-Literary Analysis of the Female Characters in the Fourth Gospel* (Collegeville, Minn.: Liturgical Press, 1998), 20.

[62] Ibid., 7–8.   [63] Ibid., 9–10.   [64] Ibid., 10–17.
[65] Ibid., 20.   [66] Ibid., 49–52.   [67] Ibid., 47–49.
[68] Ibid., 93.   [69] Ibid., 150, 160.   [70] Ibid., 106–7, 175–78.
[71] Ibid., 32–42, 69–79, 107–11, 140–41.

suggests that a reader-response approach or a performative faith perspective might enable interpreters to view John's female characters as assertive, courageous disciples.[72]

Although Fehribach provides a detailed treatment of marriage themes in John 4:4–42, 12:1–8, and 20:1–18, her chief concern is with John's similarities to popular Greco-Roman novels and conformity to first-century cultural conventions. She pays scant attention (fewer than seven pages) to John's scriptural allusions. For the most sustained treatment to date of John's allusions to biblical texts about marriage, we must refer to Winsor's book, *A King Is Bound in the Tresses*.[73] Winsor concentrates heavily on their nature and significance – at least with respect to allusions to the Song of Songs in John 12 and 20. She applies the theories of Riffaterre and Ben-Porat in identifying and interpreting them, and she suggests how they might have found their way into the narrative.

Winsor's answers fail to satisfy, however. For one thing, her method does not generate consistently compelling conclusions. Some of her proposed allusions are based only on a remote similarity. John's μνημεῖον scarcely resembles the Song's ταμίειον, John's reference to Jesus' feet hardly echoes the Song's descriptions of female feet, and the supposed corruption of τῆς στακτῆς to πιστικῆς is pure speculation. Furthermore, all but six of her proposed allusive links consist of only one verbal similarity, such as "feet" or "scent." This weakens her argument that John 12:1–3 and 20:1, 11–18 allude to the entire Song of Songs. Thirteen Johannine words or ideas with only about sixty parallels in the Song (including thirty-one references to scent alone) hardly constitute an allusion to a poem of nearly two thousand words (in Greek). Put another way, John's anointing and resurrection scenes do not readily evoke the Song as a whole, with its pastoral settings, wedding processions, and metaphorical descriptions of the human body. Scattered verbal and thematic similarities along with a couple of "ungrammaticalities" prove to be insufficient indicators. More criteria are needed.

More criteria are provided by Richard B. Hays. In his book *Echoes of Scripture in the Letters of Paul*, Hays lists seven guidelines for identifying and interpreting Paul's allusions to Scripture.[74] Like Winsor,

---

[72] Ibid., 175–84.

[73] For a summary of Winsor's argument, see above, pp. 9–10.

[74] Richard B. Hays, *Echoes of Scripture in the Letters of Paul* (New Haven: Yale University Press, 1989), 29–32.

Hays considers verbal parallels between the originating text and the evoked text as well as the significance of the evoked text for the alluding author. Unlike Winsor, Hays also stresses the frequency of verbal parallels and the rhetorical emphasis laid on the allusion. In addition, Hays' guidelines assess the impact of the allusion on the originating text, account for the plausibility of the allusion in its historical context, and evaluate its reception by a contemporary audience. Although they were compiled for understanding allusions in Paul's epistles, they can be easily adapted for use with the Fourth Gospel.

In this study, I adapt and then adopt Hays' criteria in order to investigate possible allusions to marriage texts in John the Baptist's bridegroom saying (John 3:29), the Samaritan story (John 4:4–42), the anointing scene (12:1–8), and the resurrection appearance to Mary Magdalene (20:1–18). My first concern is with John's allusions as an act of communication between an implied author and implied audience. A story's implied author is the author's persona as projected in the text. Its implied audience consists of those expected to understand the story, including its direct discourse as well as its implicit commentary.[75] Since both implied author and implied audience must be constructed primarily on the basis of evidence from the text, I focus my initial investigation on the text of the Fourth Gospel without considering other literary or historical sources. When I apply Hays' criteria to John's narrative, four allusions are confirmed: Jer. 33:10–11 in John 3:29, Gen. 29:1–20 in John 4:4–42, Song 1:12 in John 12:3, and Song 3:1–4 in John 20:1–18.

A literary analysis in accordance with Hays' criteria shows that John's implied author uses each allusion to develop a marriage metaphor describing Jesus as the Messiah and depicting Jesus' relationship with the believing community. In John 3:22–30, Jer. 33:10–11 helps to characterize Jesus as a bridegroom-Messiah who inspires joy and whose progeny will increase. The allusion to Gen. 29:1–20 in John 4:4–42 illustrates the origin of this family of faith. Here, Jesus is portrayed as a bridegroom greater than Jacob who offers eternal life, and the Samaritan woman as the bride whose testimony causes many of her fellow-citizens to believe. In John 12:1–8, Song 1:12 depicts

---

[75] The concept of implied author and audience is borrowed from Wayne Booth (*The Rhetoric of Fiction* [Chicago: University of Chicago Press, 1961], 70–71), as elaborated by Seymour Chatman (*Story and Discourse: Narrative Structure in Fiction and Film* [Ithaca, N.Y.: Cornell University Press, 1978], 148–51, 267) and Culpepper (*Anatomy*, 6–8). I use the term "implied audience" instead of "implied reader" because John addresses a group of people, as indicated by the second-person plural pronoun in John 20:31.

Jesus as the king on the couch even as he contemplates his imminent crucifixion. Finally, the search of the bride for her beloved in Song 3:1–4 provides a format for Mary Magdalene's recognition of the risen and ascending Lord.

This interpretation raises a question addressed by many previous exegetes: does John's casting female characters in the role of brides indicate that they are representative figures? Specifically, do the bride of John 3:29, the Samaritan woman, Mary of Bethany, and Mary Magdalene symbolize the people of God?[76] This issue can be addressed with the help of some recently developed guidelines for identifying and interpreting John's symbols. Craig R. Koester devotes an entire chapter of his book, *Symbolism in the Fourth Gospel*, to symbolic and representative figures.[77] According to Koester, many of John's characters can function not only as individuals in their own right but also as representatives of particular groups of people. Especially pertinent are Koester's insights into techniques by which John imparts symbolic value. For example, John might directly identify individual characters with a certain group, endow them with the distinctive traits of that group, or refer to them with plural pronouns.[78]

As I investigate John's allusions to marriage texts, then, I also explore how the Gospel incorporates these and other techniques to lend various degrees of representative value to the women who assume the role of the bride. In the process, I am careful to distinguish among different audiences. There is no explicit evidence in the Gospel to suggest that its implied audience would have understood either the bride of John 3:29 or Mary of Bethany in John 12:1–8 as a representative figure. There is, however, some indication that the Samaritan woman symbolizes the Samaritan people and that Mary Magdalene exemplifies Jesus' followers as described elsewhere in the Gospel.[79] Moreover, historical evidence shows that John's original audience may have attributed even more representative value to these four female

---

[76] Scholars who raise this question include Braun (*Jean le théologien 3.1*, 93–95), Boismard ("Aenon près de Salem," 225), Girard ("Jésus en Samarie," 304), Neyrey ("Jacob Traditions," 425–26), Jaubert ("Symbolique du puits," 63–73 and "Symbolique des femmes," 118–19), Cambe ("Influence du Cantique," 25), and Feuillet ("Recherche du Christ," 103–7 and *Mystère de l'amour divin*, 231), as well as Fehribach, Schneiders, Baril, and Origen.

[77] Craig R. Koester, *Symbolism in the Fourth Gospel* (Minneapolis: Fortress, 1995), 32–73.

[78] Ibid., 35–36.

[79] Koester reaches similar conclusions about the Samaritan woman and Mary Magdalene (ibid., 48–51, 69–70).

characters – representative value also recognized by contemporary audiences familiar with conventions whereby brides represent the people of God.

This calls into question Winsor's proposal that the Gospel alludes to the Song of Songs because the Johannine tradition values women's experience. In light of the women's roles as brides, it seems more likely that the significance of John's allusions to marriage texts lies in their contribution to some other aspect of John's message. In this study, I investigate the possibility that they help to advance the Gospel's central aim, "that you may come to believe that Jesus is the Messiah, the Son of God, and that through believing you may have life in his name" (John 20:31).[80]

That Winsor never considers this possibility is perhaps understandable, since John's concern with belief that Jesus is the Messiah is not readily apparent either in the anointing story or in the resurrection appearance (the two passages studied in her book). Messianic overtones are quite prominent, however, in the bridegroom saying and in the Samaritan story. John the Baptist prefaces his testimony by reiterating, "I am not the Messiah but I have been sent ahead of him" (John 3:28). Similarly, the Samaritan story portrays Jesus as the Messiah who offers the gift of eternal life (John 4:14, 25–26). There is even some subtle potential for messianic significance in the anointing story. If John 12:3 indeed alludes to Song 1:12, then it implicitly compares Jesus to a royal figure, "the king . . . on the couch."

Fehribach, who studies all of John's stories about women, pays much more attention to this matter. From the outset, she observes that John's main concern is to characterize Jesus and to show how those who believe become God's children.[81] She then consistently demonstrates how the allusions function to portray Jesus as the messianic bridegroom and his female followers as the women in his life.[82] What Fehribach never considers, however, is why John chooses these particular passages to illustrate this point. Betrothal stories and the Song of Songs certainly treat the subject of marriage, but what do they have to do with the Messiah, God's anointed king? What prompts John to liken the Gospel's Messiah, Jesus, to the bridegroom in certain biblical texts?

Questions concerning the messianic significance of the evoked texts can be addressed using a theory articulated by Donald Juel. In his book

---

[80] Cf. John 1:12; 3:15–16, 36; 6:40, 47; 11:25–27; 17:3.
[81] Fehribach, *Women in the Life of the Bridegroom*, 17–18.
[82] Ibid., 49–52, 93, 150, 160.

Messianic Exegesis, Juel explains why first-century believers may have imputed messianic significance to passages that make no mention of a king or an anointing. He proposes that "messianic exegesis" developed in response to a tension that lay at the heart of their faith. On the one hand, the earliest Jewish believers in Jesus (along with other first-century Jews) regarded certain biblical passages – such as Gen. 49:10–12; Num. 24:17; 2 Sam. 7:10–14; Zech. 6:12; Isa. 11; Jer. 33:14–16; and Ps. 2 – as messianic prophecies.[83] On the other hand, they believed that Jesus was the Messiah.[84] Inherent in this belief is a serious contradiction. The crucified Jesus bears no resemblance to the prophesied Messiah who "shall break [the nations] with a rod of iron" (Ps. 2:9) and "execute justice and righteousness in the land" (Jer. 33:15).[85]

Juel suggests that in order to resolve this difficulty, the first believers relied on creative exegesis of messianic prophecies. This exegesis proceeded according to accepted methods of argumentation. For example, first-century exegetes assumed that since all Scripture is God's Word, it contains one unified theological message. Therefore, they felt free to interpret one passage by means of a second if both passages share identical words or phrases.[86] Paul does this in Rom. 4:1–12, enlisting Ps. 32:1–2 to support his interpretation of Gen. 15:6 because both passages contain the verb "reckon (λογίζομαι)."

According to Juel, similar methods were used to make sense of a crucified Christ. Passages reminiscent of Jesus' career were interpreted in light of acknowledged messianic prophecies on the basis of shared vocabulary.[87] For example, Gen. 22:18 can be interpreted in light of 2 Sam. 7:12 because each verse contains the term "offspring (זֶרַע; σπέρμα)." The "offspring" of 2 Sam. 7:12, the Messiah whose kingdom God will establish, is also the "offspring" of Gen. 22:18 by whom all the nations of the earth will be blessed. This connection allows Luke's Peter to contend that all the families of the earth will be blessed through the Messiah; that is, Jesus (Acts 3:25). It also allows Paul to assert that God's promise in Gen. 22:18 refers to Abraham's "offspring," the

---

[83] Donald Juel, *Messianic Exegesis: Christological Interpretation of the Old Testament in Earliest Christianity* (Philadelphia: Fortress, 1988), 16.

[84] Ibid., 24–26.

[85] Ibid., 26.

[86] Ibid., 38–46. See also Renée Bloch, "Midrash," in *Approaches to Ancient Judaism: Theory and Practice* (trans. Mary Howard Callaway; ed. William S. Green; BJS 1; Missoula, Mont.: Scholars Press, 1978), 32; Roger Le Déaut, "Apropos a Definition of Midrash" (trans. Mary Howard), *Int* 25 (1971), 269–70.

[87] Juel, *Messianic Exegesis*, 172–73.

Christ, whose death on a tree extends the blessing of Abraham to the Gentiles (Gal. 3:13–16).[88]

Since I suspect that John alludes to a bridegroom prophecy, a betrothal story, and the Song of Songs because of their messianic significance, I use Juel's theory to explain how these portions of Scripture can be interpreted with reference to the Messiah. Each of these marriage texts can be linked with an acknowledged messianic prophecy, Ps. 45, using verbal similarities. Psalm 45 celebrates the marriage of God's anointed king, the most handsome of men. His bride, a beautiful princess, is led to his palace in a joyful procession. The scene is strongly reminiscent of the wedding celebrations in Jer. 33:10–11, Gen. 29:1–20, and especially the Song of Songs.

Other twentieth-century exegetes have analyzed the shared vocabulary between Ps. 45 and the Song of Songs. Each approaches the problem with a different aim, whether to date the Psalm, to interpret it in light of the Song of Songs, or to demonstrate the dependence of both on Neo-Assyrian literary traditions.[89] None attempts to show how, on the basis of shared vocabulary, it can be argued that the Messiah of Ps. 45 also appears in the joyful procession of Jer. 33:10–11, at the well in Gen. 29:1–20, on the couch in Song 1:12, and to his lover in Song 3:1–4. I do, and I argue that messianic interpretation of these passages may well have inspired John's allusions, thus enhancing the Gospel's depiction of Jesus as the Messiah prophesied in Scripture. According to John, this Messiah is heard by a rejoicing John the Baptist, offers eternal life at a well, is anointed for burial, and appears to a searching woman – as foretold in Jer. 33, Gen. 29, and the Song of Songs.

My conclusions thus agree with those of Origen and Hippolytus in a number of ways. Their interpretation of Israel's Scriptures shares certain similarities with the interpretation evinced by John's allusions to marriage texts. Origen's concept of "harmonious patterns" and "mysteries in agreement" is closely related to a fundamental assumption of messianic exegesis: that all Scripture presents the same unified theological message. Hippolytus' belief that Song 3:1–4 foretells the

---

[88] Ibid., 84–87.

[89] F. Dijkema, "Zu Psalm 45," *ZAW* 27 (1907): 26–32; Raymond Tournay, "Les affinités du Ps. xlv avec le Cantique des Cantiques et leur interprétation messianique," in *Congress Volume: Bonn, 1962* (VTSup 9; Leiden: Brill, 1963), 173, 210–12; Oswald Lorentz, *Das althebräische Liebeslied: Untersuchungen zur Stichometrie und Redaktionsgeschichte des Hohenliedes und des 45. Psalms* (AOAT 14/1; Butzon & Bercker, 1971), 67–70; Johannes S. M. Mulder, *Studies on Psalm 45* (Oss: Witsiers, 1972), 95, 154–55.

women's experience at Jesus' tomb coincides with John's apparent opinion that the Song is a messianic prophecy. As we shall see, there is even strong evidence that both third-century scholars recognized some of the verbal links among Gen. 29, the Song of Songs, and Ps. 45. In addition, Origen's interpretation of John 4:4–42 and 12:1–8 resembles an understanding that can be attributed to the Gospel's original audience. Specifically, his contention that the Samaritan woman and Mary of Bethany represent believers does not seem far off the mark.

Compatibility with ancient exegesis generated by obsolete methods does not render my interpretation inaccessible to contemporary audiences. In the end, I show that twenty-first-century Christians do not have to accept John's messianic interpretation of marriage texts in order to hear and appreciate the echoes. It is not necessary to understand Jer. 33:10–11, Gen. 29:1–20, Song 1:12, and Song 3:1–4 as messianic prophecies in order to realize how John's allusions to these passages enhance the Gospel's portrayal of Jesus. It is also not necessary to assert that John's female characters actually symbolize the church in order to recognize how they simply exemplify believers in relationship with Christ, thus illustrating John's theme of belief. Allusions to biblical texts about marriage in the Fourth Gospel help to portray Jesus as the expected, crucified, risen, and ascending king who offers eternal life. In addition, they enhance John's depiction of believers testifying to Jesus, recognizing his post-resurrection presence, rejoicing at his coming, and joining his growing family. By echoing Jeremiah's bridegroom prophecy, Jacob's betrothal narrative, and the Song of Songs, John harmonizes the story of Jesus with Israel's Scripture in tones that can please even the twenty-first-century ear.

2

ECHOES OF SCRIPTURE, REPRESENTATIVE FIGURES, AND MESSIANIC EXEGESIS

Echoes of Scripture in the Fourth Gospel

We cannot begin the process of identifying and interpreting John's allusions to marriage texts without some idea of what an allusion is and how it works. Wendell V. Harris offers a clear and concise definition in his *Dictionary of Concepts in Literary Criticism and Theory*. According to Harris, an allusion is "the evocation of a person, character, place, event, idea, or portion of text through quotation (exact or approximate), implicit reference through similarity, explicit reference, or echo. Such evocation or suggestion is intended to lead the reader to bring some aspect of the referent to bear at that point of the originating text."[1] He further explains that "allusion is presumed to enrich meaning, pleasure being derived from the economy with which it does so."[2] In Harris' terms, the proposed allusions to be evaluated in this study evoke a portion of Israel's Scriptures by means of implicit reference through similarity.

This definition begs for immediate qualification. Who inscribes implicit references, and for whom do those references evoke a portion of a text? Who leads what reader to associate the referent with the originating text? In order to understand an allusion, it is first necessary to define its author and audience.

Once we have defined author and audience, we can then follow the basic approach suggested by Harris' two-part definition. First, we must identify the allusion. Since it consists of "the evocation of a . . . portion of text [by means of] . . . implicit reference through similarity," we must recognize and delineate similarities between the originating text and some referent, or evoked text. Second, we must interpret the allusion. According to Harris, it serves "to lead the reader to bring some aspect of

---

[1] Wendell V. Harris, "Allusion," *Dictionary of Concepts in Literary Criticism and Theory* (New York: Greenwood, 1992), 10.
[2] Ibid., 11.

the referent to bear at that point of the originating text." Therefore, we must discern how the similarities between the allusion and its referent enrich the originating text's meaning.

This basic approach presents several difficulties. One concerns how allusions are identified. An implicit reference through similarity is more obscure than an exact quotation. How does one determine that an apparent similarity to another text constitutes an allusion?[3] A second difficulty involves identifying the evoked text. If the allusion corresponds to more than one precursor text, how does one decide which text serves as the best referent? Finally, there is the difficulty of understanding the relationship between the allusion and its referent. Which aspects of the evoked text can profitably be brought to bear on the originating text?

Difficulties in identifying and interpreting allusions cannot be definitively resolved, but they can be negotiated by applying appropriate guidelines. Hays has admirably performed this task. He proposes seven tests for identifying and interpreting allusions to Scripture in Paul.[4] I have adapted and adopted these criteria, making a few modifications to account for the differences between Paul's epistolary discourse, treated by Hays, and John's narrative discourse, examined here. Because Paul and John employ different rhetorical strategies, they make slightly different uses of allusions.

I have also modified Hays' guidelines in order to clarify the identity of the Gospel's author and audience. Questions of the historical plausibility of an allusion necessarily concern the Gospel's original author and audience, while the issue of satisfaction with a given interpretation involves the understanding of a contemporary audience. Most of the following guidelines, however, can be applied to the implied author and audience.

---

[3] This question is raised with reference to the Fourth Gospel by Barnabas Lindars ("The Place of the Old Testament in the Formation of New Testament Theology," *NTS* 23 [1976], 65) and Herman N. Ridderbos (*The Gospel According to John: A Theological Commentary* [trans. John Vriend; Grand Rapids: Eerdmans, 1997], 112).

[4] Hays, *Echoes of Scripture*, 29–32. John Hollander, upon whose theory Hays models his approach, distinguishes between allusion and echo. For Hollander, an allusion is an author's fragmentary or paraphrastic citation of a text familiar to his or her audience, whereas an echo is an allusion recognized by a reader but not necessarily intended by the author (*The Figure of Echo: A Mode of Allusion in Milton and After* [Berkeley: University of California Press, 1981], 64). Due to the hypothetical nature of Paul's original audiences, Hays makes no such distinction (*Echoes of Scripture*, 29). Due to the hypothetical nature of John's author and audience, original or implied, I also do not distinguish the terms in this way.

Guidelines for identifying and interpreting allusions

Availability

This guideline for identifying allusions concerns the availability of the proposed referent to both implied author and implied audience. If the proposed referent was not available to the implied author, then he or she cannot have alluded to it. Similarly, if it was not available to the implied audience, then the implied author cannot have expected them to understand the supposed allusion.[5] Whether an author could have intended an allusion to a particular referent thus depends on the availability of the proposed referent, at least to that author.

If Israel's Scriptures were not available to John's implied author, it would be a waste of time and energy to proceed any further. It is relatively easy to settle this matter. Israel's Scriptures were certainly available to the Fourth Evangelist. In fact, they were available in three languages. Every book in the canon had been written in Hebrew and translated into Greek by the beginning of the first century B.C.E., well before the events related in the Gospel.[6] In addition, public reading of the Hebrew Scriptures was usually accompanied by a translation into the vernacular (see Neh. 8:8). In Palestine, this led to the development of Aramaic Targums.

Israel's Scriptures were not only available to the Fourth Evangelist; they were also known to him.[7] He provides thirteen formal citations of texts that can be readily identified.[8] He obviously assumes their importance for his audience.[9]

These observations raise a further question: does John refer to a Hebrew Bible or to a Greek or Aramaic translation? This question can be answered only in part. John certainly knew at least some biblical

---

[5] Hays, *Echoes of Scripture*, 29.

[6] On the dating of the Septuagint, see Emanuel Tov, "The Septuagint," in *Mikra: Text, Translation, Reading and Interpretation of the Hebrew Bible in Ancient Judaism and Early Christianity* (ed. Martin Jan Mulder; CRINT, sec. 2, vol. 1; Philadelphia: Fortress, 1988), 162.

[7] I use a masculine pronoun to designate the Gospel's implied author since John 21:24 indicates that he is a man. For the sake of convenience, I will occasionally refer to him as "John."

[8] Isa. 40:3 in John 1:23; Ps. 69:9 in John 2:17; Exod. 16:4 and Ps. 48:23–25 in John 6:31; Isa. 54:13 in John 6:45; Ps. 82:6 in John 10:34; Ps. 118: 25–26 in John 12:13; Zech. 9:9 in John 12:15; Isa. 53:1 in John 12:38; Isa. 6:10 in John 12:40; Ps. 41:9 in John 13:18; Pss 35:19 and 69:4 in John 15:25; Ps. 22:18 in John 19:24; Zech. 12:10 in John 19:37.

[9] Culpepper, *Anatomy*, 219–20.

books in a Greek translation.[10] Four of his citations correspond closely to extant versions: Ps. 69:9 in John 2:17; Ps. 82:6 in John 10:34; Isa. 53:1 in John 12:38; Ps. 22:18 in John 19:24.[11]

It is possible that John's implied author might also have known Hebrew and Aramaic versions. That he knows at least some Hebrew and Aramaic is evident from his use of terms like "Rabbi" (1:38), "Messiah" (1:41; 4:25), and "Rabbouni" (20:16). That some of his audience knows only Greek is evident from the fact that he follows these terms with a Greek translation.[12]

Evidence for the implied author's familiarity with Hebrew or Aramaic Scriptures can be gleaned from those citations that do not exactly conform to any extant Greek text. Unfortunately, that evidence is somewhat difficult to interpret. Several scholars theorize that John sometimes provides his own Greek translation of a Hebrew or Aramaic source. Both Braun and Edwin D. Freed point out that some of John's formula citations resemble the wording of the Masoretic Text or one of the Targums.[13] Günter Reim and M. J. J. Menken also suppose that John occasionally reverts to the Hebrew Bible.[14] Bruce G. Schuchard, on the other hand, concludes that John exclusively cites a Greek text, often editing it to suit his purposes. To complicate the issue, Schuchard agrees that John probably knew Hebrew and Aramaic traditions. Still, he argues that the Evangelist cited only the Greek text known to his audience.[15]

---

[10] It is impossible to determine exactly which Greek version (or versions) John knew. The Greek text reproduced in this study is taken from *Septuaginta* (ed. Alfred Rahlfs; Stuttgart: Deutsche Bibelgesellschaft, 1979). Significant variants are discussed in Rahlfs' critical notes, as well as notes by Joseph Ziegler in *Jeremias, Baruch, Threni, Epistula Jeremiae* (Vetus Testamentum graecum auctoritate Academiae Scientiarum Gottingensis editum 15. Göttingen: Vandenhoeck & Ruprecht, 1957). I refer to these variants in the footnotes.

[11] Edwin D. Freed, *Old Testament Quotations in the Gospel of John* (SNT 11; Leiden: Brill, 1965), 126. Psalm chapter and verse numbers differ in the LXX. For example, the verses reckoned as Pss 69:9, 82:6, and 22:18 in the NRSV are reckoned as Pss 68:10, 81:6, and 21:19 in the LXX. Unless otherwise noted, I refer to the standard reckoning used in English translations.

[12] Ibid., 218–19.

[13] Braun, *Jean le théologien 2*, 3–21; Freed, *OT Quotations*, 26.

[14] Günter Reim, *Studien zum alttestamentlichen Hintergrund des Johannesevangeliums* (SNTSMS 22; Cambridge: Cambridge University Press, 1974), 90; Maarten J. J. Menken, *Old Testament Quotations in the Fourth Gospel: Studies in Textual Form* (CBET 15; Kampen: Pharos, 1996), 205–6.

[15] Bruce G. Schuchard, *Scripture within Scripture: The Interrelationship of Form and Function in the Explicit Old Testament Citations in the Gospel of John* (SBLDS 133; Atlanta: Scholars Press, 1992), 151–56.

It is not necessary to settle this matter for the purposes of this study. Since John's implied author alludes to the Scriptures in Greek for the benefit of a Greek-speaking audience, a Greek Bible should be considered the only possible allusive referent. His possible familiarity with a Hebrew Bible is a factor – and a minor factor, at that – only for considering how he interprets the evoked texts.[16]

Volume

This criterion for identifying allusions focuses on how they attract an audience's attention. Hays briefly mentions three ways:

(a) *Correspondence*; that is, the degree of correspondence between allusion and referent. According to Harris, correspondence between an originating text and a precursor text constitutes the allusion. According to Hays, the greater the degree of correspondence, the clearer the allusion.[17] If an allusion corresponds to more than one precursor text, the text to which it corresponds the most should be preferred as the referent.

Hays rightly assumes that an epistler like Paul chiefly uses diction and syntax to establish a verbal correspondence with a precursor text.[18] An evangelist like John can likewise allude by means of verbal correspondence. Of course, the LXX necessarily constitutes the precursor text for any verbal correspondence between John's Gospel and Israel's Scriptures.

An evangelist like John is not limited to allusion by means of verbal correspondence, however. Narrative discourse permits the evocation of other details – such as plot, characters, and setting – by means of "circumstantial correspondence."[19] Unlike verbal correspondence, circumstantial correspondence does not require that the precursor text share the language of the originating text. It depends only on idiosyncratic elements of a precursor story or scene.

The allusion to Ps. 69:21 in John 19:28–30 provides a good example of both verbal and circumstantial correspondence. John 19:28–30 reads as follows:

---

[16] See below, pp. 111, 113, 116, 117. The Hebrew text reproduced in this study is taken from *BHS*.

[17] Hays, *Echoes of Scripture*, 29.

[18] Ibid.

[19] Robert L. Brawley makes a similar point when discussing correspondence between Luke's narrative and Israel's Scriptures (*Text to Text Pours Forth Speech: Voices of Scripture in Luke-Acts* [Indiana Studies in Biblical Literature 18; Bloomington: Indiana University Press, 1995], 13).

> After this, when Jesus knew that all was now finished, he said
> (in order to fulfill the scripture), "I am thirsty (διψῶ)." A jar
> full of sour wine (τοῦ ὄξους) was standing there. So they put
> a sponge full of the wine (ὄξους) on a branch of hyssop and
> held it to his mouth. When Jesus had received the wine (τὸ
> ὄξος), he said, "It is finished."

It is generally agreed that this passage echoes Ps. 69:21:

> They gave me poison for food,
> and for my thirst they gave me vinegar to drink (ὄξος εἰς τὴν
> δίψαν).[20]

The allusion is marked in part by the reiteration of two significant
words from the evoked text, the verb διψῶ and the noun ὄξος. In
addition, each passage depicts similar circumstances. In both scenes,
the ὄξος is given to a suffering man by an anonymous group of
tormentors. Here, circumstantial correspondence may be John's way
of showing that this episode does indeed fulfill the Scripture.

It should be noted that this circumstantial correspondence serves to
strengthen the connections already established by two verbal links. It
would be much more difficult to argue that John alludes to Ps. 69:21 if
the words διψῶ and ὄξος did not appear in the narrative. Circumstantial
correspondence alone does not constitute a clear allusion. Nevertheless,
it considerably enhances the volume of verbal correspondence, and may
even draw attention to the echo.

The volume of various allusions in the Fourth Gospel can be profitably compared to the volume of those same allusions in one or more of
the first three Gospels. Sometimes, certain aspects of a Johannine story
that resemble a passage from Israel's Scriptures may fail to appear in
that story's Synoptic parallels. This phenomenon serves as an additional
indicator of two possibilities: either John's implied author has added
these details in order to stress an allusion, or a common tradition
contained certain allusive details that John has retained. This holds true
whether similarities among John and the other Gospels are attributed to
direct dependence or shared sources.[21] For example, Matthew (27:48),

---

[20] See, e.g., NA[27], 785.

[21] The issue is a matter of some debate. According to Frans Neirynck, John's sources
include the Synoptic Gospels ("John and the Synoptics," in *L'évangile de Jean: Sources,
rédaction, théologie* [ed. Marinus de Jonge; BETL 44; Louvain: Louvain University Press,
1977], 106). Peder Borgen counters that John's sources included traditions known also to
the Synoptic Evangelists ("John and the Synoptics," in *The Interrelations of the Gospels*
[ed. David L. Dungan; BETL 95; Louvain: Louvain University Press, 1990], 408–37.) For

Mark (15:36), and Luke (23:36) all report that the dying Jesus was given sour wine (ὄξος) to drink. Apparently, all four Gospels somehow share a source that includes this episode. The Synoptic accounts differ slightly from John's version of the story, however. None of them reiterates the word ὄξος three times, as does John. In addition, none of them uses the word διψῶ or indicates that Jesus' thirst fulfilled the Scriptures. John's deviations from the Synoptic accounts indicate that John lays particular stress on this allusion.

It should be noted that John's implied audience would have recognized how John alone stresses this allusion only if they had access to another passion narrative. Deviations from the Synoptic accounts do not necessarily mark an allusion for an implied audience. They simply provide evidence that the story was made to conform to an allusive referent.

Another way to judge volume involves allusions that correspond closely with their precursor texts. Such allusions may seem somewhat awkward in the context of the originating text, especially when that context relates a supposedly cohesive story. Instead of harmonizing with John's account, these allusions resound to the strains of someone else's tale. This phenomenon may be termed "dissonance." Dissonant details often contrast so strongly with the originating text that they become powerful signals of an allusion. They may also serve as clear indicators of its precursor text. The absence of dissonant details does not preclude the presence of an allusion. Their presence, however, draws attention to the figure of speech at work.[22]

The criterion of correspondence not only aids in identifying an allusion; it also serves as a starting point for interpretation. Areas of explicit or "stated" correspondence establish an initial relationship between the originating and precursor texts. Once established, this relationship may suggest instances of "unstated" correspondence; that is, aspects of the precursor text not explicitly evoked in the originating text, yet similar in some way. Corresponding details, both stated and unstated, then indicate which aspects of the referent may profitably be brought to bear on the originating text.[23]

---

a review of the issues, see D. Moody Smith, *John among the Gospels: The Relationship in Twentieth-Century Research* (Minneapolis: Fortress, 1992).

[22] See also Riffaterre, *Semiotics*, 5, 164–65. Riffaterre refers to this phenomenon as "ungrammaticalities." Brawley notes it (*Text to Text*, 14), and Winsor uses it as one of her chief criteria (*A King Is Bound*, 8–9). Hays makes no mention of it, perhaps because Paul never uses it.

[23] Hays uses the term "unstated correspondence" to refer to metalepsis (*Echoes of Scripture*, 20).

(b) *Prominence*. It is more likely that an author would allude to a familiar text than to an obscure referent. Prominence increases plausibility. The more prominent the precursor text, the stronger the allusion to that text.[24]

Of course, we cannot establish the prominence of a text based on a proposed allusion to that text and then use prominence as a criterion to confirm the presence of that allusion. Other evidence must indicate the prominence of a proposed referent. For example, if the evidence suggests that John's implied author regards a proposed referent as a messianic prophecy, then the prominence of that referent can be confirmed. As we shall see, this argument can be made in the case of Ps. 69:21, echoed in John 19:28–30. John probably alludes to Ps. 69 because of its messianic significance.

(c) *Rhetorical emphasis*. Presumably, an author might highlight an allusion by means of strategic placement.[25] Paul might emphasize an allusion by placing it at a rhetorical climax in his argument. John, on the other hand, might do so by locating it at a focal point in his narrative or by several repetitions of an important word from the evoked text. John emphasizes the allusion to Ps. 69:21 in at least three ways. First, it appears near the climax of the story. Jesus is about to die; he knows that all is now finished (John 19:28). Second, the narrator explicitly states that when Jesus says, "διψῶ," he fulfills the Scripture (John 19:28). Third, the word ὄξος is repeated three times (John 19:29–30). These emphases add to the evidence for the allusion.

Recurrence

Hays suggests that a proposed allusion whose referent or its context is frequently cited by Paul merits additional consideration.[26] Recurrence provides additional evidence for the importance (or prominence) of a precursor text to an implied author. Psalm 69 offers a good example of a text cited more than once in the Fourth Gospel, as John explicitly quotes it on two occasions (Ps. 69:9 in John 2:17; Ps. 69:4 in John 15:25). On the basis of this evidence, a case can be made that Ps. 69 was important to John. Therefore, it is not improbable that he alludes to it in his crucifixion scene.

This test neither confirms proposed allusions that do conform nor rules out those that do not conform. If a proposed allusion's precursor

---

[24] Ibid., 30.   [25] Ibid.   [26] Ibid.

text or its immediate context is cited frequently in the Fourth Gospel, however, this can add to the evidence supporting the allusion's authenticity.

Thematic coherence

This first test for a proposed interpretation considers how well that interpretation coheres with the context of the allusion's originating text. Does it enhance the themes developed both in the passage containing the proposed allusion and in the broader context of the entire book?[27] In the case of Ps. 69:21 in John 19:28–30, the answer is clear: this allusion helps John to accomplish his primary agenda. It indicates that Jesus fulfills a messianic prophecy, so that John's audience "may believe that Jesus is the Messiah" (John 20:31).

John's allusions are of course capable of enhancing more than just the Gospel's themes. They can also help depict a setting, portray a character, and illustrate the plot. They can add to a scene's irony or contribute to a narrative motif. They can even relate aspects of John's story to concepts evoked by a precursor text, thus facilitating the creation of a symbol or metaphor.

The criterion of thematic coherence assumes that an allusion's consonance with the discourse of a text enriches that text's meaning. A thorough exploration of thematic coherence thus constitutes the primary interpretive task. Accordingly, my interpretation investigates how John's allusions to marriage texts enhance the Gospel's settings, characters, plot, ironies, themes, motifs, symbols, and metaphors.

Hays also considers how images and ideas from the precursor text within its context illuminate the argument of the originating text.[28] Here I depart from his approach. I question whether this is an appropriate way to understand John's allusions. What controls John's intertextual practice is not the images and ideas present in a precursor passage but rather his interpretation of the evoked text and how that interpretation suits his purposes. As we shall see, John alludes to Ps. 69:21 because he regards this verse as a messianic prophecy and because it aptly describes an event in the life of Jesus. He is not primarily concerned with the mood of the psalm as a whole.[29]

---

[27] Ibid.   [28] Ibid.

[29] See below, pp. 43–44. Elisabeth A. Johnson takes a similar approach in her analysis of biblical allusions in Luke's birth narrative ("Barrenness, Birth, and Biblical Allusions in Luke 1–2" [Ph.D. diss., Princeton Theological Seminary, 2000], 16–19).

Historical plausibility

Hays presents this test as a second guideline for interpreting allusions. "Could [the author] have intended the alleged meaning effect?" he asks. "Could his readers have understood it? . . . This test, historical in character, necessarily requires hypothetical constructs of what might have been intended and grasped by particular first-century figures."[30] This is the only criterion that involves reconstructing John's original author and audience – their historical setting, their interpretation of the evoked texts, their understanding of the allusion – on the basis of outside sources. Such constructs need not be elaborate. They must only render the proposed allusion and its interpretation historically plausible. For John as well as for Paul, I contend with Hays that they ought to account for his Jewish identity. They should demonstrate that "his readings could hold a respectable place within the discourse of Israel's faith."[31]

History of interpretation

"Have other readers, both critical and precritical, heard the same echoes?" asks Hays.[32] If others have recognized the same allusions I perceive, this indicates that my proposals are perhaps not so far-fetched. Someone else agrees that they constitute reasonable inferences from the text or plausible wordplays by its implied author.

This criterion is useful mostly for positive confirmation. As Hays points out, it "should rarely be used as a negative test to exclude proposed echoes that commend themselves on other grounds."[33] Hays also avers that whereas this test provides confirmation for identifying allusions, it is of little use in interpreting them.[34] My interpretation will certainly have to contend with the interpretations of others. Since I have a different perspective and may use different methods, however, it will not necessarily agree with them.

Satisfaction

Finally, and perhaps most importantly, the proposed allusion and its interpretation need to make sense. They must offer "a good account of

---

[30] Hays, *Echoes of Scripture*, 30.   [31] Ibid., 31.
[32] Ibid.   [33] Ibid.   [34] Ibid.

the experience of a contemporary community of competent readers."[35]
Can we tune our ears to echoes generated nearly two thousand years
ago? Will we resonate with their frequencies, or do our different
conventions put us on another wavelength altogether?

Representative figures in the Fourth Gospel

In the process of identifying and interpreting John's allusions to marriage texts, two important issues emerge. The first has to do with Hays'
criterion of thematic coherence (which evaluates the way an allusion
enhances the discourse of its originating text) and involves the role
played by John's female characters. Are they representative figures, as
so many scholars assert?[36] If so, what or whom do they represent? How
does any representative value cohere with John's allusions to marriage
texts?

Harris does not define "representative figure" in his dictionary. The
term is used by Raymond F. Collins, who equates representative
figures with "symbolic personages."[37] Harris does define a symbol –
as "anything that, through convention, resemblance, or association, is
recognized as representing or standing for a second thing."[38]

Again, this definition must be qualified. The passive verb *is recognized* indicates that symbolic value is attributed by audiences. It takes
an audience to recognize conventions. It takes an audience to be
familiar enough with a symbolic referent to realize its resemblance to
or its association with a symbol. Therefore, a crucial step in interpreting
symbols is identifying their audience.

As a type of symbol, then, a representative figure is a character
understood by a particular audience to represent something or someone
else; that is, to designate a symbolic referent. According to Harris,
representative figures can be recognized in three ways: they conform
to conventions of symbolic representation, they resemble their symbolic
referents, or they can be associated with their referents by some other
means. According to Koester, John uses all three ways in various
fashions to develop symbols and representative figures in the Fourth

---

[35] Ibid., 32.   [36] See above, p. 16, n. 76.

[37] Raymond F. Collins, "The Representative Figures of the Fourth Gospel," *DRev* 94
(1976), 27; repr. in *These Things Have Been Written: Studies in the Fourth Gospel*
(Louvain Theological and Pastoral Monographs 2; Louvain: Peeters, 1990). Collins
believes that John's characters were initially developed by a homilist who used them to
typify various faith responses to Jesus ("Representative Figures," 29–32).

[38] Harris, "Symbol," *Dictionary of Concepts*, 398.

Gospel. In effect, Koester delineates various aspects of convention, resemblance, and association as he discusses criteria for recognizing John's symbols and representative figures.

Convention

One of the ways for a given audience to identify a symbol is for them to perceive that it conforms to some convention of symbolic representation. Conventions develop when the resemblance between two different entities is easily discerned and consistently exploited. It becomes common to use one (usually the more concrete entity) as a symbol of the other (usually the more abstract). Knowledge of such conventions enables interpreters to recognize many symbols, including representative figures.

Koester explains John's use of convention in terms of his reliance on several conventional Jewish symbols. Like other Jewish authors, John uses light to symbolize God, life, and understanding (e.g., 1:1–9; 3:19–21; 7:52; 8:12; 9:5; 11:9–10; 12:35–36, 46). Darkness, on the other hand, represents evil, death, and ignorance (e.g., 1:5; 3:2, 19). Bread refers to spiritual sustenance (6:1–59), the vine stands for God's people (15:1–17), and the shepherd indicates their leader or leaders (10:11–18).[39]

Koester does not extend his observations to conventions regarding representative figures. Such conventions can be recognized, however. For example, many interpreters believe that several characters in Jewish literature symbolize a Jewish community in dire straits. Daniel is thought to represent Jews whose religious practices were proscribed by Antiochus IV, while Judith seems to personify a Jewish group attacked by a Gentile army.[40] Esther, Mordecai, and Susanna apparently symbolize Diaspora Jews threatened by pogroms and endangered by assimilation.[41] Interestingly, the man born blind in John 9 is often

---

[39] Koester, *Symbolism*, 233–34. See also Severino Pancaro, *The Law in the Fourth Gospel: The Torah and the Gospel, Moses and Jesus, Judaism and Christianity According to John* (*NovTSup* 42; Leiden: Brill, 1975), 454–87.

[40] Louis F. Hartman, *The Book of Daniel* (AB 23; Garden City: Doubleday, 1978), 61; Amy-Jill Levine, "Sacrifice and Salvation: Otherness and Domestication in the Book of Judith," in *No One Spoke Ill of Her: Essays on Judith* (ed. James C. Vanderkam; Atlanta: Scholars Press, 1992), 18–23.

[41] Sidnie Ann White, "Esther: A Feminine Model for Jewish Diaspora," in *Gender and Difference in Ancient Israel* (ed. Peggy L. Day; Minneapolis: Fortress, 1989), 166–73; Amy-Jill Levine, "'Hemmed in on Every Side': Jews and Women in the Book of Susanna," in *Reading From This Place* (ed. Fernando F. Segovia and Mary Ann Tolbert;

understood in terms of this convention. He is thought to represent Johannine believers whose faith in Jesus comes under scrutiny.[42] An ancient or modern audience familiar with a convention whereby an oppressed yet courageous protagonist represents the persecuted faithful might be inclined to recognize its use in John 9.

It should be noted that conformity to convention does not automatically impart representative value. Similarities between the man born blind and Daniel or Judith do not establish him as a symbol. Other factors must also be considered.

Resemblance

A second way to identify a symbol is to recognize how it resembles its symbolic referent. In his discussion of representative figures, Koester notes that John endows them with distinctive traits. These distinctive traits fit them for representative roles.[43] In fact, they cause John's characters to resemble various groups of people known to his audience, thus enabling them to exemplify those groups. For example, the healing of the man born blind qualifies him to represent Johannine believers whose encounter with Jesus has led them from the darkness of unbelief to the light of faith.[44] His blindness is easily recognized as symbolic, given John's symbolic use of blindness in John 9:4–5, 39–41. It adds to the evidence that the man functions as a representative figure.

While a character's resembling a particular group might enhance representative value, it does not guarantee that the character symbolizes that group. It may indicate some other degree of representation. It is possible for a character to exemplify or typify a group without necessarily standing in as its symbol. Koester explains these three levels of representation with respect to the Fourth Gospel's characters. First, they are significant in their own right, as unique individuals in the Gospel's story. Second, they may represent groups of people known to John's author and audience. Third, they can typify a response to Jesus

---

Minneapolis: Fortress, 1995), 175–90. George W. E. Nicklesburg argues that Esther, Daniel 3 and 6, and Susanna are stories of the vindication and exaltation of a righteous person who remains faithful during persecution (*Resurrection, Immortality, and Eternal Life in Intertestamental Judaism* [HTS 26; Cambridge, Mass.: Harvard University Press, 1972], 48–58).

[42] This idea was first proposed by J. Louis Martyn (*History and Theology in the Fourth Gospel* [Nashville: Abingdon, 1968], 30–59).

[43] Koester, *Symbolism*, 35.   [44] Ibid., 65.

described elsewhere in the narrative.[45] It should be noted that only the second level is strictly symbolic.[46] A type is not necessarily a symbolic representative. In addition, it is possible for a character to exemplify a group of people without symbolizing that group.[47] The strongest indicators of strictly symbolic value are characteristics that, understood literally, make little or no sense.[48]

Such characteristics include anachronistic situations. If a representative figure resembles a group thought to have existed in John's day and not in Jesus', certain characteristics of that figure may seem awkward within the context of John's story about Jesus. In his book *History and Theology in the Fourth Gospel*, J. Louis Martyn points out such an anachronism in the story of the man born blind. He notes that the Jews articulate an official policy concerning those who confess that Jesus is the Messiah: they are put out of the synagogue (v. 22; cf. 12:42; 16:2). Martyn suggests that this policy was actually instated, not during Jesus' lifetime, but in John's day.[49]

This theory is not universally accepted. Reuven Kimelman points out that there is no other unambiguous historical evidence for Jewish exclusion of Christians. Jews who believed in Jesus may have left their synagogues under their own volition.[50] The most we can say about passages like John 9:22; 12:42; 16:2 is that they reflect the subjective experience, if not the actual situation, of Johannine believers.[51] This sense of marginalization undoubtedly provides the background for John's story of the man born blind. Martyn writes, "In the two-level drama of John 9 the man born blind plays not only the part of a Jew

---

[45] Ibid., 35. The idea that John's characters typify a response to Jesus has been articulated by Eva Krafft ("Die Personen des Johannesevangeliums," *EvT* 16 [1956]: 18–32) and Raymond Collins ("Representative Figures," 31), and developed by Culpepper (*Anatomy*, 145–48).

[46] See my review of Craig R. Koester, *Symbolism in the Fourth Gospel*, *Koinonia Journal* 9 (1997), 190.

[47] Teresa Okure contends that John's characters function as examples without symbolizing anything (*The Johannine Approach to Mission: A Contextual Study of John 4:1–42* [WUNT 31; Tübingen: Mohr Siebeck, 1988], 111, n. 63). While not all of John's characters represent someone or something else, convincing arguments can be (and have been) made that some of them do.

[48] Cf. Koester, *Symbolism*, 8. As David W. Wead avers, one should be cautious of finding symbols where the text does not call attention to them (*The Literary Devices in John's Gospel* [Theologischen Dissertationen 4; Basel: Reinhart, 1970], 27).

[49] Martyn, *History and Theology*, 30–59.

[50] Reuven Kimelman, "*Birkat Ha-Minim* and the Lack of Evidence for an Anti-Christian Jewish Prayer in Late Antiquity," in *Jewish and Christian Self-Definition* (ed. E. P. Sanders et al.; Philadelphia: Fortress, 1981), II:226–44, 391–403.

[51] Reinhartz, *Befriending the Beloved Disciple*, 39–50.

in Jerusalem healed by Jesus of Nazareth, but also the part of Jews known to John who have become members of the separated church because of the messianic faith."[52] Because they have confessed openly that Jesus is the Messiah, they feel excluded from the synagogue – as is the man born blind.

Koester agrees with Martyn that representative figures often face anachronistic situations. Some, like the man born blind, are put out of the synagogue. Others must cope with Jesus' absence, another situation more characteristic of John's community than of Jesus' disciples. Lazarus' grieving sisters complain that, had Jesus been present, their brother would not have died (11:21, 32); Jesus' disciple Thomas has difficulty believing without seeing (20:24–29); even the man born blind must endure an interrogation without knowing Jesus' whereabouts (9:12). According to Koester, these figures exemplify the struggles of believers living between the resurrection and the Parousia.[53]

An obvious anachronistic situation thus indicates a character's representative value. It also highlights its resemblance to its symbolic referent. In the case of the man born blind, it establishes him as a representative of those separated from the synagogue because they confess that Jesus is the Messiah.

Association

Harris' third way to identify a symbol is to recognize ways the symbol is associated with its referent. Koester points out two ways that John uses to associate his representative figures with particular groups of people. First, he comments that John often introduces a character by identifying him or her as a group member. Second, he contends that when John refers to such characters using the plural pronouns ἡμεῖς or ὑμεῖς, it further implies that they represent that group.[54] John thus uses both direct identification and plural references to associate a representative character with a familiar group. Since it makes little or no sense to use plural pronouns to refer to an individual, they constitute another strong indicator of representative value.

Koester shows how the character of Nicodemus illustrates both techniques. John 3:1 introduces Nicodemus as "a Pharisee" and "a leader of the Jews," thus identifying him with the Pharisees and Jewish

---

[52] Martyn, *History and Theology*, 41.
[53] Koester, *Symbolism*, 35–36, 64–66, 70–71.
[54] Ibid., 35.

authorities as a group. In verse 2, Nicodemus speaks for this group by using the first-person plural pronoun ἡμεῖς. Jesus reciprocates in vv. 11–12 by addressing him with the second-person plural pronoun ὑμεῖς.[55] It makes little sense for Jesus to address Nicodemus in the plural unless Nicodemus is the representative of a group. The pronoun ὑμεῖς indicates that Nicodemus represents the Pharisees. His representative value is further confirmed by his direct identification as a Pharisee and his self-reference in the plural.

I would suggest a third means of associating a representative figure with a symbolic referent: allusion to a biblical character already considered to be a representative figure. By associating one of his characters with a representative figure from Scripture, John transfers the representative value of that figure to his own character. John's portrayal of Nathanael provides a good example. In John 1:47, Jesus identifies Nathanael as "an Israelite in whom there is no deceit." This identification suggests that Nathanael may indeed represent all such Israelites. Jesus then tells Nathanael, "You will see (ὄψεσθε) heaven opened and the angels of God ascending and descending upon the Son of Man" (John 1:51). Jesus addresses Nathanael in the plural, further indicating his representative function.[56] In addition, John alludes to Gen. 28:12, which describes Jacob's vision at Bethel in very similar terms. This allusion associates Nathanael with Jacob, Israel's patriarch and premier representative. John thus invites audiences aware of Jacob's representative value to transfer it to Nathanael. Like Jacob, Nathanael also represents Israel – as indicated by Jesus' greeting in verse 47.

Messianic exegesis in the Fourth Gospel

The question of representative value as an aspect of thematic coherence is not the only issue raised in the process of identifying and interpreting John's allusions to marriage texts. A second has to do with the criterion of prominence. Why does John allude to certain texts about marriage? Why were they important to him? In order to answer this question, we must try to determine how he interprets them.

Much has been written about how John interprets Israel's Scriptures, a good deal of it in the wake of pioneering research by C. H. Dodd, Barnabas Lindars, and C. K. Barrett. In his book *According to the Scriptures*, first published in 1952, Dodd sets forth the biblical

---

[55] Ibid., 45–46.   [56] See also ibid., 68.

testimonia used by the first Christians to articulate their theology.[57] Lindars' 1961 monograph, *New Testament Apologetic*, examines the stages of interpretation that ensued as each passage was used to answer various arguments against Christian precepts.[58] Both Dodd and Lindars contend that the New Testament writers were chiefly interested in theological concepts that could be gleaned from Israel's Scriptures and applied to the life and work of Jesus.[59] Meanwhile, Barrett had already laid a foundation for understanding John's theology as the exposition of a comprehensive understanding of biblical themes such as redemption (John 1:29) and sanctification (John 7:37).[60] Successive studies have built on this foundation by exploring how John develops the theology of Israel's Scriptures.[61]

I wish to experiment with a different approach. As John R. Donahue observes, "Biblical theology has always been the child of the marriage of reigning exegetical methods to theological questions of a given period."[62] This suggests that the enterprise of understanding the

---

[57] C. H. Dodd, *According to the Scriptures: The Substructure of New Testament Theology* (London: Nisbet, 1952).

[58] Barnabas Lindars, *New Testament Apologetic: The Doctrinal Significance of the Old Testament Quotations* (Philadelphia: Westminster, 1961).

[59] Dodd, *According to the Scriptures*, 126–33; Lindars, *New Testament Apologetic*, 16–17.

[60] C. K. Barrett, "The Old Testament in the Fourth Gospel," *JTS* 48 (1947): 155–69.

[61] See, e.g., Richard Morgan, "Fulfillment in the Fourth Gospel: The Old Testament Foundations," *Int* 11 (1957), 164; Merrill C. Tenney, "The Old Testament and the Fourth Gospel," *BSac* 120 (1963): 300–308; C. H. Dodd, *Historical Tradition in the Fourth Gospel* (Cambridge: Cambridge University Press, 1965), 31–49; C. F. D. Moule, "Fulfillment Words in the New Testament: Use and Abuse," *NTS* 14 (1968), 302; D. Moody Smith, "The Use of the Old Testament in the New," in *The Use of the Old Testament in the New and Other Essays* (ed. J. M. Efird; Durham, N.C.: Duke University Press, 1972), 53–54; C. van der Waal, "The Gospel According to John and the Old Testament," *NeoT* 6 (1972): 28–47; Wayne A. Meeks, "'Am I a Jew?' Johannine Christianity and Judaism," in *Christianity, Judaism, and Other Greco-Roman Cults: Part 1, New Testament* (ed. Jacob Neusner; SJLA 12; Leiden: Brill, 1975), 173–76; Schneiders, "Resurrection Narrative," I:xxxv; Richard N. Longenecker, *Biblical Exegesis in the Apostolic Period* (Grand Rapids: Eerdmans, 1975), 152–57; D. A. Carson, "John and the Johannine Epistles," in *It Is Written: Scripture Citing Scripture* (ed. D. A. Carson and H. G. M. Williamson; Cambridge: Cambridge University Press, 1988), 245–64; Martin Hengel, "Die Schriftauslegung des 4. Evangeliums auf dem Hintergrund der urchristlichen Exegese," *Jahrbuch zur biblische Theologie* 4 (1989): 249–88; Hanson, *Interpretation of Scripture*, 171 and *Prophetic Gospel*, 246; Schuchard, *Scripture within Scripture*, 155–56; Johannes Beutler, "The Use of 'Scripture' in the Gospel of John," in *Exploring the Gospel of John* (ed. R. Alan Culpepper and C. Clifton Black; Louisville: Westminster John Knox, 1996), 147; Andreas Obermann, *Die christologische Erfüllung der Schrift im Johannesevangelium: Eine Untersuchung zur johanneischen Hermeneutik anhand der Schriftzitate* (WUNT 2/83; Tübingen: Mohr Siebeck, 1996).

[62] John R. Donahue, "The Changing Shape of New Testament Theology," *HBT* 11 (1989), 21.

theological interpretation of Israel's Scriptures in the Fourth Gospel should begin with an accurate identification of the theological questions that prompted it and the exegetical methods that yielded it. The distillation of theological themes and typological patterns in order to develop various points of Christian doctrine reflects the exegetical methods and theological issues of modern scholarship, but not necessarily those of the Fourth Gospel.

John's theological questions

Not one of the scholars who continue the work of Dodd and Barrett with respect to John's Gospel presumes the central importance of the confession that Jesus is the Messiah. For John, however, this confession is the primary theological issue. "Was Jesus the Christ? And how could he be the Christ, he who, in his (supposed) descent, conduct, and death on the cross in no respect conformed to what [John's contemporaries] pictured to themselves, or could picture to themselves, as the Messiah?"[63]

John certainly believes that Jesus is indeed the Messiah. He peppers his Gospel with declarations to that effect. In John 1:41, Andrew tells his brother Simon, "'We have found the Messiah' (which is translated Anointed)." In John 4:25–26, the Samaritan woman says, "'I know that Messiah is coming' (who is called Christ)." Jesus replies, "I am he, the one who is speaking to you." In John 11:27, Martha of Bethany confesses, "Yes, Lord, I believe that you are the Messiah, the Son of God, the one coming into the world." Most significantly, Jesus' messianic identity lies at the heart of John's stated purpose: "that you may believe that Jesus is the Messiah, the Son of God" (John 20:31).

John uses two words for Messiah: Μεσσίας and χριστός. Μεσσίας is a Greek transliteration of the Hebrew מָשִׁיחַ, which means "anointed" – χριστός in Greek. According to Israel's Scriptures, kings (1 Sam. 16:1–13; 2 Sam. 5:3; 1 Kings 1:39; 2 Kings 11:12; 23:30), priests (Lev. 4:3, 5, 16; Ps. 133:2), and prophets (1 Kings 19:18) were anointed with oil to symbolize their consecration. For John, the term "Messiah" clearly has royal connotations.[64] John's Jesus is never explicitly portrayed as an anointed priest. He is called a prophet, but only three times (John 4:19; 6:14; 9:17). Moreover, each of these acknowledgments precedes a more conclusive declaration: Jesus is "the Messiah"

---

[63] Ridderbos, *Gospel According to John*, 10.
[64] Cf. Juel, *Messianic Exegesis*, 9–11.

(4:25–26); the "Holy One of God" (6:69); the "Son of Man" (9:35–38). In contrast, John consistently portrays Jesus, the "anointed one," as a king. He introduces royal imagery early in the narrative when Nathanael declares, "You are the King of Israel!" (John 1:49). Jesus' kingship then comes to the fore as he enters Jerusalem and is tried and executed there.[65] When he rides into town on a colt, a crowd hails him as "the King of Israel" (John 12:15). His trial before Pilate concerns whether he is "the King of the Jews" (18:33–38), it is as "the King of the Jews" that Pilate offers to release him (18:39), and it is as "King of the Jews" that the soldiers mock him (19:2–5). Finally, Jesus is placarded "King of the Jews" as he hangs on the cross (19:19).

John's Jesus does not resemble the kind of royal Messiah expected by other Roman subjects – a Messiah who would defeat Israel's oppressors and restore David's dynasty. *Fourth Ezra*, written ca. 100 C.E., foretells the advent of a Davidic Messiah who will condemn the Romans for their wickedness and save the remnant of Israel (*4 Ezra* 12:31–34; cf. 7:28–29; 11:37–12:1; 13:3–13, 25–52; 14:9).[66] More predictions come from the author of the *Psalms of Solomon*, who apparently survived Pompey's invasion of Jerusalem (*Pss. Sol.* 2:1, 2, 26–29; 8:16–18; 17:12).[67] *Psalms of Solomon* 17 prophesies salvation from Gentile oppressors by a victorious king, a descendant of David (v. 21), the "Lord Messiah" (v. 32). Biblical prophecies about a Davidic king – sometimes an anointed king – are marshaled to help describe this Messiah. He will "smash the arrogance of sinners like a potter's jar" and "shatter all their substance with an iron rod" (v. 23) as does the Lord's anointed in Ps. 2:9.[68] "He will strike the earth with the word of his mouth" (v. 36) like the shoot from Jesse's stump prophesied in Isa. 11:4.[69]

---

[65] Cf. ibid., 12–13.

[66] The date of *4 Ezra* is not widely disputed. See Bruce M. Metzger, "4 Ezra," in *OTP* I:520. As Michael E. Stone observes, the function of the Messiah in *4 Ezra* is judicial, not military ("The Question of the Messiah in 4 Ezra," in *Judaisms and Their Messiahs* [ed. Jacob Neusner, William S. Green, and Ernest Frerichs; Cambridge: Cambridge University Press, 1984], 217). I would point out that this does not make him any less royal.

[67] Robert B. Wright, "Psalms of Solomon," *OTP* II:641.

[68] All English translations from the *Psalms of Solomon* 17 are borrowed from Wright, as are the references to Israel's Scriptures (*OTP* II:665–68).

[69] Other extant texts that refer to a royal deliverer but lack the word "Messiah" include *T. Jud.* 24; 4QFlor; 4QpIsa[a] III, 11–25; and 1Q28b. They cite such passages as Num. 24:17; 2 Sam. 7:10–14; Ps. 2:1; Ps. 45:4, 7; Isa. 11:1–5; and Amos 9:11. For an overview of messianic expectations as expressed in the literature of Early Judaism, see James H. Charlesworth, "From Messianology to Christology: Problems and Prospects," in *The Messiah: Developments in Earliest Judaism and Christianity* (ed. James H. Charlesworth; Minneapolis: Fortress, 1992), 3–35 and "Messianology in the Biblical Pseudepigrapha," in

Nothing in Ps. 2 or Isa. 11 – and nothing in other royal texts such as Num. 24:17, Jer. 33:14–16, and Zech. 6:12 – suggests that the Messiah will be executed by Gentiles. John must explain why Jesus, whom he claims is the Messiah, God's anointed king, meets his end on a Roman cross. The Fourth Gospel offers ample evidence that its implied author "searches the Scriptures" (John 5:39) for passages like Ps. 22:18 and Ps. 69:4, 9, 21 that support his belief.[70] He then interprets them as messianic prophecies using exegetical techniques that were popular in his day.[71]

John's exegetical techniques

Biblical interpreters in John's day began with a fundamental assumption: a belief in the theological unity of the Scriptures. In her authoritative article on midrash, Renée Bloch describes their conviction: "The Bible . . . comes from God in all of its parts and it therefore offers a broad context to which one should always return."[72] She then summarizes their exegetical approach: "[Their] goal [was] primarily practical: to define the lessons for faith and for the religious way of life contained in the biblical text."[73] Roger Le Déaut concurs: "Midrash . . . is first of all the response to the question: What does Scripture want to say for the life of today? And no effort is spared – even at the price of methods which are strange to us – to allow it to make its response."[74]

Over the centuries, attempts have been made to classify the "strange methods" of ancient interpreters. One catalogue, listing seven exegetical techniques, is attributed to the Pharisee Hillel.[75] This catalogue terms the first technique *qal vahomer* ("light and heavy"). It describes a method by which a principle applicable in an inconsequential circumstance can be transferred to a weightier situation. The second category,

---

Qumran-Messianism: Studies on the Messianic Expectations in the Dead Sea Scrolls (ed. James H. Charlesworth, Hermann Lichtenberger, and Gerbern S. Oegema; Tübingen: Mohr Siebeck, 1998), 21–52; Lichtenberger, "Messianic Expectations and Messianic Figures in the Second Temple Period," in *Qumran-Messianism*, 9–20.

[70] Cf. Nils A. Dahl, "The Johannine Church and History," in *Current Issues in New Testament Interpretation* (ed. William Klassen and Graydon F. Snyder; New York: Harper, 1962), 129–36.

[71] Cf. Juel, *Messianic Exegesis*, 13–15, 60, 172–73.

[72] Bloch, "Midrash," 32.

[73] Ibid.

[74] Le Déaut, "Apropos a Definition of Midrash," 270.

[75] *t. Sanh.* 7.11; *'Abot R. Nat.* A § 37. For a helpful summary of these seven techniques, see Craig A. Evans, *Noncanonical Writings and New Testament Interpretation* (Peabody, Mass.: Hendrickson, 1992), 117–18.

gezerah shawah ("equivalent regulation"), shows how one text may be interpreted by means of a second if both texts share a word or phrase. Since the Bible "comes from God in all of its parts," Scripture is used to interpret Scripture.[76]

John's exegetical techniques are similar to those of his contemporaries. Frédéric Manns points out arguments of John's Jesus that may be classified as examples of *qal vahomer*. In John 10:34–36, Jesus contends that since Ps. 82:6 declares that those who received the law were called "gods," it is not blasphemy for God's sanctified emissary to call himself "God's Son."[77] In the same vein, Jesus maintains in John 7:22–23 that if it is legal to circumcise on the Sabbath, then it is also legal to heal on the Sabbath.[78] Additionally, the Evangelist's citation of both Ps. 118:25–26 and Zech. 9:9 in John 12:13–15 may be understood as the result of *gezerah shawah*. Psalm 118:26 invokes a blessing on "the one who comes (הַבָּא; ὁ ἐρχόμενος) in the name of the Lord," while Zech. 9:9 announces, "Lo, your king comes (יָבוֹא; ἔρχεται) to you." John apparently associates these passages because both contain the verb to come (בּוֹא; ἔρχομαι).[79] This technique of interpreting one passage in light of another using shared vocabulary offers ancient interpreters a way to impart messianic significance to a text that is not ostensibly about the Messiah. All that is needed is familiarity with accepted messianic texts that contain the necessary words.

Messianic texts

John's implied author certainly seems to have been familiar with texts considered to be messianic prophecies by other first-century Jews. He applies several such texts to Jesus. One of the first is Isa. 11:1–16, a prophecy about a shoot from the stump of Jesse, a branch upon whom the spirit (τὸ πνεῦμα) of the Lord will rest (ἀναπαύσεται). This prophecy is used to describe the Messiah in 4QFlor 1–3 I, 11; 4QpIsaᵃ 8–10 III, 11–25; 1Q28b V, 24–46; *1 Enoch* 49:3; 62:3; *T. Levi* 18:5, 7; and *Pss. Sol.* 17:36–37.[80] In the Fourth Gospel, John the Baptist

---

[76] Bloch, "Midrash," 32.

[77] Frédéric Manns, "Exégèse rabbinique et exégèse johannique," *RB* 92 (1985), 532.

[78] Ibid., 532–33.

[79] Ibid., 533. Of the three Synoptic Gospels, only Matthew actually quotes both Ps. 118:25–26 and Zech. 9:9 (Matt. 21:5–9). Unlike John, however, Matthew does not cite the passages in consecutive sentences.

[80] Only *Pss. Sol.* uses the term "Messiah." It is clear, however, that the other passages refer to a similar royal redeemer.

testifies, "I saw the Spirit (τὸ πνεῦμα) descending from heaven like a dove, and it remained (ἔμεινεν) on him" (1:32: cf. Matt. 3:16). John the Baptist's testimony indicates that Jesus is the Messiah foretold in Isa. 11:2.

Later in the Gospel, some of the people ask, "Surely the Messiah does not come from Galilee, does he? Has not the scripture said that the Messiah is descended from David (ἐκ τοῦ σπέρματος Δαυὶδ) and comes from Bethlehem, the village where David lived?" (7:42). Here is an apparent reference to God's promise to David in 2 Sam. 7:12, "I will raise up your offspring (τὸ σπέρμα) after you, who shall come forth from your body, and I will establish his kingdom." The Evangelist also seems to allude to Mic. 5:2: "But you, O Bethlehem of Ephrathah, . . . from you shall come forth for me one who is to rule in Israel."[81] Evidence indicates that both of these texts were regarded as messianic prophecies. For example, Qumran exegetes composed a midrash on 2 Sam. 7:10–14 in which they identified David's offspring as the eschatological "branch of David" (4QFlor 1–3 I, 11–12). In Matt. 2:3–6, the chief priests and scribes quote Mic. 5:2 to show King Herod that the Messiah will be born in Bethlehem. In John 7:42, John apparently alludes to familiar messianic prophecies to indicate that Jesus' origins do not conform to the people's expectations.

Finally, John uses Ps. 89 to show that Jesus' death does not conform to the people's expectations, either. Psalm 89 was composed in response to 2 Sam. 7:10–14, first describing God's faithfulness to David (vv. 1–37), whom God has "anointed (מְשַׁחְתִּיו; ἔχρισα)" with holy oil (v. 20), and then lamenting his dynasty's decline (vv. 38–51). The argument of John 12:34 presumes that this psalm, like 2 Sam. 7:10–14, was regarded as a messianic prophecy. Here the crowd states, "We have heard from the law that the Messiah remains forever (ὁ Χριστὸς μένει εἰς τὸν αἰῶνα)." They allude to Ps. 89:36, "His seed remains forever (τὸ σπέρμα αὐτοῦ εἰς τὸ αἰῶνα μενεῖ)."[82] (Note that their question implicitly affirms that "the seed" of Ps. 89:36 – and 2 Sam. 7:14 – is understood to be the Christ.[83]) Because of this prophecy, the crowd does not expect the Messiah to be lifted up (that is, crucified). Ironically, Jesus later assures his disciples that he will indeed remain with them (John 15:4–5). John affirms that the Messiah will remain forever, but only after he is lifted up.

---

[81] Juel, *Messianic Exegesis*, 77.
[82] LXX Ps. 88:37; my translation.
[83] Juel, *Messianic Exegesis*, 107–8.

Messianic exegesis

John not only alludes to texts considered messianic in first-century Jewish circles; he also echoes texts about suffering individuals identified as messianic by other early Christian exegetes. Among these are Pss 22 and 69. Juel shows how both of these psalms can be interpreted in light of Ps. 89 on the basis of shared vocabulary. Psalm 89 refers to David as God's "servant (עֶבֶד; δοῦλος)" (vv. 3, 20, 39). As it mourns the decline of David's dynasty, the psalm declares, "He has become the scorn (הָיָה חֶרְפָּה; ἐγενήθη ὄνειδος) of his neighbors" (Ps. 89:41). Juel points out several factors that connect Pss 22 and 69 with Ps. 89. For one, all three have to do with David. Psalms 22 and 69 are psalms of David, and Ps. 89 is all about David. Like Ps. 89, Ps. 69 concerns a "servant (עֶבֶד; παῖς)" (v. 17). In addition, both Pss 22 and 69 feature the noun חֶרְפָּה, translated in Greek either as ὄνειδος or ὀνειδισμός.[84] In Ps. 22:6, the petitioner is "scorned by others (חֶרְפַּת אָדָם; ὄνειδος ἀνθρώπου)"; in Ps. 69:7, 9–10, 19–20, he has received "insults (חֶרְפַּת; ὀνειδισμός)." Because of these similarities, first-century exegetes could argue that the sufferers of Pss 22 and 69 can be identified with the Messiah of Ps. 89.

John applies both of these laments to Jesus. He agrees with the Synoptic Evangelists in his passion narrative by quoting Ps. 22:18 in John 19:24, thus indicating that the crucified Jesus is the suffering Messiah whose clothes are divided.[85] He also agrees with the Synoptic Evangelists when he alludes to Ps. 69:21 in John 19:29–30, thereby portraying the crucified Jesus as the suffering Messiah who is given sour wine to drink.[86] John cites Ps. 69:9 in his temple-cleansing account (John 2:17). The Jesus who rampages in the temple reveals himself as the zealous Messiah of Ps. 69. Psalm 69 is quoted one other time in the Fourth Gospel, this time to describe the world's response to the Messiah. In John 15:25, Jesus uses Ps. 69:4 to explain, "They hated me without a cause."[87]

John's references to Pss 22 and 69 can therefore be understood as the fruit of messianic exegesis, evidence of an interpretive tradition inherited by the Fourth Evangelist. Belief that Jesus is the Messiah inspires recognition of shared vocabulary between a royal psalm

---

[84] Ibid., 110–11.
[85] Cf. Mark 15:24; Matt. 27:35; Luke 23:34.
[86] Cf. Mark 15:36, Matt. 27:48, and Luke 23:36.
[87] Psalm 22 is also used to describe Jesus in 1 Pet. 5:8 and Heb. 2:12. Psalm 69 is similarly cited in Acts 1:20 and Rom. 11:9–10; 15:3.

(Ps. 89) and laments that can describe how Jesus lived and died (Pss 22 and 69). The Fourth Evangelist evokes all three of these texts in his narrative, relying on Israel's Scriptures to understand a crucified Messiah and to explain his rejection.

It is my contention that John evokes Jer. 33:10–11, Gen. 29:1–20, and the Song of Songs in a similar fashion. These passages can be linked to a messianic psalm, Ps. 45, on the basis of shared vocabulary. John's implied author either makes these connections himself or inherits this tradition of messianic exegesis, and then uses the prophecies to illustrate how Jesus lived and died. His voice is heard in Judea, he meets a woman at a well, he is perfumed with nard, and he becomes the object of a woman's nocturnal search.

Identifying and interpreting John's allusions

In the following chapters, I incorporate Hays' guidelines into a three-part process for investigating John's allusions to Israel's Scriptures. The first part uses evidence from the Gospel text to explore how its implied author alludes to certain passages and how those allusions enhance his narrative. It begins with identifying allusions using the criteria of correspondence, rhetorical emphasis, and recurrence. (The availability of Israel's Scriptures is assumed, and the history of interpretation is considered throughout the process.) Particular attention is paid to the frequency of corresponding features between the originating and precursor texts. Instances of dissonance are also noted. Then, once an allusion is identified, its thematic coherence with John's narrative can be described. Corresponding details (both stated and unstated) are studied in order to determine how they enhance the Gospel's settings, characters, plot, ironies, themes, motifs, symbols (including representative figures), and metaphors. Chapter 3 performs these tasks for allusions in John 3:22–30 and 4:4–42, while Chapter 4 deals with John 12:3 and 20:1–18.

Chapter 5 presents the second part of the process, which concerns the suitability of the proposed allusions for John's implied author and involves the criterion of prominence. The significance of the evoked texts for John's implied author is investigated. Specifically, evidence for messianic significance either inherited or invented by that author is presented in accordance with Juel's concept of messianic exegesis.

The third part, in Chapter 6, considers the impact of John's allusions on audiences other than the implied audience. Because this part employs the tests of historical plausibility and satisfaction, it involves constructs of historical author and historical audiences with special attention to their exegetical traditions. A reconstruction of the original audience is offered, and their possible understanding of John's allusions is explored. The potential perspective of a contemporary audience is then taken into account. In the end, we want some sense of whether our exegetical method, married to our theological questions, has produced a satisfactory interpretation.

3

THE REVELATION OF THE BRIDEGROOM-MESSIAH: ALLUSIONS TO JEREMIAH 33:10–11 AND GENESIS 29:1–20

The Fourth Evangelist's first concern is to introduce Jesus. His opening chapters involve both explaining who Jesus is and describing how people respond to him.[1] The prologue (1:1–18) sets this two-part agenda. It begins by identifying Jesus as "the Word" (1:1, 14) and "the light" (1:4–9). It then turns to the messianic designation "Christ" (1:17), but not before characterizing human response to Jesus:

> He was in the world, and the world came into being through him; yet the world did not know him. He came to what was his own, and his own people did not accept him. But to all who received him, who believed in his name, he gave power to become children of God, who were born, not of blood or of the will of the flesh or of the will of man, but of God. And the Word became flesh and lived among us, and we have seen his glory, the glory as of [the Father's only Son], full of grace and truth. (1:10–14)[2]

Subsequent stories follow the agenda set in the prologue. When Jesus appears on the scene in 1:29–51, John adds further revelations of his identity and begins to describe his encounters with various people. Initially, the response to Jesus is quite positive. People begin to recognize that he is the Messiah. John the Baptist confesses, "I am not the Messiah" (1:20), and then goes on to suggest that Jesus is (1:26–34). The Baptist's disciple Andrew tells his brother Simon, "We have found the Messiah" (1:41). Finally, Nathanael confesses, "You are the Son of God! You are the King of Israel!" (1:49).

---

[1] See also Barnabas Lindars, *The Gospel of John* (NCB 43; Grand Rapids: Eerdmans, 1972), 123; Culpepper, *Anatomy*, 89–90.

[2] The reading in brackets is given as an alternate to the NRSV's translation of μονογενοῦς παρὰ πατρὸς. Use of the definite article should be preferred, given the Gospel's dominant concern with "the Father" (cf. 1:18). John's Jesus emanates the glory of the Messiah, the Son of God – not that of a father's only son.

The agenda of revelation and response continues immediately after Nathanael's confession with John 2:1–11, where Jesus and his disciples attend a wedding in Cana. When the wine runs out, Jesus miraculously transforms more than one hundred gallons of water to replenish the supply. John reports that "this, the first of his signs . . . revealed his glory, and his disciples believed in him" (2:11). As explained in John 1:10–13, Jesus comes to his own people and his disciples believe in his name. His first sign reveals his glory – glory as of the Father's only Son, as anticipated in John 1:14.[3] In some way, Jesus' transformation of water into wine demonstrates that he is indeed the Messiah.[4]

The text does not explicitly state why this particular sign indicates Jesus' messianic identity, however.[5] John apparently assumes that his audience will make the connection, perhaps based on some traditional association between the Messiah and wine.[6] Such an association is provided by two biblical prophecies. One of these, Jacob's blessing for Judah at the end of Genesis (49:10–12), features Judah's royal descendant clothed with a wine-soaked garment:

> The scepter shall not depart from Judah,
>> nor the ruler's staff from between his feet,
> until tribute comes to him;
>> and the obedience of the peoples is his.
> Binding his foal to the vine
>> and his donkey's colt to the choice vine,
> he washes his garments in wine
>> and his robe in the blood of the grapes;
> his eyes are darker than wine,
>> and his teeth whiter than milk.[7]

---

[3] See also Marie-Joseph Lagrange, *L'Évangile selon S. Jean* (3rd edn; *Ebib*; Paris: Gabalda, 1927), 60; Hoskyns, *Fourth Gospel*, 199; Lindars, *Gospel of John*, 132.

[4] For a history of interpretation of John 2:1–12, see Ignace de la Potterie, *Mary in the Mystery of the Covenant* (trans. Bertrand Buby; New York: Alba, 1992), 161–63. My opinion about the story's central message is shared by Raymond E. Brown, who wisely points out that it does not emphasize the wine as a replacement for ritual water, Mary's intercessions, or the reactions of the steward or the bridegroom as much as it emphasizes Jesus' glory (*John I–XII*, 103–4). See also Lagrange, *Évangile selon S. Jean*, 60; Rudolf Schnackenburg, *The Gospel According to St. John* (trans. Kevin Smyth et al.; New York: Herder & Herder, 1968–75), I:323, 337; Raymond Collins, "Cana (John 2:1–12): The First of His Signs or the Key to His Signs?" in *These Things Have Been Written*, 162; repr. from *ITQ* 47 (1980): 79–95; Hengel, "Wine Miracle," 87; La Potterie, *Mary*, 192–93.

[5] See also Hengel, "Wine Miracle," 87.

[6] See also La Potterie, *Mary*, 193.

[7] NRSV. The LXX of v. 10 is slightly different, but this does not change how the prophecy associates the Messiah with wine.

More significantly, the final oracle in Amos (9:11, 13–14) links the restoration of the Davidic king with an eschatological abundance of wine:

> On that day I will raise up
>   the booth of David that is fallen,
> and repair its breaches,
>   and raise up its ruins,
>   and rebuild it as in the days of old . . .
> The time is surely coming, says the LORD,
>   when the one who plows shall overtake the one who reaps,
>   and the treader of grapes the one who sows the seed;
> the mountains shall drip sweet wine,
>   and all the hills shall flow with it.
> I will restore the fortunes of my people Israel,
>   and they shall rebuild the ruined cities and inhabit them;
> they shall plant vineyards and drink their wine,
>   and they shall make gardens and eat their fruit.[8]

The idea that the Messiah's advent is accompanied by an abundance of wine finds further support in *2 Baruch* (written ca. 100–120):

> And it will happen that when all that which should come to pass in these parts has been accomplished, the Anointed One will begin to be revealed . . . The earth will also yield fruits ten thousandfold. And on one vine will be a thousand branches, and one branch will produce a thousand clusters, and one cluster will produce a thousand grapes, and one grape will produce a cor of wine.   (*2 Bar.* 29:3, 5–6)[9]

Those who minted coins during the Jewish War (64–73) also apparently believed in this tradition. The vine was a common motif, symbolizing the messianic expectations of the revolutionaries.[10]

---

[8] Several commentators also cite passages like Hos. 2:19–20; 14:7; Isa. 25:6–8; Jer. 2:2; 31:12 (see, e.g., Brown, *John I–XII*, 105; Francis J. Moloney, *The Gospel of John* [SP 4; Collegeville, Minn.: Liturgical Press, 1998], 66). Whereas these prophecies refer to an eschatological abundance of wine, they do not explicitly mention the Messiah. Unless they are interpreted in light of prophecies that do mention the Messiah, they provide no precedent for associating the Messiah with wine.

[9] Trans. A. F. J. Klijn, "(Syriac Apocalypse of) Baruch," in *OTP* I:630. See Collins, "Cana," 174, n. 44.

[10] Hengel, *Wine Miracle*, 132–35; Ya'akov Meshorer, *Jewish Coins of the Second Temple Period* (Tel Aviv: Am Hassefer, 1967), 154–69, Plates XIX–XXVIII.

It is not at all clear that *2 Baruch* and the vine motif on Jewish coins were familiar to John's implied author. Nevertheless, they do indicate that at least some of his contemporaries associated the advent of the Messiah with abundant wine. This lends support to the idea that John makes the same connection. Jesus' miraculous provision of six large jars of wine in John 2:1–12 most likely fulfills messianic expectations based on Gen. 49:10–12 and Amos 9:11, 13–14. In this way, it confirms that Jesus is in fact the prophesied Messiah – as previously claimed by John the Baptist, Andrew, and Nathanael (John 1:34, 41, and 49).[11]

In showing that Jesus provides the wine for a wedding celebration, John is also able to hint that the Messiah is a bridegroom – a concept that receives more attention in John 3:29. The hint comes by way of irony. Jesus' disciples presumably know the source of the new wine supply (2:11), as do the servants who drew the water (2:9). John's audience, having observed the entire process, is also in on the secret. In contrast, the steward of the feast remains blissfully ignorant. John exploits this ironic situation by reporting the steward's compliments to the bridegroom: "Everyone serves the good wine first, and then the inferior wine after the guests have become drunk. But you have kept the good wine until now" (2:10). John's audience realizes that the steward ought to acknowledge, not their host, but Jesus. Indeed, he has acknowledged Jesus without realizing it. As Duke observes, "Readers accustomed to thinking of Jesus as bridegroom (from . . . previous readings of 3:29) will know that though the steward addresses the wrong man, he is quite right to praise the bridegroom."[12] John hints that the Messiah who provides an abundance of good wine is a bridegroom.[13]

It should be noted that, at this stage in the story, John offers no more than a hint. There is very little evidence to sustain interpretations that

[11] See also Brown, *John I–XII*, 105; Schnackenburg, *Gospel According to St. John*, I:338; George W. MacRae, *Invitation to John: A Commentary on the Gospel of John with Complete Text from the Jerusalem Bible* (Garden City: Doubleday, 1978), 48; Collins, "Cana," 172–73; Hengel, "Wine Miracle," 100–101; Ronald J. Feenstra, "Hills Flowing with Wine: A Meditation on John 2:1–11," *Reformed Journal* 38, no. 4 (April 1988): 9–10.

[12] Duke, *Irony*, 83–84. See also Alfred Plummer, *The Gospel According to S. John* (CGTSC; Cambridge: Cambridge University Press, 1892), 86; Winandy, "Cantique et le NT," 170; La Potterie, *Mary*, 177, 198. Augustine reaches a similar conclusion (*Tract. Ev. Jo.* 9.2, in *NPNF*[1] 7:63). In contrast, Ridderbos detects no such hint (*Gospel According to John*, 109).

[13] See also Collins, "Cana," 173–74; Staley, *Print's First Kiss*, 90, 101 n. 35; cf. Schneiders, *Revelatory Text*, 187; Stibbe, *John*, 46, 61; Fehribach, *Women in the Life of the Bridegroom*, 30–31.

take the Cana story for a messianic wedding celebration.[14] The messianic
bridegroom is not clearly identified, and his bride is not yet introduced.
Their wedding banquet is never described, either here or elsewhere in the
Gospel. As Staley points out, John 2:1–11 gives very little away.[15]

"The bridegroom's voice"

Shortly after the steward at Cana unwittingly hints that Jesus is a bridegroom, a reliable witness – John the Baptist – intentionally implies it:[16]

> No one can receive anything except what has been given from
> heaven. You yourselves are my witnesses that I said, "I am not
> the Messiah, but I have been sent ahead of him." He who has
> the bride is the bridegroom. The friend of the bridegroom, who
> stands and hears him, rejoices greatly at the bridegroom's
> voice. For this reason my joy has been fulfilled. He must
> increase, but I must decrease.   (John 3:28–30)

This enigmatic saying raises several questions. Why does John suddenly liken Jesus to a bridegroom? Who is "the bride," and how does
Jesus "have" her? What is meant by "the friend of the bridegroom"?
Why does John mention "the bridegroom's voice" when the passage
never indicates that Jesus is speaking?

Several scholars suggest that John is using a metaphor for the spiritual marriage between God and God's people – a metaphor based on
prophecies such as Hos. 1–3; Jer. 2:2; Isa. 61:10; and the Song of Songs
interpreted allegorically.[17] This would account for the reference to

---

[14] Alfred F. Loisy (*Le quatrième Évangile: Les épîtres dites de Jean* [Paris: Picard,
1906], 283) and Braun (*Jean le théologien 3.1*, 81) argue that, together with John 3:29, the
Cana story symbolizes the new covenant, the marriage of the Messiah and his people, that
supersedes the Jewish rites of purification mentioned in John 2:3. Several other commen-
tators contend that John 2:1–12 foreshadows the eschatological wedding banquet proph-
esied in passages like Isa. 25:6–8 and Matt. 22:1–14 – see, e.g., Plummer, *Gospel
According to S. John*, 86; Bauer, *Johannes-Evangelium*, 47; R. H. Lightfoot, *St. John's
Gospel: A Commentary* (ed. C. F. Evans; Oxford: Clarendon, 1956), 100; Sanders,
Commentary, 114; Lindars, *Gospel of John*, 123–33. According to Adolf Smitmans,
Hippolytus was one of the first to propound this interpretation (*Das Weinwunder von
Kana: Die Auslegung von Jo 2,1–11 bei den Vätern und heute* [BGBE 6; Tübingen: Mohr
Siebeck, 1966], 207–17; see Hippolytus, Εἰς τὸ ᾆσμα, Frag. 17).

[15] Staley, *Print's First Kiss*, 90.

[16] See also Marsh, *Saint John*, 196.

[17] See, e.g., B. F. Westcott, *The Gospel According to St. John* (London: Murray, 1892),
129; Plummer, *Gospel According to S. John*, 102; Loisy, *Quatrième Évangile*, 338;
Joachim Jeremias, *Jesus als Weltvollender* (BFCT 33, no. 4; Gütersloh: Bertelsmann,
1930), 22–32; Hoskyns, *Fourth Gospel*, 249; Bauer, *Johannes-Evangelium*, 63;
C. K. Barrett, *The Gospel According to St. John* (London: SPCK, 1955), 185–86;
Boismard, "Ami de l'époux," 291; Brown, *John I–XII*, 156; Marsh, *Saint John*, 196.

marriage in general, and mention of the bridegroom and bride in particular. It would even explain why John the Baptist, the Messiah's forerunner, styles himself as the bridegroom's friend. Still, it cannot be claimed that John's implied author bases his references to marriage on the metaphor in these passages, since he never betrays knowledge of its existence.[18] Moreover, the metaphor delineates no role for "the bridegroom's voice."

This last difficulty is often solved with reference to an interpretation made popular by Joachim Jeremias. In his *TNDT* article "νύμφη, νυμφίος," Jeremias stresses that a Jewish bridegroom's friend (שׁוֹשְׁבִין) was responsible for conducting him to the bridal chamber and, upon the consummation of the marriage, displaying the tokens of the bride's virginity. In the same way, he contends, John the Baptist joyfully presents a purified people to the Messiah.[19] It seems unlikely that the Fourth Evangelist meant to convey this notion, however, as he does not otherwise emphasize the responsibilities of "the friend of the bridegroom." Indeed, the Gospel pays only a little attention to John the Baptist's role in preparing people for the coming of the Messiah (1:23). Much more stress is laid on his function as a witness to Jesus (1:7–8, 26–27, 29–36). A more convincing solution must be sought.

Feuillet and Cambe offer one that accounts for the distinctive phrasing of the Baptist's saying: "the bride (τὴν νύμφην)," "the bridegroom (νυμφίος)," "the friend of the bridegroom (ὁ φίλος τοῦ νυμφίου)," and "the bridegroom's voice (τὴν φωνὴν τοῦ νυμφίου)" are mentioned because the saying alludes to the Scriptures. They suggest several possible evoked texts. Especially compelling for Cambe and Feuillet are the similarities between John 3:29 and the Song of Songs. Both observe a connection to Song 2:8–14 and 5:2–6, two passages that describe a joyful response to the voice of the beloved.[20] The former passage begins with the bride's exclamation, "The voice of my beloved!" (Song 2:8). He leaps over the mountains, looks into her window, and beckons her to "arise, . . . and come away" (Song

---

[18] As to whether John's original author and audience might have known this metaphor, see below, pp. 132–34, 142.

[19] Jeremias, "νύμφη, νυμφίος," in *TDNT*, IV:1101.

[20] Feuillet, "Symbolisme de la colombe," 540; "Cantique et l'Apocalypse," 334, n. 8; "Recherche du Christ," 106; *Mystère de l'amour divin*, 231; and *Jesus and His Mother*, 12; Cambe, "Influence du Cantique," 13.

2:10, 13). In the latter passage, he begs, "Open to me, my sister, my love" (Song 5:2). Her response: "My soul failed me when he spoke" (Song 5:6).

An allusion to either of these passages is not likely, however. The only verbal parallel is the word "voice (φωνή)," found in John 3:29, Song 2:8, and Song 5:2. Moreover, circumstantial correspondence is somewhat inexact. Whereas the Song's joyful response comes from the bride (2:8; 5:5–6), the Gospel's emanates from the bridegroom's friend.

Stronger parallels link John 3:29 with Song 8:13:

> O you who dwell in the gardens,
>> my companions are listening for your voice;
> let me hear it.[21]

Cambe explores these parallels in some detail. He acknowledges that the MT uses a female second-person pronoun to indicate the garden dweller (הַיּוֹשֶׁבֶת) whose voice (קוֹלֵךְ) is desired, thus rendering it an unlikely candidate for an evoked text. The LXX offers a better possibility. Here, the garden dweller (ὁ καθήμενος) is a man.[22]

Cambe asserts that, in echoing Song 8:13, John likens Jesus to this man. "The bridegroom's voice (τὴν φωνὴν τοῦ νυμφίου)" in John 3:29 belongs to the Song's lover (τῇ φωνῇ σου). In addition, John's "friend of the bridegroom (ὁ φίλος τοῦ νυμφίου)" then assumes the role of the Song's "companions (ἑταῖροι)." John the Baptist hears the voice of the bridegroom-Messiah, and his joy is fulfilled.[23]

These parallels are intriguing. Nevertheless, the proposed allusion to Song 8:13 is relatively weak. Verbal correspondence between John 3:29 and Song 8:13 consists of only two words: the noun φωνή and the verb ἀκούω. Circumstantial correspondence strengthens the first verbal parallel: John 3:29 features the bridegroom's voice just as Song 8:13

---

[21] Feuillet, "Symbolisme de la colombe," 540; "Cantique et l'Apocalypse," 334, n. 8; "Recherche du Christ," 106; *Mystère de l'amour divin*, 231; and *Jesus and His Mother*, 12; Cambe, "Influence du Cantique," 15.

[22] Cambe, "Influence du Cantique," 15. See also Joüon, *Cantique des cantiques*, 331–32; Winandy, "Cantique et le NT," 167; Braun, *Jean le théologien 3.1*, 101–2; Feuillet, *Mystère de l'amour divin*, 231.

[23] Cambe, "Influence du Cantique," 15. See also Joüon, *Cantique des cantiques*, 331–32; Feuillet, "Recherche du Christ,"106; *Mystère de l'amour divin*, 231; and *Jesus and His Mother*, 12; Braun, *Jean le théologien 3.1*, 93, 99–103. Winandy attributes the allusion, not to an association of Jesus with the Song's bridegroom, but to an association of joy with marriage ("Cantique et le NT," 171–72). He argues that John 3:29 mentions marriage, not in order to develop a metaphor associating Jesus with a bridegroom, but in order to illustrate John the Baptist's joy. I agree with Winandy, but I think it is still necessary to explain why John refers to marriage and not to some other joyful occasion.

refers to the voice of the Song's lover. The subject of the verb ἀκούω, however, does not match. In John 3:29, the bridegroom's friend hears him (ὁ φίλος . . . ἀκούων αὐτοῦ). In Song 8:13, ἀκούω appears in the imperative mood. The subject is the bridegroom, and the object is the bride (ἀκούτισόν με). The more exact parallel to the listening friend in John 3:29 is not a verbal parallel with the bride who wishes to hear, but rather a circumstantial parallel with the listening companions (ἑταῖροι προσέχοντες).[24]

This instance of circumstantial correspondence does offer some reinforcement to the tenuous verbal link provided by the noun φωνή. Circumstantial correspondence also includes the presence of a bride. She is the presumed speaker of LXX Song 8:13, and according to John 3:29 the bridegroom has her. Nevertheless, the correspondence ends here. John 3:22–30 says nothing about dwelling in the gardens or a bride who hears. It refers to a comrade but does not reiterate the word ἑταῖροι. If John echoes Song 8:13, he echoes only one phrase: ἑταῖροι προσέχοντες τῇ φωνῇ σου.

Verbal correspondence between John 3:29 and some of Jeremiah's prophecies is somewhat more compelling. As Cambe points out, Jeremiah explicitly mentions "the voice of the bride and the voice of the bridegroom." In Jer. 7:32–34, 16:9, and 25:10, as well as in Bar. 2:23, these voices cease when the Lord destroys Jerusalem and the neighboring cities of Judah:

> Therefore, the days are surely coming, says the LORD, when it will no more be called Topheth, or the valley of the son of Hinnom, but the valley of Slaughter: for they will bury in Topheth until there is no more room. The corpses of this people will be food for the birds of the air, and for the animals of the earth; and no one will frighten them away. And I will bring to an end the sound of mirth and gladness, the voice of the bride and bridegroom in the cities of Judah and the streets of Jerusalem; for the land shall become a waste. (Jer. 7:32–34)

> For thus says the LORD of hosts, the God of Israel: I am going to banish from this place, in your days and before your eyes, the voice of mirth and the voice of gladness, the voice of the bridegroom and the voice of the bride. (Jer. 16:9)

---

[24] Indeed, Winandy recognizes only one common word: φωνή ("Cantique et le NT," 172).

> And I will banish from them the sound of mirth and the sound
> of gladness, the voice of the bridegroom and the voice of the
> bride, the sound of the millstones and the light of the lamp.
>
> (Jer. 25:10)

> I will make to cease from the towns of Judah and from the
> region around Jerusalem the voice of mirth and the voice of
> gladness, the voice of the bridegroom and the voice of the bride,
> and the whole land will be a desolation without inhabitants.
>
> (Bar. 2:23)

In Jer. 33:10–11, they resume at the restoration:

> Thus says the LORD: In this place of which you say, "It is a waste
> without human beings or animals," in the towns of Judah and
> the streets of Jerusalem that are desolate, without inhabitants,
> human or animal, there shall once more be heard the voice of
> mirth and the voice of gladness, the voice of the bridegroom and
> the voice of the bride, the voices of those who sing, as they bring
> thank offerings to the house of the LORD:

> "Give thanks to the LORD of hosts,
>   for the LORD is good,
>   for his steadfast love endures forever!"

> For I will restore the fortunes of the land as at first, says
> the LORD.

The prophet uses these voices to symbolize God's favor towards his
people.[25]

The Fourth Gospel reiterates important terms from these prophecies.
John 3:29 mentions "the bridegroom's voice (τὴν φωνὴν τοῦ
νυμφίου)" while Jeremiah refers to "the voice of the bridegroom
(φωνὴ νυμφίου)." The only difference is that John has the definite
article.[26] Furthermore, a bride is mentioned in all six texts: "the voice
of the bride (φωνὴ νύμφης)" in Jeremiah and Baruch and "he who has
the bride (ὁ ἔχων τὴν νύμφην)" in the Fourth Gospel.

The fact that both John and Jeremiah mention "the bridegroom's
voice" and "the bride" is significant. For one thing, the phrase "the

---

[25] Cambe, "Influence du Cantique," 14; cf. also Bernard, *Critical and Exegetical Commentary*, I:31; Jeremias, *Jesus als Weltvollender*, 28–29; Bauer, *Johannes-Evangelium*, 63;
Winandy, "Cantique et le NT," 168; Hengel, "Wine Miracle," 101–2; Zimmermann and
Zimmermann, "Freund des Bräutigams," 126.

[26] No extant Greek manuscript of Jeremiah includes it.

bridegroom's voice" is somewhat dissonant, as John 3:22–30 never mentions that Jesus is speaking or that John the Baptist is listening to him. It signals the possibility of an allusion – of necessity, an allusion to Jeremiah, as the phrase is found nowhere else in the LXX. An audience familiar with Scripture might think first of Jeremiah upon hearing "τὴν φωνὴν τοῦ νυμφίου." For another thing, the explicit terms "bride" and "bridegroom" forge a stronger connection to Jeremiah's prophecies than to the Song of Songs. While these terms are central to John the Baptist's saying as well as to Jer. 7:34; 16:9; 25:10; 33:11 and Bar. 2:23, they are only implicit in Song 8:13.

A third instance of verbal and circumstantial correspondence links John 3:22–30 more specifically with Jer. 7:34 and 33:10–11. Jeremiah's prophecies concern "the towns of Judah (ἐκ πόλεων Ιουδα; ἐν πόλεσιν Ιουδα)" (Jer. 7:34; 33:10), and John's Jesus is baptizing in "the Judean countryside (εἰς τὴν Ἰουδαίαν γῆν)" (John 3:22).[27] All three of these passages thus feature the voice of a bridegroom and the presence of a bride in the region around Jerusalem.

John 3:22–30 is not similar to Jer. 7:34 – or its counterparts, Jer. 16:9; 25:10; Bar. 2:23 – in any other respect. John the Baptist celebrates the presence of the bridegroom and the bride. People are flocking to Judea to be baptized by Jesus, causing John the Baptist to rejoice because his joy has been fulfilled. Jeremiah 7:34, on the other hand, warns of the impending absence of bridegroom and bride. The land will become a waste, and the voices of mirth and gladness will cease.

Circumstantial and verbal correspondence with Jer. 33:10–11 is much stronger. In addition to the three instances already noted, two more parallels link this prophecy to John the Baptist's bridegroom saying. First, the verb ἀκούω appears in both passages. According to Jer. 33:10, the celebrating voices "shall once more be heard (ἔτι ἀκουσθήσεται)."[28] According to John the Baptist, the friend of the bridegroom "stands and hears him (ἀκούων αὐτοῦ)."

The second additional parallel concerns the festive atmosphere. John the Baptist rejoices in John 3:29, while the voices of mirth and gladness return with the bridegroom and the bride in Jer. 33:10–11. John establishes a close, though not exact, verbal parallel between the Baptist's saying and Jeremiah's prophecy. Jeremiah speaks of "the voice of mirth and the voice of gladness (φωνὴ εὐφροσύνης καὶ φωνὴ

---

[27] Again, the passage reckoned as Jer. 33:1–13 in the MT as well as in the NRSV appears at Jer. 40:1–13 in the LXX. The word Ιουδα is spelled without diacritical marks.
[28] One witness (א*) reads "ετι ακουσετε."

χαρμοσύνης)," while John the Baptist "rejoices greatly (χαρᾷ χαίρει)" so that his "joy (ἡ χαρὰ) has been fulfilled." The noun χαρά, the verb χαίρω, and the adjective χαρμόσυνος share the same root. John the Baptist's rejoicing can be understood as a reference to the φωνὴ χαρμοσύνης of Jer. 33:11.[29]

In summary, six instances of verbal and circumstantial correspondence link John 3:22–30 with Jer. 33:10–11. First, both locate the action in "Judea (᾽Ιουδαῖα)" or "Judah (Ιουδα)." Second, both feature the unusual phrase "the bridegroom's voice (τὴν φωνὴν τοῦ νυμφίου; φωνὴ νυμφίου)." Third, both depict the bridegroom in the company of a "bride (νύμφη)." Fourth, both celebrate the presence of the matrimonial couple (as opposed to Jer. 7:34; 16:9; 25:10; and Bar. 2:23, which foretell their absence). Fifth, both state that someone hears (ἀκούω) the bridegroom's voice. Sixth, both associate the bridegroom with "joy (χαρά)" and "gladness (χαρμόσυνος)." Song of Songs 8:13, on the other hand, displays only three corresponding features: a man's "voice (φωνή)," listening friends, and the presence of a bride. An allusion to Jer. 33:10–11 seems much more probable than an allusion to Song 8:13.

The similarities between John 3:22–30 and Jer. 33:10–11 serve as a starting point for interpretation. John reiterates important words from Jeremiah's prophecy in order to indicate its fulfillment. According to Jeremiah, the voice of the bridegroom will once more be heard in the towns of Judah. The passive verb, however, does not specify who will do the hearing.[30] According to the Fourth Gospel, it is John the Baptist. He hears the voice of the bridegroom, Jesus, who is baptizing in the countryside of Judea.

In addition, John uses two elements of the prophecy to illustrate two themes of his own story about Jesus. The following interpretation will discuss each in turn. First, John builds on the theme of marriage introduced in John 2:1–11 by identifying Jesus as Jeremiah's bridegroom and by mentioning a bride. Second, John the Baptist becomes the first character in this Gospel who rejoices because of Jesus. John 3:22–30 thus adds to the account of Jesus' revelation and human response by portraying Jesus as a bridegroom-Messiah and delineating the role of John the Baptist. The Messiah's voice, heard by his friend John the Baptist, causes him to rejoice – as prophesied in Jeremiah 33:10–11.

---

[29] One codex (A) attests a variant reading: "φωνη χαρμονης." The possibility that John knew this reading does not detract from my point.

[30] The variant ετι ακουσετε attested by ℵ* is equally ambiguous, but less apt to be understood as a prophecy about John the Baptist.

The bridegroom and the bride

John the Baptist's saying portrays Jesus as both Messiah and bridegroom. In his answer to his disciples' observation that "all are going to [Jesus]" (v. 27), John the Baptist implies that Jesus is the Messiah. "You yourselves are my witnesses that I said, 'I am not the Messiah, but I have been sent ahead of him,'" he declares (3:28). His disciples should not expect that everyone will come to them when Jesus is around. John the Baptist is only the Messiah's forerunner; Jesus is the Messiah himself.

John the Baptist then adds, almost as if he were quoting a proverb, "He who has the bride is the bridegroom" (3:29). This confirms what was hinted in the Cana story: Jesus, the Messiah, is like a bridegroom.[31] At Cana, Jesus does what the Gospel's implied audience expects of the Messiah – and what the steward expects of the bridegroom – when he provides a copious supply of wine. In the Judean countryside, Jesus the Messiah is again compared to a bridegroom. What is more, the phrase "the bridegroom's voice" indicates that Jesus is not just any bridegroom. It alludes to Jer. 33:10–11, implying that Jesus is that bridegroom whose return is prophesied by Jeremiah.[32]

John the Baptist recognizes Jesus as the bridegroom because Jesus "has" the bride. At this stage of the narrative, it is not exactly clear what "having the bride" means. The only thing that Jesus (the bridegroom) seems to have but that John the Baptist (the bridegroom's friend) lacks is the people who are going out to Jesus. Perhaps "the bride" means "followers."

This interpretation is certainly consistent with the marriage metaphor developed in passages like Hos. 1–3 and Jer. 2:2 to represent the relationship between God and God's people – a metaphor that several New Testament authors apply to Christ and the church.[33] At this point in the narrative, however, it is not yet clear whether John is developing

---

[31] See also Barrett, *Gospel According to St. John*, 186; Marsh, *Saint John*, 196; Schneiders, *Revelatory Text*, 187 and *Written That You May Believe*, 35; Duke, *Irony*, 101; Stibbe, *John*, 60–61.

[32] It should be noted that Jeremiah never indicates that this bridegroom is the Messiah. I will argue that this connection was made by John.

[33] See 2 Cor. 11:2; Eph. 5:22–32; Rev. 21:2, 9; 22:17. Those who interpret John 3:29 in light of this metaphor include Plummer (*Gospel According to S. John*, 102), Léon Zander ("Le Précurseur selon le P. Boulgakof," *Dieu vivant* 7 (1949), 105), Boismard ("Ami de l'époux," 291), Sanders (*Commentary*, 134), Feuillet ("Symbolisme de la colombe," 539–40), and Schneiders (*Written That You May Believe*, 35). Those who contend that the bride in John 3:29 does not represent the church include Lagrange (*Évangile selon S. Jean*, 95), Rudolf Bultmann (*The Gospel of John: A Commentary* [trans. G. R. Beasley-Murray;

such a metaphor. The only indication so far that the bride of John 3:29 might have some representative value is the brief but mysterious affirmation that Jesus "has" her. The idea is not pursued any further in this passage. As Boismard observes, the main purpose of John 3:29 is not to identify the bride, but rather to give the sign for recognizing the bridegroom.[34]

The voice of gladness

In Jer. 33:11, the voice of the bridegroom and the voice of the bride are accompanied by "the voice of gladness (φωνὴ χαρμοσύνης)." In John 3:29, it is John the Baptist, the bridegroom's friend, who "rejoices greatly (χαρᾷ χαίρει)" and whose "joy (ἡ χαρὰ) has been fulfilled." This parallel allows the Evangelist to delineate the role of John the Baptist. He is not the Messiah, but rather the Messiah's forerunner (v. 28). If Jesus is like a bridegroom, then John is like the bridegroom's friend (v. 29). He is no longer the center of attention, the one to whom "all are going out" (v. 26).[35] Instead, he identifies himself with the "voice of gladness" that accompanies the voice of the bridegroom in Jer. 33:10–11.

In doing so, he joins the ranks of those who rejoice at the coming of Jesus. They include Abraham, who "rejoiced (ἠγαλλιάσατο) that he would see [Jesus'] day; he saw it and was glad (ἐχάρη)" (John 8:56). They also include Jesus' disciples, who "rejoiced (ἐχάρησαν) when they saw" the risen Jesus (John 20:20; cf. 16:20–22). Here, the voice of gladness belongs to John the Baptist. He recognizes that Jesus is the Messiah, the prophesied bridegroom, and rejoices to hear his voice.

The Johannine Jesus at Jacob's well

"He must increase, and I must decrease," concedes John the Baptist as he fades from the narrative (3:30). Just as a bridegroom marries a bride and then begets children, so Jesus will elicit belief in more and more people. We soon learn that Jesus is indeed gaining a greater number of followers than is his forerunner (4:1). His success in Judea becomes the occasion for a journey through Samaria (4:3–4). John 4:4–42 then

---

Philadelphia: Westminster, 1971], 173–74, n. 11), Lindars (*Gospel of John*, 167), and Ridderbos (*Gospel According to John*, 147, n. 131).

[34] Boismard, "Ami de l'époux," 291.

[35] See also Zimmermann and Zimmermann, "Freund des Bräutigams."

fulfills John the Baptist's final prophecy. In a scene reminiscent of biblical betrothal narratives, the bridegroom-Messiah adds to his increase with a host of Samaritan believers.[36]

Israel's Scriptures include three stories in which the meeting of a man and a woman at a well leads to a betrothal. In Gen. 24:1–67, the man is Abraham's servant and the woman is Rebekah; in Gen. 29:1–20, Jacob meets Rachel; in Exod. 2:15–22, Moses defends Zipporah and her sisters. Various scholars have proposed that each of these stories, either alone or in combination, is the text evoked in John 4:4–42.[37] In addition, critics have suggested two other allusive referents. First, Hoskyns and Friedrich point out that Josephus (*Ant.* 2.257) retells the story of Moses and Zipporah in terms that recall John's well scene.[38] Josephus' Moses sits upon a well in the vicinity of a city – just as Jesus, at noon, sits on a well near the city of Sychar (John 4:5–6).[39] Second, many agree that John 4:4–42 is a "betrothal type-scene." John simply follows a familiar story-telling convention used also in Gen. 24:1–67, Gen. 29:1–20, and Exod. 2:15–22.[40]

The criterion of availability eliminates the possibility that John alludes to Josephus or to some extra-biblical tradition known to Josephus. It is not at all clear that such sources were available to John's implied author. On the other hand, the criterion of recurrence confirms the possibility of allusions to any one of the three biblical stories. Although none of them actually appears elsewhere in John, their main characters do. Abraham, who initiates the action in Gen. 24, becomes the subject of a crucial dispute in John 8:31–59. Jacob, the bridegroom of Gen. 29, receives some attention in a conversation between Jesus and Nathanael that alludes to Jacob's vision at Bethel (John 1:51; cf. Gen. 28:12).[41] Finally, John refers to Moses a number of times (1:17, 45; 3:14; 5:45–46; 6:32; 7:19, 22–23; 9:28–29).

---

[36] See also Carmichael, "Marriage and the Samaritan Woman," 335.

[37] See above, p. 6.

[38] Hoskyns, *Fourth Gospel*, 263; Friedrich, *Wer ist Jesus?*, 25.

[39] Friedrich, *Wer ist Jesus?*, 25.

[40] See above, p. 7. For an argument that minimizes the likelihood and significance of any allusions to well-betrothal narratives in John 4:4–42, see Okure, *Johannine Approach to Mission*, 87–89 (see also Lindars, *Gospel of John*, 179–80; Moloney, *Gospel of John*, 121). Similarly, John Painter contends that the parallels between John 4:4–42 and the well-betrothal narratives are insufficient to establish it as a betrothal type-scene (*The Quest for the Messiah: The History, Literature, and Theology of the Johannine Community* [Edinburgh: T&T Clark, 1991], 165–66).

[41] Carmichael also notes a connection between John 1:51 and 4:4–42 ("Marriage and the Samaritan Woman," 337). It leads Jennifer K. Berenson Maclean to propose that "John 1–4 as a whole must be understood in light of the entire Jacob narrative" ("The Divine

To which of the three narratives, if any, does John's story most closely correspond? In matters of syntax, it bears no marked resemblance to any of them. John repeats no characteristic or unusual phrase. On the other hand, several details of plot, characters, setting, and diction in John 4:4–42 match similar details in Gen. 24, Gen. 29, and Exod. 2. The stage is set when the traveling man stops at a well (φρέαρ) and a woman (γυνή) comes (ἔρχομαι) to draw (ἀντλέω) water (John 4:4–7; Gen. 24:10–15; 29:1–9; Exod. 2:15–16).[42] One of them then draws water from the well and gives it to the other (this procedure is discussed in John 4:7–15, and enacted in Gen. 24:16–20; 29:10; Exod. 2:17). Next, the woman rushes home to tell her family about the stranger at the well (John 4:28–29; Gen. 24:28; 29:12; Exod. 2:18–19). Finally, the family offers hospitality to the stranger (John 4:40; Gen. 24:29–33; 29:13–14; Exod. 2:18–19).[43] The "betrothal type-scene" construct proposed by Alter is derived from these similarities in plot, characters, and setting. Therefore, it also shares these features with John 4:4–42.[44]

The two Genesis stories include three further details present in John 4 but absent from Exod. 2, as well as from the hypothetical type-scene. First, whereas all four biblical accounts mention the woman's father or ancestor (πατήρ), only John and Genesis emphasize her eligibility in terms of both her ethnic heritage and her marital status.[45] The Samaritan woman's family background is stressed in John 4:7, 9, 12, and 20, and her marital status is the subject of John 4:17–18. In Gen. 24, Abraham's servant searches specifically for a woman from Abraham's family (vv. 3–4). The narrator reveals Rebekah's identity as the grand-daughter of Abraham's brother in v. 15, and the servant learns it in v. 24. Her family background and its importance to Abraham are

---

Trickster: A Tale of Two Weddings in John," in *A Feminist Companion to John* [ed. Amy-Jill Levine; London: Sheffield Academic Press, 2003], I:51). She is especially concerned with parallels between John 2:1–12 and the "mythic pattern" of Gen. 29:1–20 ("Divine Trickster," 61–72). These parallels, however, do not constitute an allusion as I have defined it.

[42] The word φρέαρ appears in Gen. 24:11, 20, 62; Gen. 29:2–3, 8, 10; Exod. 2:15; John 4:11,12; γυνή in Gen. 24:36–40, 44, 51, 67; Gen. 29:21, 28; Exod. 2:21, 22; John 4:7, 9, 11 (in some manuscripts), 15, 17, 19, 25, 27, 28, 39, 42; ἔρχομαι in Gen. 29:6, 9; Exod. 2:15; John 4:7; ἀντλέω in Gen. 24:13, 20, 43; Exod. 2:17, 19; John 4:7, 15.

[43] Each of these parallels is also noted by Braun (*Jean le théologien 3.1*, 93–95), Bonneau ("Woman at the Well"), Boismard ("Aenon près de Salem," 223–25), Boismard and Lamouille (*Évangile de Jean*, III:136), Dagonet (*Femme de Samarie*, 47–50), Girard ("Jésus en Samarie," 302–3), and Staley (*Print's First Kiss*, 100). They contradict the contention that John 4:4–42 contains no hint of an allusion to well-betrothal stories.

[44] Alter, *Art of Biblical Narrative*, 51–58.

[45] The word πατήρ occurs in Gen. 24:23; Gen. 29:9, 12; Exod. 2:16, 18; John 4:12, 20.

rehearsed once more during the servant's tale (vv. 37–38, 47–48). In addition, the narrator notes that Rebekah is a beautiful virgin (v. 16). Likewise, Rachel's eligibility is emphasized in Gen. 29:1–20. When Jacob arrives at the well in search of his uncle Laban, he immediately discovers that Rachel is Laban's daughter (vv. 4–5). The kinship of Jacob and Laban is stressed throughout the narrative, especially in v. 10 where the phrase "his mother's brother Laban" appears three times (see also vv. 12–15). Rachel's beauty is also mentioned (v. 17). It should be noted that both Genesis betrothal stories stress the heritage of the maiden because the patriarchs Isaac and Jacob must perpetuate the family through Abraham's kin. The children of Israel must not have a Canaanite mother (Gen. 24:3, 37; 28:1–5).[46]

A second distinctive feature shared by John 4, Gen. 24, and Gen. 29 is the hidden identity of the traveler. The Samaritan woman immediately knows that Jesus is a Jew (John 4:9), but does not learn that he is the Messiah until they have discussed living water (John 4:26). Abraham's servant introduces himself only after Rebekah has given him a drink, watered his camels, identified herself, and offered hospitality (Gen. 24:22–27). Similarly, Jacob rolls the stone from the well and waters Laban's flock before he reveals his identity to Rachel (Gen. 29:10–12). The maiden does not realize the traveler's significance until water is drawn and shared. Her rushing off to report to her family occurs immediately after she learns his identity (John 4:28–29; Gen. 24:27–28; 29:12). Presumably her interest in him has been heightened.

Finally, the woman's account of the traveler's actions and identity generates further intense interest at home. In all three stories, someone comes to the well to meet the traveler. In John 4, many citizens of Sychar arrive at the well to welcome Jesus (v. 30). In Gen. 24, Laban is eager to receive the servant of his great-uncle Abraham who has lavished such valuable gifts on his sister Rebekah (vv. 29–33).[47] In Gen. 29, he rushes out to greet his sister Rebekah's son and to offer him hospitality (vv. 13–14). Apparently Laban has as much to gain from alliances with Abraham's family as do Israel's patriarchs from marriages with Abraham's kinswomen.

---

[46] Dagonet notes a similar concern with the woman's background in both Gen. 24:23 and John 4:16 (*Femme de Samarie*, 50). Okure regards the Samaritan woman's marital status as a disparity that weakens the echo of well-betrothal narratives rather than as a similarity that strengthens it (*Johannine Approach to Mission*, 88). See also Painter, *Quest for the Messiah*, 166; Cook, "Wells, Women, and Faith," 15–17.

[47] Braun also notes the parallel between John 4:30 and Gen. 24:29 (*Jean le théologien 3.1*, 93, n. 4). See also Boismard, "Aenon près de Salem," 224; Boismard and Lamouille, *Évangile de Jean*, 136.

John 4 shares certain characteristics with Gen. 24 alone. Whereas three words (φρέαρ, γυνή, and πατήρ) appear in John 4, Gen. 24, and Gen. 29, six words that occur in both John 4 and Gen. 24 are absent from Gen. 29. Only Gen. 24 mentions the traveler's arrival in a πόλις (v. 10; cf. John 4:5).[48] Only Gen. 24 refers to the well as a πηγή (vv. 13, 16, 29, 30, 42, 43, 45; cf. John 4:6, 14).[49] Only Gen. 24 actually uses the words ἀντλέω (vv. 13, 20, 43; cf. John 4:7, 15), ὕδωρ (vv. 11, 13, 17, 32, 40; cf. John 4:10, 11, 13–15), ὑδρία (vv. 14–18, 20, 43, 45, 46; cf. John 4:28), and πίνω (vv. 14, 18, 19, 22, 44, 46; cf. John 4:7, 9, 10, 12–14).[50] Only in Gen. 24 does the woman use the terms ἄνθρωπος, λάλω, and μοι in her report (Gen. 24:30; cf. John 4:29).[51]

Another similarity shared by John 4 and Gen. 24 alone involves the request for a drink of water. In John 4:7, Jesus tells the Samaritan woman, "Give me a drink." In Gen. 24:17, Abraham's servant makes a similar request of Rebekah: "Please let me sip a little water from your jar." The story repeats this request twice: once in v. 14 when the servant prays, and once in v. 43 when he explains his errand to Laban.[52] In contrast, Gen. 29 contains no such request. Jacob does not want water from Rachel. Instead, he is eager to provide water for her.[53]

---

[48] Braun, *Jean le théologien 3.1*, 93, n. 4. See also Boismard, "Aenon près de Salem," 223; Boismard and Lamouille, *Évangile de Jean*, 136; Dagonet, *Femme de Samarie*, 49; Girard, "Jésus en Samarie," 302.

[49] Braun, *Jean le théologien 3.1*, 93, n. 4. See also Boismard, "Aenon près de Salem," 225; Dagonet, *Femme de Samarie*, 49. Boismard observes that Jesus sits by the well (ἐκαθέζετο οὕτως ἐπὶ τῇ πηγῇ) in John 4:6 just as Abraham's servant stands by the spring (ἐγὼ ἔστηκα ἐπὶ τῆς πηγῆς) in Gen. 24:13 (Boismard, "Aenon près de Salem," 223, 225; Boismard and Lamouille, *Évangile de Jean*, 136; Girard, "Jésus en Samarie," 302). Jesus' position, however, is actually more similar to that of Moses, who also sits by the well (ἐκάθισεν ἐπὶ τοῦ φρέατος) in Exod. 2:14. See Derrett, "Samaritan Woman's Pitcher," 254. There is no support for Derrett's conclusion that both Jesus and Moses sit to indicate their superiority. Similar arguments cannot be made about Jesus and Jacob, as Gen. 29 never describes Jacob's posture.

[50] Bonneau points out that both John 4 and Gen. 24 contain the words γυνή, ἀντλέω, ὕδωρ, φρέαρ, and ὑδρία ("Woman at the Well," 1254). The verb ἐκπορεύομαι does not appear in John 4, as he claims. The verb μένω does occur in both John 4:40 and Gen. 24:55, as he indicates, but in different contexts.

[51] Braun, *Jean le théologien 3.1*, 93, n. 4. See also Boismard, "Aenon près de Salem," 224; Boismard and Lamouille, *Évangile de Jean*, 136; Dagonet, *Femme de Samarie*, 50; Girard, "Jésus en Samarie," 303.

[52] Braun, *Jean le théologien 3.1*, 93, n. 4. See also Sanders, *Commentary*, 141; Boismard, "Aenon près de Salem," 224–25; Boismard and Lamouille, *Évangile de Jean*, 136; Dagonet, *Femme de Samarie*, 49; Girard, "Jésus en Samarie," 303.

[53] Some have also pointed out other, less compelling, parallels between John 4 and Gen. 24. Rebekah receives gifts in Gen. 24:22 while John's Jesus speaks of "the gift of God" in John 4:10 (Braun, *Jean le théologien 3.1*, 93, n. 4; see also Dagonet, *Femme de Samarie*, 50). Both Gen. 24:19 and John 4:12 mention watering animals (Girard, "Jésus en Samarie," 303). Both Gen. 24:26 and John 4:20–24 refer to worship (Girard, "Jésus en

Other traits are shared by John 4 and Gen. 29 alone. One concerns the time of day. It is "about noon (ὥρα ἦν ὡς ἕκτη)" when Jesus sits by the well near Sychar (John 4:6).[54] Similarly, Jacob arrives at the well near Haran when "it is still broad daylight (ἔτι ἐστὶν ἡμέρα πολλή)" (Gen. 29:7).[55] Abraham's servant, on the other hand, does not reach the well until sometime "toward evening (τὸ πρὸς ὀψέ)" (Gen. 24:11).[56]

A second similarity between John 4:4–42 and Gen. 29:1–20 has to do with the arrival of the woman. John 4:7 reads, "A Samaritan woman came (ἔρχεται) to draw water." Genesis 29:9 relates that "Rachel came (ἤρχετο) with her father's sheep." In Gen. 24:15, however, we see Rebekah "coming out (ἐξεπορεύετο) with her water jar on her shoulder" (cf. vv. 13, 45). Genesis 24 uses a different verb.

Another, more significant, element of John 4 finds a parallel in Gen. 29 alone: both stories feature the patriarch Jacob (Ἰακωβ). Jacob is the main character of Gen. 29:1–20. In John 4, Jesus meets the Samaritan woman, a descendant of Jacob (v. 12), at Jacob's well (v. 6), near the field that Jacob gave to his son Joseph (v. 5). John's story thus mentions Jacob three times, twice in the first three verses.[57] Moreover, the Samaritan woman explicitly compares Jesus to Jacob in verse 12: "Are you greater than our ancestor Jacob, who gave us the well?"[58] This comparison is strengthened if we recall that Jesus, a man on a journey, has just been identified as a bridegroom (John 3:29). In Gen. 29, Jacob is also a man on a journey who becomes a bridegroom. In Gen. 24, however, the bridegroom never travels to the well. The mysterious stranger who courts Rebekah is the servant of the bridegroom's father.

The parallel between Jesus and Jacob, along with the rhetorical emphasis placed on it, is the strongest indicator that John 4:4–42 alludes most directly to Gen. 29:1–20. Indeed, four elements at the start

---

Samarie," 303). Both Abraham's servant (Gen. 24:33) and Jesus (John 4:31–32) refuse to eat (Boismard, "Aenon près de Salem," 224–25; Boismard and Lamouille, *Évangile de Jean*, 136; Girard, "Jésus en Samarie," 303; Staley, *Print's First Kiss*, 101–2; Dagonet, *Femme de Samarie*, 50). Not only do these corresponding details lack verbal similarities, they also do not fit into the plot of John 4 in the same way as they do in the plot of Gen. 24.

[54] This translation assumes that John counts the hours from 6:00 a.m. For an argument in support of this position, see Brown, *John I–XII*, 75.

[55] See also Carmichael, "Marriage and the Samaritan Woman," 336–37; Jones, *Symbol of Water*, 97.

[56] See also Bligh, "Jesus in Samaria," 336; Carmichael, "Marriage and the Samaritan Woman," 336–37.

[57] See also Conway, *Men and Women*, 108.

[58] Sanders and Carmichael also note that mention of Jacob in John 1:51 and 4:12 establishes a link with Gen. 29 (Sanders, *Commentary*, 140–41; Carmichael, "Marriage and the Samaritan Woman," 337).

of John's story provide an immediate connection with the beginning of Gen. 29. The first is the mention of Jacob (John 4:5–6). The second is the appearance of a man on a journey (John 4:3–6). Third, the man arrives at a well (John 4:6). Fourth, it is the middle of the day (John 4:6). Jesus is most reminiscent of Jacob, the bridegroom who journeys to a well at noon (Gen. 29:1, 2, 7).[59]

To be sure, Gen. 24 contains more verbal parallels with John 4 than does Gen. 29. John's use of πόλις, πηγή, ἀντλέω, ὕδωρ, ὑδρία, πίνω, ἄνθρωπος, λάλω, and μοι, however, is not as distinctive as his three-fold mention of Jacob. Moreover, John repeats none of these words in an unusual phrase unique to Gen. 24. He does not even explicitly echo the servant's thrice-repeated request for a drink:

> Please offer your jar that I may drink (ἐπίκλινον τὴν ὑδρίαν σου, ἵνα πίω). (Gen. 24:14)

> Please let me sip a little water from your jar (πότισόν με μικρὸν ὕδωρ ἐκ τῆς ὑδρίας σου). (Gen. 24:17)

> Please give me a little water from your jar to drink (πότισόν με μικρὸν ὕδωρ ἐκ τῆς ὑδρίας σου). (Gen. 24:43)

> Give me a drink (δός μοι πεῖν). (John 4:7)

In fact, one could argue that because the exchange of water in John 4:10–15 involves Jesus' offer of living water to the Samaritan woman, it more closely resembles Jacob's watering Rachel's sheep in Gen. 29:10.

The shared elements of Gen. 29:1–20 and John 4:4–42 offer strong evidence that John alludes to this story.[60] They outweigh any similarities between John 4:4–42 and Gen. 24:1–67, Exod. 2:15–22, and the type-scene construct. (Incidentally, one could argue that the main reason John 4:4–42 resembles these three well scenarios is because they in turn resemble Gen. 29:1–20.) The shared elements of Gen. 29:1–20 and John 4:4–42 may be summarized as follows: the encounter of a traveling man ('Ιακωβ, in Gen. 29) and a woman (γυνή – Jacob's descendant, in John 4) who comes (ἔρχομαι) to a well (φρέαρ – Jacob's well, in John 4) is followed by their sharing a drink of water. The woman's family background (in John 4, descent from her πατήρ Jacob) and marital status is emphasized. When the man finally discloses his

---

[59] See also Staley, *Print's First Kiss*, 101.
[60] They are sufficient to challenge Painter's skepticism (see *Quest for the Messiah*, 165–66).

identity, the woman runs home to tell her family. A relative then hurries back to the well to greet the man and to offer hospitality.

There is also one important difference: unlike the Genesis story, John's account does not end with a promise of marriage. Instead, it concludes with the woman's fellow-citizens coming to faith in Jesus (4:39–42). Here John develops an unstated correspondence between marriage and belief.[61] This suggests an interesting line of interpretation.[62] In the Samaritan story, corresponding elements from Gen. 29:1–20 become vehicles for some of John's central themes. Specifically, the well water, Rachel's eligibility, Jacob's self-disclosure, Rachel's reporting to family members, the offer of hospitality, and the new relationship between Jacob and Rachel enhance the Johannine themes of eternal life, the fatherhood of God, Jesus' messianic identity, testimony, remaining, and believing. I will discuss each element in turn to show how John borrows details from Gen. 29 to reveal Jesus as the Jewish Messiah who offers eternal life to apostate Samaritans. The woman bears witness to Jesus, and many come to believe. Just as Jacob's meeting Rachel at a well, their sharing a drink, his revelation of his identity, her report to her family, and the family's offer of hospitality eventually lead to the births of the twelve patriarchs (Gen. 29:31–30:24; 35:16–21), so also Jesus' meeting a woman at a well, his offer of eternal life, his revelation of his identity, her witness, and his remaining in Sychar produce a family of faith – a family in which all Jacob's children worship the Father in spirit and in truth.

The drink of water

The first feature of Gen. 29:1–20 to acquire a new meaning in John 4:4–42 is the drink of water. The subject of water and drinking dominates the conversation between Jesus and the woman from v. 7 through v. 15. Jesus initiates the conversation by asking the woman for a drink (v. 7).[63] When the woman wonders at the audacity of such a

---

[61] Cf. also Carmichael, "Marriage and the Samaritan Woman," 335; Jones, *Symbol of Water*, 92.

[62] Contra Okure, to whom the absence of a betrothal in John 4 suggests that John does not make a strong connection between the Samaritan account and well-betrothal stories (*Johannine Approach to Mission*, 88). The fact that John changes some of the details of Gen. 29:1–20 does not decrease the possibility that he alludes to it. Staley comes closer to the mark when he identifies John's story as a parody (*Print's First Kiss*, 98–102).

[63] Carmichael suggests that Jesus' request is tantamount to a proposal, given the associations in Prov. 5:15 and Song 4:15 between water and female sexuality ("Marriage

request, Jesus indicates that he is able to provide her with "living water (ὕδωρ ζῶν)" (vv. 9–10). Because he links his ability to do so with the gift of God and his own identity, one might conclude that he means something other than running water from a spring. The woman, however, remains ignorant of Jesus' identity; she merely wonders how he will draw water without a vessel (v. 11). Jesus finally explains that he does not refer to the water in Jacob's well.[64] Whoever drinks the water that Jesus gives will never thirst again, for the water that Jesus gives will become in that person a spring of water welling up into "eternal life (ζωὴ αἰώνιος)" (v. 14).

The Fourth Gospel has already described Jesus as the source of eternal life. "In him was life (ζωή)," declares the prologue (1:4). According to John 3:15–16, 36, whoever believes in Jesus has "eternal life (ζωὴ αἰώνιος)." John will reiterate this teaching in 5:24–26; 10:10, 28; 12:25; 14:19; 17:2–3; and 20:31. He will also illustrate it using metaphors such as "the bread of life" (6:33–58), "words of life" (6:63, 68), "the light of life" (8:12), "the resurrection and the life" (11:25–27), and "the way, the truth and the life" (14:6). Living water reappears in John 7:38–39, when Jesus announces that "rivers of living water (ποταμοὶ . . . ὕδατος ζῶντος)" will flow out of the hearts of those who believe in him. John explains that Jesus is referring to the Spirit, to be received after Jesus' glorification.[65]

John 4:7–15, then, alludes to Gen. 29:10 in order to illustrate what has just been explained in John 1 and 3, as well as to introduce further elaboration in John 5–20. By identifying the drink of water from the Genesis story with the Johannine concept of "eternal life," John is able to portray Jesus as the giver of water that becomes a spring of eternal life. The one who asks for a drink in v. 7 ("δός μοι πεῖν") is asked for a drink in v. 15 ("δός μοι τοῦτο τὸ ὕδωρ"). Note that water

and the Samaritan Woman," 336). This interpretation seems unlikely, however, as John does not emphasize these associations.

[64] According to Jaubert, Jacob's well symbolizes the law of Moses ("Symbolique du puits"; see also Braun, *Jean le théologien 3.1*, 90–92; Bonneau, "The Woman at the Well," 1256–57). Since John's implied author does not betray familiarity with targumic and rabbinic tradition associating wells with the Law, this symbolism can only be attributed to an original author.

[65] For a discussion of the Johannine theme of eternal life, see C. H. Dodd, *The Interpretation of the Fourth Gospel* (Cambridge: Cambridge University Press, 1953), 148–49. Studies of water as a symbol in John's Gospel include Culpepper, *Anatomy*, 192–95; Koester, *Symbolism*, 155–84; Jones, *Symbol of Water*; Michael A. Daise, "'Rivers of Living Water' as New Creation and New Exodus: A Traditio-Historical Vantage Point for the Exegetical Problems and Theology of John 7:37–39" (Ph.D. diss., Princeton Theological Seminary, 2000), 88–107.

is never actually drawn from the well and shared, as in Gen. 29:10. Jacob waters the sheep belonging to Rachel's father, but Jesus has something more than water to offer the Samaritan woman and her fellow-citizens.[66]

The woman's eligibility

A second element from Gen. 29:1–20 to appear in John's narrative is the woman's eligibility. This includes both her heritage and her marital status.[67] It is easy to see how John highlights the Samaritan woman's heritage in order to enhance the theme of God's fatherhood. As with Rachel, her family background receives special emphasis. Indeed, the story of her initial encounter with Jesus is dominated by their ethnic difference. It mentions three times that she is a Samaritan (vv. 7, 9), and twice contrasts her nationality to that of Jesus (v. 9).[68] When Jesus offers her living water (v. 10), she again refers to her ancestry: "Are you greater than our ancestor (τοῦ πατρὸς ἡμῶν) Jacob?" (v. 12). Then, following a discussion of her marital status (vv. 16–18), the topic of Jewish and Samaritan differences re-emerges.[69]

The ensuing conversation involves a play on the word "father" (πατήρ)." "Our ancestors (οἱ πατέρες ἡμῶν) worshiped on this mountain," declares the Samaritan woman, "but you (ὑμεῖς) say that the place where people must worship is Jerusalem" (v. 20). Her comment provides Jesus with the opportunity to distinguish worship by Samaritan ancestors (οἱ πατέρες ἡμῶν) from worship of the Father (ὁ πατήρ). The Father (ὁ πατήρ) will be worshiped neither on Mount Gerizim nor on Mount Zion (v. 21). True worshipers will worship the Father (ὁ πατήρ) in spirit and in truth; in fact, the Father (ὁ πατήρ) seeks such worshipers (v. 23).

John uses the wordplay to show that true worship of God transcends Jewish and Samaritan ancestral worship. In this way, he adds an

---

[66] See also Staley, *Print's First Kiss*, 101–2.

[67] John's emphasis on the woman's "adulterous" sexual history and her "foreign" ethnicity lead Jane S. Webster to compare her to the "strange woman" of Prov. 7; 9:13–18 ("Transcending Alterity: Strange Woman to Samaritan Woman," in *A Feminist Companion to John*, I:126–42). These parallels, however, do not constitute an allusion as I have defined it.

[68] Olsson's structural analysis also underscores John's emphasis on Samaritan identity (*Structure and Meaning*, 138–47).

[69] Carmichael contends that the woman emphasizes the common ancestry of Samaritans and Jews ("Marriage and the Samaritan Woman," 337). John, however, lays more stress on Jewish and Samaritan differences.

interesting twist to his echo of Gen. 29. Rachel's heritage is a matter of some concern to Jacob, since Jacob must marry a descendant of Abraham. Jesus, however, is not similarly concerned about the heritage of the Samaritan woman. More important than the Samaritan ancestor (τοῦ πατρὸς ἡμῶν) Jacob is the Father (ὁ πατήρ), God.[70]

It is less easy to interpret John's references to the woman's marital status. These references begin with v. 16, when Jesus asks her to call her husband. The woman initially confesses that she has no husband (v. 17). Jesus, however, reveals that she has had five husbands, and currently lives with a man to whom she is not married (v. 18). The woman's response: "Sir, I see that you are a prophet" (v. 19).

Interpretations of John 4:16–18 fall into three categories, two literal and one symbolic. Many commentators contend that Jesus' observation about husbands reveals her moral deficiency. This explains why she has come to the well alone in the middle of the day: her illicit behavior has made her a social outcast, so that she does not join the other women at the normal evening hour. It also explains the ensuing discussion of worship in vv. 20–24: the embarrassed woman has changed the subject. Several such commentators conclude that Jesus' conversation with the Samaritan woman shows that he welcomes sinners, as well as women and people of marginalized ethnic groups.[71]

This interpretation fails to account for the fact that the discussion about the woman's sexual morality in vv. 17–18 seems somewhat out of place. The subject is virtually absent from the rest of the Gospel.[72] The Samaritan story certainly does not treat it in much more detail.[73] The only other clear allusion to the woman's marital status is her exclamation in vv. 29 and 39: "Come and see a man who told me everything I have ever done!" This leads other scholars to argue that Jesus' comment about husbands emphasizes not the woman's depravity, but rather Jesus' prophetic ability. This interpretation explains the woman's immediate realization that Jesus is a prophet (v. 19), as well as her testimony that Jesus has told her everything she has ever done (vv. 29, 39). It also accounts for her turning the discussion to worship

---

[70] See also Bernard, *Critical and Exegetical Commentary*, I:147; Cook, "Wells, Women, and Faith," 16–17.

[71] See, e.g., Plummer, *Gospel According to S. John*, 107, 110–11; Lagrange, *Évangile selon S. Jean*, 110; Brown, *John I–XII*, 171; Schnackenburg, *Gospel According to St. John*, I:433; Friedrich, *Wer ist Jesus?*, 36–38; Sanders, *Commentary*, 144–49.

[72] It turns up elsewhere only in John 7:53–8:11, a passage that does not appear in the earliest manuscripts and was probably added later.

[73] See also Lindars, *Gospel of John*, 186; Black, "Rhetorical Criticism," 273.

(v. 20): she expects that a prophet will be able to make an authoritative pronouncement on the subject.[74]

It does not, however, explain why Jesus introduces the topic of husbands in the first place. This topic seems like an intrusion. Up until v. 16, the story highlights the differences between Jews and Samaritans as Jesus offers the woman a drink of living water. In vv. 19–26, the discussion again concerns differences between Jews and Samaritans, this time as a way to introduce Jesus as the Messiah. Moreover, the questions about Jewish and Samaritan worship raised in verses 20–24 constitute the centerpiece of the narrative and provide the backdrop for the Samaritans' confession in v. 42.[75] These questions now take the stage, yet the conversation about husbands is never resolved. The woman never calls the man who is not her husband. Instead, she summons her fellow-citizens (vv. 28–29). She and her love life then recede into the background. Her marital status seems to be beside the point.

A symbolic interpretation of the six men is more consonant with the story's emphasis on Samaritan ancestry and religious identity.[76] The five husbands are thought to represent the five cults brought into Samaria after the Assyrian conquest. According to 2 Kings 17:30–31, "The people of Babylon made Succoth-benoth, the people of Cuth made Nergal, the people of Hamath made Ashima; the Avvites made Nibhaz and Tartak; the Sepharvites burned their children in the fire to Adrammelech and Anammelech, the gods of Sepharvaim." The sixth man represents the form of Yahwism described in 2 Kings 17:32: "They also worshiped the LORD and appointed from among themselves all sorts of people as priests of the high places, who sacrificed for them in the shrines of the high places." The situation is summarized in 2 Kings 17:41: "So these nations worshiped the LORD, but also served their carved images; to this day their children and their children's children continue to do as their ancestors did."[77]

---

[74] See, e.g., Bultmann, *Gospel of John*, 187; Lindars, *Gospel of John*, 186; Gail R. O'Day, *The Word Disclosed: John's Story and Narrative Preaching* (St. Louis, Mo.: CBP Press, 1987), 42–43 and "John," in *The Women's Bible Commentary* (ed. Carol A. Newsom and Sharon H. Ringe; Louisville: Westminster John Knox, 1992), 296; Black, "Rhetorical Criticism," 273; Ridderbos, *Gospel According to John*, 158–62; Moloney, *Gospel of John*, 127.

[75] Bligh outlines this story as a five-point chiasm, locating vv. 16–26 at the center ("Jesus in Samaria," 329). See also Cahill, "Narrative Art," 42.

[76] See also Cahill, "Narrative Art," 43; Schneiders, *Revelatory Text*, 190 and *Written That You May Believe*, 139–40.

[77] According to Eberhard Nestle, the connection between the five husbands and the five cults was perceived by a thirteenth-century copyist ("Die fünf Männer des

If the six men represent Samaritan religions, then the Samaritan woman represents the Samaritan people. Indeed, the Evangelist emphasizes the resemblance. The woman is identified as a Samaritan (vv. 7, 9). She associates herself with her people by referring to "our ancestor (τοῦ πατρὸς ἡμῶν) Jacob" (v. 12) and "our ancestors (οἱ πατέρες ἡμῶν)" who worshiped on Mount Gerizim (v. 20). Jesus himself addresses her with the plural ὑμεῖς in vv. 21–22.[78]

The resemblance of the woman to Samaritans and the men to Samaritan religions is quite striking. It does not, however, conclusively indicate that they symbolize those entities. Resemblance does not always imply representation. For example, Jesus is identified as a Jew (v. 9) and is referred to using the plural pronouns ὑμεῖς and ἡμεῖς (vv. 20–22), but he does not symbolize Jews. The most that can be said is that the woman with her six men exemplifies the Samaritans with their six religions, as described in 2 Kings 17.

This observation suggests the possibility of a fourth way to interpret John 4:18: as part of an allusion to 2 Kings 17. In addition to the parallel between the six men and the six religions, the allusion is marked by three instances of verbal and circumstantial correspondence. First,

---

samaritanischen Weibes," *ZNW* 5 [1904]: 166–67). Twentieth-century proponents of this view include Loisy (*Quatrième Évangile*, 354), Bauer (*Johannes-Evangelium*, 75), Hoskyns (*Fourth Gospel*, 258, 265–66), Dodd (*Interpretation*, 313), Barrett (*Gospel According to St. John*, 235), Oscar Cullmann ("Samaria and the Origins of the Christian Church: Who Are the ἄλλοι of John 4.38?" in *The Early Church* [ed. A. J. B. Higgins; London: SCM Press, 1956], 187–88), Boismard ("Aenon près de Salem," 225–26), Marsh (*Saint John*, 216), Otto Betz ("'To Worship God in Spirit and in Truth': Reflections on John 4, 20–26," in *Standing Before God: Studies on Prayer in Scriptures and in Tradition* [ed. Asher Finkel and Lawrence Frizzell; trans. Nora Quigley; New York: Ktav, 1981], 56–58), Schneiders (*Revelatory Text*, 190 and *Written That You May Believe*, 139–40), and Fehribach (*Women in the Life of the Bridegroom*, 68–69). Opponents point out that the account of Samaritan origins in 2 Kings 17:30–31 associates traditional Samaritan religion with seven deities, not five or six (see, e.g., Bernard, *Critical and Exegetical Commentary*, I:143–44; Schnackenburg, *Gospel According to St. John*, I:433). Defenders claim that the five husbands refer, not to the seven deities, but to the five cults (see, e.g., Bligh, "Jesus in Samaria," 336). In his article "'The Savior of the World,'" Koester circumvents this problem by pointing out that the seven deities in 2 Kings were introduced by five nations. He then argues that the five husbands represent the five nations mentioned in this passage, and that the sixth man, who is not the woman's husband, refers to the Roman empire ("'The Savior of the World' [John 4:42]," *JBL* 109 [1990], 675–77). He makes the case that John 4:1–42 has strong political connotations as well as religious concerns. I would point out that any political connotations in this story are not as explicit as its religious significance. There is no evidence to support Derrett's opinion that the five husbands represent the five senses through which passion has enslaved the woman ("The Samaritan Woman's Pitcher," 255).

[78] Koester, *Symbolism*, 48, 50. See also Fehribach, *Women in the Life of the Bridegroom*, 58–61.

both passages are primarily concerned with Samaritan and Jewish differences – in particular, differences about the proper worship of Israel's God. The word προσκυνέω, which appears nine times in John 4:20–24, occurs twice in the reiteration of the first commandment found in 2 Kings 17:35–36: "You shall not worship other gods or bow yourselves (προσκυνήσετε) to them or serve them or sacrifice to them, but you shall worship the LORD, who brought you out of the land of Egypt with great power and with an outstretched arm; you shall bow yourselves (προσκυνήσετε) to him, and to him you shall sacrifice."[79] According to 2 Kings 17, the Samaritans break the first commandment in two ways: they worship other gods (vv. 29, 41) and they worship Israel's God in illegitimate shrines (v. 32). Clearly, Jesus and the Samaritan woman are endeavoring to interpret this commandment in John 4:20–24: should God be worshiped in Jerusalem or on Mount Gerizim?[80]

A second similarity between John 4 and 2 Kings 17 involves the fact that both attribute Jewish and Samaritan differences to ancestral customs. The Samaritan woman refers to "our ancestors (οἱ πατέρες ἡμῶν)" who worshiped on Mount Gerizim (John 4:20). Likewise, 2 Kings 17:41 affirms that the Samaritans continue to practice the customs of "their ancestors (οἱ πατέρες αὐτῶν)."[81]

A third and even more striking parallel is that both John 4 and 2 Kings 17 state that the Samaritans do not know Israel's God. According to 2 Kings 17:26, Samaritan immigrants from Babylon, Cuthah, Avva, Hamath, and Sepharvaim suffer lion attacks because they "do not know (οὐκ ἔγνωσαν) the law of the god of the land." Similarly, Jesus tells the Samaritan woman, "You worship what you do not know (οὐκ οἴδατε)" (John 4:22).[82]

If John 4:4–42 indeed alludes to 2 Kings 17, then there is no need to postulate symbolism in John 4:18. John is simply making a comparison. The Samaritan woman with her six men is like the Samaritan people with their six religions. They practice the customs of their ancestors, who worshiped the gods of five foreign cults and who still do not know Israel's God. This comparison allows Jesus to assure the woman that it

---

[79] 2 Kings 17 is found in the LXX at 4 Kgdms 17.
[80] See also Betz, "To Worship God," 56.
[81] See also ibid., 58.
[82] See also ibid., 56. Betz goes on to liken Jesus to the Israelite priest who saves the Samaritans by teaching them about true worship (2 Kings 17:27–28). For Betz, this explains Jesus' claim in John 4:22 that "salvation is from the Jews." This connection is somewhat tenuous, however, as the priest was from Israel and not from Judah.

no longer matters whether God is worshiped in Jerusalem or on Mount Gerizim. True worshipers worship in spirit and in truth (John 4:21–24).

The Samaritan woman claims to be a descendant of Jacob. Unlike Rachel, however, she is not portrayed as a beautiful virgin.[83] Her previous marriages and current liaison resemble the ancestral worship of her people. Her heritage and her "marital status" hardly make her eligible for a relationship with a Jewish Messiah.[84] According to Jesus, however, her eligibility has less to do with her ancestor Jacob than with the Father, God. Furthermore, worship of that Father in spirit and in truth makes her "marital history" obsolete. One greater than Jacob offers living water to a religious renegade, a Samaritan daughter of Jacob, at Jacob's well.[85] His offer trivializes the ancestor who gave her people the well (v. 12) as well as the ancestors who worshiped on Mount Gerizim (v. 20). The most important ancestor now is the Father who seeks true worshipers (v. 23).

The man's identity

The third element from Gen. 29 featured in John 4 is the traveler's hidden identity. In the Genesis story, Jacob reveals who he is after the sharing of water (Gen. 29:10–12). Here, Jesus identifies himself after a conversation about living water (John 4:25–26). Unlike Jacob, however, Jesus does not introduce himself by name. He rather indicates that he is the Messiah, the Christ.

This is the first time that John's Jesus states his messianic identity.[86] It is not the Fourth Gospel's first reference to Jesus as Messiah, however. Andrew tells his brother Simon, "'We have found the Messiah' (which is translated Anointed)" (1:41). Nathanael confesses, "Rabbi, you are the Son of God! You are the King of Israel!" (1:49). As we have seen, Jesus' provision of wine for the wedding at Cana (2:1–11) indicates that he is the prophesied Messiah, as does John the Baptist's bridegroom saying (3:22–30).[87] Everything concerning Jesus' identity that has been stated or implied so far in the narrative is confirmed by

---

[83] See also Strauss, *Life of Jesus*, 308; Braun, *Jean le théologien 3.1*, 93–95; Sanders, *Commentary*, 141; Dagonet, *Femme de Samarie*, 50, n. 1; Culpepper, *Anatomy*, 136; Duke, *Irony*, 102–3; Girard, *Jésus en Samarie*, 303; Staley, *Print's First Kiss*, 101.

[84] This particular point remains valid even if the five husbands are interpreted more literally.

[85] See also Neyrey, "Jacob Traditions," 426.

[86] It is not the last. In John 17:3, Jesus calls himself "Jesus Christ."

[87] See above, pp. 49–50, 57–58.

Jesus' revelation to the Samaritan woman. "'I know that Messiah is coming' (who is called Christ)," she remarks (4:25). Jesus replies, "I am he, the one who is speaking to you" (4:26).

Not only does the exchange in John 4:25–26 allow Jesus to affirm his messianic identity as previously hinted by the Evangelist and stated by Andrew, Nathanael, and John the Baptist, it also constitutes the climax of the Samaritan story.[88] In fact, the revelation of the traveler's identity is the turning point of both Gen. 29:1–20 and John 4:4–42. In Gen. 29, Jacob's introducing himself leads directly to Rachel's report, Laban's offer of hospitality, and the eventual betrothal of Jacob and Rachel (vv. 12–20). Laban's family welcomes Jacob into their household because he is Rebekah's son. Similarly, the revelation of Jesus' identity in John 4 results in the Samaritan woman's testimony, an invitation for Jesus to remain in Sychar, and the eventual belief of many citizens (vv. 25–42). The Samaritans welcome Jesus because they recognize that he is the Messiah.

The woman's report

The Johannine theme of witness is developed in the woman's report to her relatives, a fourth element of Jacob's betrothal story. In Gen. 29:12, Rachel runs home to tell Laban about his sister's son Jacob. In John 4:28–29, the Samaritan woman goes back to the city to tell the people about Jesus. Her departure immediately follows Jesus' self-disclosure. Indeed, his identity is the subject of her report: "He cannot be the Messiah, can he?" (v. 29).

The Evangelist terms her action "testimony (μαρτυρούσης)" (v. 39). The Samaritan woman's testimony joins that of John the Baptist and Jesus in illustrating the prologue's assertion that testimony leads either to belief or unbelief. According to John 1:7–8, John the Baptist came "as a witness (εἰς μαρτυρίαν) to testify (ἵνα μαρτυρήσῃ)" to Jesus, "so that all might believe (ἵνα πάντες πιστεύσωσιν)" (cf. 15, 19, 32). John 3:11–12 tells how Nicodemus and those like him do not receive Jesus' testimony (τὴν μαρτυρίαν); they do not believe (οὐ πιστεύετε) (cf. 3:32; 6:31–38; 8:13–18). In contrast, John 4:39 shows that many Samaritans from Sychar believe in Jesus because of the woman's

---

[88] Verse 26 closes the section on worship designated by Bligh and Cahill as the center of this story (see n. 75 above). Schnackenburg also identifies v. 26 as the narrative's climax (*Gospel According to St. John*, I:442).

testimony (ἐπίστευσαν εἰς αὐτὸν . . . διὰ τὸν λόγον τῆς γυναικὸς μαρτυρούσης). Just as Rachel's report about Rebekah's son eventually leads to their betrothal, so the Samaritan woman's testimony about the Messiah leads to belief.

The offer of hospitality

In the meantime, the woman's family improves their acquaintance with the traveler. In both Gen. 29 and John 4, a rush to the well and an offer of hospitality follow the woman's report about the man's identity. Laban runs out to the well to greet his sister's son and to bring him home (Gen. 29:13). Similarly, the Samaritan townspeople flock to meet Jesus at the well. "Come and see (δεῦτε ἴδετε) a man who told me everything I have ever done!" exclaims the woman (v. 29). "So when the Samaritans came to him, they asked him to stay (μεῖναι) with them; and he stayed (ἔμεινεν) there two days" (v. 40).[89]

Here the Evangelist takes up a theme introduced in John 1:35–39, where John the Baptist's testimony motivates some of his disciples to follow Jesus: the theme of staying or abiding. "Look, here is the Lamb of God!" declares John (v. 36). The disciples ask Jesus, "Where are you staying (ποῦ μένεις)?" (v. 38). "Come and see (ἔρχεσθε καὶ ὄψεσθε)," replies Jesus (v. 39).[90] "They came and saw where he was staying (μένει), and they remained (ἔμειναν) with him that day" (v. 39). This theme is of course consummately developed in the vine analogy of John 15. Meanwhile, in John 4, the offer of hospitality from Gen. 29 becomes the Johannine invitation to stay, a crucial step towards familiarity with Jesus.[91]

---

[89] I have chosen not to include a detailed analysis of vv. 8, 27, 31–38. The parallel narrative about the disciples does not properly form a part of the betrothal scene, but rather serves as a foil to it. It concerns food instead of living water (vv. 31–34), and describes God's work in Samaria using harvest imagery (35–38).

[90] Both ℵ and A read "ἔρχεσθε καὶ ἴδετε." External and internal evidence, however, favors "ἔρχεσθε καὶ ὄψεσθε." This reading is preserved in 𝔭[66], 𝔭[75], and B. The variant can be explained as an attempt to harmonize John 1:39 with John 4:29.

[91] See also Barrett, *Gospel According to St. John*, 204; Brown, *John I–XII*, 510–12; Raymond Collins, "Discipleship in John's Gospel," in *These Things Have Been Written: Studies in the Fourth Gospel* (Louvain: Peeters, 1990); repr. from *Emmanuel* 91 (1985): 248–55; Gary M. Burge, *The Anointed Community: The Holy Spirit in the Johannine Tradition* (Grand Rapids: Eerdmans, 1987), 54–56; Sharon H. Ringe, *Wisdom's Friends: Community and Christology in the Fourth Gospel* (Louisville: Westminster John Knox, 1999), 76.

The betrothal

Genesis 29:1–20 ends with the betrothal of Jacob and Rachel (vv. 15–20). John 4:4–42 ends, not with betrothal, but with belief.[92] At first, "Many Samaritans from that city believed (ἐπίστευσαν) in him because of the woman's testimony" (v. 39). Later, "Many more believed (ἐπίστευσαν) because of his word. They said to the woman, 'It is no longer because of what you said that we believe (πιστεύομεν), for we have heard for ourselves, and we know that this is truly the Savior of the world'" (vv. 41–42).

Belief serves as a fitting conclusion to the Samaritan story. It fulfills the agenda set in the prologue and followed in the narrative so far. Jesus comes into the world, but some do not accept him. There are those, however, "who believed (τοῖς πιστεύουσιν) in his name" (John 1:12). When Jesus performs his first sign, "his disciples believed (ἐπίστευσαν) in him" (2:11). More people "believed (ἐπίστευσαν) in his name" (2:23) when they saw his signs in Jerusalem. In the same way, Jesus' sojourn in Samaria also results in belief.

In addition, belief necessarily concludes the Samaritan story because it is the means for attaining the eternal life promised by Jesus in John 4:14. We learn this in John 3:15, when Jesus tells Nicodemus, "The Son of Man must be lifted up, that whoever believes (πᾶς ὁ πιστεύων) in him may have eternal life." The Gospel continues with John 3:16, "For God so loved the world that he gave his only Son, so that everyone who believes (πᾶς ὁ πιστεύων) in him may have eternal life."[93] John reiterates this teaching right before the Samaritan story: "Whoever believes (ὁ πιστεύων) in the Son has eternal life" (3:36). In order to receive the water that springs up to eternal life (4:14), of course the Samaritan woman and the citizens of Sychar must come to believe.

Jacob's betrothal serves as a metaphor for Samaritan belief, but not in the sense that Jesus and Samaritan believers are now bound together in a love relationship similar to that enjoyed by Jacob and Rachel. What makes this betrothal an appropriate metaphor for the Samaritan story has very little to do with the couple's love. It has more to do with their anticipated offspring. To be sure, Gen. 29 mentions Jacob's love for Rachel (vv. 18, 20, 30), but its main purpose is to describe the

---

[92] Cahill proposes that the reader familiar with the type-scene format will expect an actual betrothal ("Narrative Art," 47). Stibbe, however, rightly points out that since Jesus is a symbolic bridegroom in John 2:1–11 and 3:29, one might anticipate a symbolic betrothal in John 4:4–42 (*John*, 69).

[93] It is not clear whether John 3:16 is spoken by Jesus or added by the Evangelist.

beginnings of a family.[94] The betrothal of Jacob to Rachel eventually results in births (Gen. 29:31–30:24). In a sense, then, Gen. 29 narrates the origins of Israel. Similarly, when the Samaritan woman meets one greater than Jacob at Jacob's well, a family of faith is established. The citizens of Sychar believe, and receive power to become children of God (cf. 1:12). They experience the birth that Jesus describes to Nicodemus (3:3–7).[95] As prophesied by John the Baptist, Jesus the bridegroom continues to increase (3:30). His encounter with a Samaritan woman produces spiritual offspring.[96]

John 4:4–42, then, develops John's depiction of Jesus' revelation and human response by describing Jesus' interaction with Samaritan believers in terms of Gen. 29:1–20. The story about Israel's origins through the patriarch Jacob provides the outline for a story about the origins of belief in one greater than Jacob among Jacob's Samaritan descendants. It provides an exquisite setting for the depiction of the Jewish Messiah Jesus, who draws sacrilegious Samaritans to himself. It also illustrates six Johannine themes. The betrothal-scene features of drinking water and the traveler's self-disclosure help to portray Jesus as the Christ, the source of eternal life. Themes of testifying, remaining, and believing, enacted in the woman's report to her relatives and her family's receiving the stranger, characterize the woman as a witness to Jesus and the Samaritans as believers who receive her testimony. Finally, the theme of the woman's eligibility, effected in the Samaritan story by her descent from Jacob and her several previous marriages, reveals that the fatherhood of God transcends the ethnic and religious distinctions between Jew and Samaritan as portrayed in 2 Kings 17. Jacob's apostate offspring become God's faithful children when the Johannine Jesus visits Jacob's well.

Excursus: the Johannine Jesus in Israel's wilderness

A comparison of John 4 with John 6 both supports and illuminates the interpretation of John 4 offered here. John 6 develops several of the themes present in John 4, such as eternal life, the fatherhood of God, the messianic identity of Jesus, and belief. Whereas John 4

---

[94] See also Carmichael, "Marriage and the Samaritan Woman," 337; cf. Fehribach, *Women in the Life of the Bridegroom*, 56–58.

[95] See also Carmichael, "Marriage and the Samaritan Woman," 333; Cahill, "Narrative Art," 47.

[96] See also Carmichael, "Marriage and the Samaritan Woman," 335.

elaborates these themes in a Samaritan setting, however, John 6 concerns a group of Jews.

In both scenes, the theme of eternal life appears in connection with a potent religious symbol. In John 4, Jesus sits by Jacob's well (4:6), an important aspect of Samaritan ancestral heritage. He claims that he can give the Samaritan woman living water (ἔδωκεν ἄν σοι ὕδωρ ζῶν) (4:10). The Samaritan woman reminds Jesus of "our ancestor (τοῦ πατρὸς ἡμῶν) Jacob, who gave (ἔδωκεν)" her people the well and drank from it himself (4:12). Jesus, however, proposes to infuse this ancestral relic with life. He explains to the Samaritan woman that everyone who drinks water from Jacob's well will thirst again, but that those who drink the water that he will give (δώσω) will have eternal life (ζωὴν αἰώνιον) (4:13–14). His offer elicits an eager response from the woman: "Sir, give me this water (κύριε, δός μοι τοῦτο τὸ ὕδωρ)" (4:15).

The same dynamics, reinforced by much of the same vocabulary, operate in John 6. Jesus has just fed a crowd (6:1–14), recalling an important aspect of Jewish ancestral heritage: God's provision of manna in the wilderness. He admonishes the crowd to work "for the food that endures for eternal life (ζωὴν αἰώνιον), which the Son of Man will give you (ὑμῖν δώσει)" (6:27). The Jews remind Jesus that "our ancestors (οἱ πατέρες ἡμῶν) ate the manna in the wilderness" (6:31). Jesus, however, proposes to infuse this ancestral tradition with life. His Father can give (ὁ πατήρ μου δίδωσιν) true bread from heaven – bread that gives life (ζωὴν διδοὺς) to the world (6:32–33). He later explains to the Jews that their ancestors ate manna and died, but the one who eats the true bread from heaven "will live forever (ζήσει εἰς τὸν αἰῶνα)" (6:49–50, 58). His offer elicits an eager response from the crowd: "Sir, give us this bread always (κύριε, πάντοτε δός ἡμῖν τὸν ἄρτον τοῦτον)" (6:34).[97]

Both John 4 and John 6 involve the same wordplay on "father (πατήρ)." As we have seen, the Samaritan woman in John 4 makes two references to her ancestry: one to "our ancestor (τοῦ πατρὸς ἡμῶν) Jacob" (4:12) and one to "our ancestors (οἱ πατέρες ἡμῶν)" who worshiped on Mount Gerizim (4:20). This enables Jesus to distinguish worship by Samaritan ancestors (οἱ πατέρες ἡμῶν) from worship of the Father (ὁ πατήρ), whom "true (ἀληθινοὶ) worshipers" will worship in spirit and in truth (4:21–24).

---

[97] See also Pancaro, *Law*, 477; Ridderbos, *Gospel According to John*, 156–57.

Likewise, the crowd in John 6 displays a concern with "our ancestors (οἱ πατέρες ἡμῶν)" who ate the manna (6:31). According to Jesus, however, "it is my Father (ὁ πατήρ μου) who gives you the true (ἀληθινόν) bread from heaven" (6:32). In John 6, as in John 4, the traditions of "the ancestors (οἱ πατέρες)" are contrasted to true (ἀληθινός) worship and the true (ἀληθινός) bread from "the Father (ὁ πατήρ)."[98]

John 4 and John 6 share a concern with Jesus' identity. Initially, his words and actions lead to the supposition that he is a prophet. Jesus' remark about the six men in her life causes the Samaritan woman to declare, "Sir, I see that you are a prophet (προφήτης)" (4:19). Similarly, his miraculous feeding of a large crowd results in the belief that "This is indeed the prophet (ὁ προφήτης) who is to come into the world" (6:14).[99] Eventually, Jesus' messianic identity is affirmed. Jesus himself reveals his identity to the Samaritan woman. In response to her statement, "I know that Messiah is coming," Jesus replies, "I am he" (4:25–26). In John 6, the confession of Jesus' messianic identity falls to Peter: "We have come to believe and know that you are the Holy One of God" (6:69).

Finally, both John 4 and John 6 are interested in belief as a response to Jesus. In John 4, Jesus' offer of eternal life, his affirmations about his Father, and his revelation of his identity lead to widespread belief: "Many Samaritans from that city believed (ἐπίστευσαν) in him" (4:39; cf. vv. 41–42). The Galilean crowd, however, remains skeptical. Jesus reminds them, "You have seen me and yet do not believe (οὐ πιστεύετε)" (6:36). He acknowledges that even some of his disciples "do not believe (οὐ πιστεύουσιν)" (6:64). In the end, Simon Peter speaks for the twelve: "We have come to believe (πεπιστεύκαμεν)" (6:69). Upon learning that Jesus identifies himself with the manna from heaven, the Galilean crowd is less ready to accept his offer of eternal life. Jesus has come to his own people, and his own people have not accepted him (cf. John 1:11). On the other hand, to the Samaritans, "who received him, who believed in his name, he gave power to become children of God" (John 1:12).

---

[98] See also Pancaro, *Law*, 477.

[99] Here the crowd is almost certainly thinking of the prophet foretold by Moses in Deut. 18:15–22. Jesus has just fed them with bread; surely he is the prophet like Moses, through whom God provided manna in the wilderness. See also Pancaro, *Law*, 478.

4

THE GLORIFICATION OF THE BRIDEGROOM-MESSIAH: ALLUSIONS TO SONG 1:12 AND SONG 3:1–4

John 2:1–4:42 introduces Jesus as the bridegroom-Messiah. At Cana in Galilee (2:1–11), he provides abundant wine for a wedding feast, assuming the role of the bridegroom and fulfilling messianic prophecy. At Aenon in Judea (3:22–30), John the Baptist hints that Jesus is the bridegroom foretold by Jeremiah. At Sychar in Samaria (4:4–42), Jesus imitates Jacob at the well and establishes a family of faith. As Jesus reveals his messianic identity, he gains more and more followers. His disciples believe in him (2:11), people flock to be baptized by him (3:23, 30), and the citizens of Sychar declare that he is the Savior of the world (4:42). In terms of John 1:11–13, many receive him, believe in his name, and become God's children.

John 4:43–10:42 continues with the program outlined in John 1:11–13 and initiated in John 1:19–4:42. After Jesus leaves Samaria, however, he faces more rejection than reception. A few come to believe, such as the royal official (4:53) and the man born blind (9:35–38). Most, however, do not accept Jesus. They argue with him about his identity and his mission (5:1–47; 6:1–71; 7:1–52; 8:12–59; 9:13–41; 10:22–39) and they look for an opportunity to do away with him (7:1, 44; 8:20, 59; 10:31, 39). He comes to his own, and his own do not receive him.

In John 11–12, a transition occurs. With the raising of Lazarus, Jesus' own death and resurrection come to the fore. Then, as Jesus enters Jerusalem, the narrative begins to focus both on the circumstances that lead to his execution as well as on the implications of his departure for his disciples. John's final two references to marriage texts emerge in this context. In John 12:3, an allusion to Song 1:12 portrays Jesus as the bridegroom-Messiah facing crucifixion. Lastly, an allusion to Song 3:1–4 in John 20:1, 11–18 provides the format for Mary Magdalene's recognition of the risen and ascending Lord.

The king on the couch

By the end of John 11, Jesus' opponents have formulated a plan. Because Jesus has raised Lazarus from the dead, they fear that everyone will believe in him, thus prompting the Romans to destroy both the temple and the nation (11:48). Now the narrative moves inexorably towards Jesus' execution. After the council conspires to put Jesus to death (11:53), he withdraws for a while to Ephraim, a town near the wilderness (11:54). Six days before Passover, however, he returns to Bethany, where they celebrate his arrival with a dinner (12:1–2). As Jesus reclines at table with Lazarus, "Mary took a pound of costly perfume made of pure nard, anointed Jesus' feet, and wiped them with her hair. The house was filled with the fragrance of the perfume" (12:3).

Several texts have been proposed as allusive referents for this scene. Hanson suggests that John 12 evokes Hag. 2:6–9, a passage that never mentions marriage:

> For thus says the LORD of hosts: Once again, in a little while, I will shake the heavens and the earth and the sea and the dry land; and I will shake all the nations, so that the treasure of all nations shall come, and I will fill this house with splendor, says the LORD of hosts. The silver is mine, and the gold is mine, says the LORD of hosts. The latter splendor of this house shall be greater than the former, says the LORD of hosts; and in this place I will give prosperity, says the LORD of hosts.

Hanson points out six parallels between Hag. 2:6–9 and John 12. First, both are associated with a character called "Jesus" or "Joshua" (Hag. 2:4; John 12:1). Second, the thundering voice from heaven in John 12:28–29 is reminiscent of the shaking in Hag. 2:6–7. Third, the Greeks who seek Jesus in John 12:20 are like the nations who bring their treasure in Hag. 2:7. Fourth, the fragrance that fills the house in John 12:3 calls to mind the splendor that fills the house in Hag. 2:7. Fifth, Judas' concern for money in John 12:4–6 parallels the silver and gold mentioned in Hag. 2:8. Finally, God glorifies Jesus as foreshadowed in John 12:23, just as he restores the temple in Hag. 2:9. Hanson concludes that John understands Hag. 2:6–9 as a prophecy of Jesus' death, burial, and resurrection, as well as Gentile inclusion, and accordingly alludes to it in John 12.[1]

---

[1] Hanson, *Interpretation of Scripture*, 118–21.

This proposed allusion, however, lacks sufficient verbal correspondence and rhetorical emphasis. Two of the suggested parallels do not even display convincing circumstantial correspondence. First, the "voice from heaven" that reminds bystanders of "thunder" or the voice of "an angel" – a loud noise overheard by a local crowd – does not immediately call to mind the physical shaking of "the heavens and the earth and the sea and the dry land" (Hag. 2:6). Second, Judas' concern with "denarii" and "the common purse" (John 12:4–6) seems to have very little to do with the "silver" and the "gold" claimed by Israel's God (Hag. 2:8).

As for the four parallels that do contain similar circumstances, verbal correspondence is scant. According to John 12:3, "The house was filled with the fragrance of the perfume (ἡ δὲ οἰκία ἐπληρώθη ἐκ τῆς ὀσμῆς τοῦ μύρου)." In Hag. 2:7, God declares, "I will fill this house with splendor (πλήσω τὸν οἶκον τοῦτον δόξης)." In John 12:23, 28, the Son of Man is "glorified (δοξασθῇ)" by the Father. In Hag. 2:9, God restores "the splendor (ἡ δόξα) of the temple." In these two cases, three words are similar but not exactly the same (οἰκία and οἶκός; πληρόω and πίμπλημι; δόξα and δοξάζω). A third circumstantial parallel has no verbal correspondence: whereas John 12:20 refers to "Greeks (Ἕλληνές)," Hag. 2:7 mentions "nations (ἔθνη)." Only one word is repeated verbatim: John 12 is about "Jesus (Ἰησοῦς)" (John 12:1); Hag. 2:6–9 is addressed to "Joshua (Ἰησοῦς)" (Hag. 2:4).

Of these four verbal similarities, two are not compelling. John's mention of Jesus is by no means a direct reminder of Haggai's Joshua, and Jesus' glorification in John 12:23, 28 hardly constitutes an unqualified reference to the splendor of the temple in Hag. 2:9. Moreover, these supposed allusions to Haggai are so scattered throughout John 12 as to render them virtually unrecognizable. The closest similarity exists between John 12:3 and Hag. 2:7, in which the cognates οἰκία/οἶκὸς and πληρόω/πίμπλημι are used to describe the filling of a house. Another, stronger allusion must be sought.

Winsor observes a number of possible connections between John 12:3 and the Song of Songs.[2] Only two of them, however, consist of more than one parallel. One of these links John 12:3 to Song 7:5 (6): "Your head crowns you like Carmel, and your flowing locks are like purple; a king is held captive in the tresses." Winsor proposes this allusion because in both John 12:3 and Song 7:5 (6), a "king [is] the

---

[2] See above, pp. 9–10.

object of the hair's 'action.'"[3] In Song 7:5 (6), the king is enthralled by his lover's tresses; in John 12:3, Mary of Bethany wipes the Messiah's perfumed feet with her hair.

Although both passages do feature somewhat similar circumstances, they do not feature similar words. Most significantly, whereas John mentions Mary's "hair" (ταῖς θριξὶν αὐτῆς), the Song of Songs refers to the woman's "tresses" (παραδρομαῖς). Moreover, the hair performs a different action in each text. Song of Songs 7:5 (6) concerns allure, while John 12:3 involves anointing. Neither verbal nor circumstantial correspondence between John 12:3 and Song 7:5 (6) suffices to constitute an allusion.

A much better case can be made for an allusion to Song 1:12, "While the king was on his couch, my nard gave forth its fragrance." This allusion, proposed by Winsor as well as by Cambe, Jacques Winandy, Bauer, and Origen before her, is marked by a slight but significant verbal correspondence.[4] There are only two exact verbal parallels. Their striking nature, however, makes up for their small number. The first of these is the term νάρδος. Mary of Bethany anoints Jesus with "a pound of costly perfume made of pure nard (λίτραν μύρου νάρδου πιστικῆς πολυτίμου)."[5] Νάρδος appears in the LXX only in the Song of Songs: twice in Song 4:13–14, and once in Song 1:12, which refers to "my nard (νάρδος μου)."[6]

The second verbal parallel is the word ὀσμή. In John 12:3, "the fragrance of the perfume (τῆς ὀσμῆς τοῦ μύρου)" fills the house. Ὀσμή commonly occurs in the LXX with reference to the pleasing odor of a sacrifice (e.g., Gen. 8:21; Exod. 29:18; Lev. 1:9, 13, 17; 2:2). Only four times does it indicate the fragrance of perfume. Three of those references are found in Song 1:3–4 and Jer. 25:10. They all contain a variation of the phrase ὀσμὴ μύρου, as found in John 12:3. The reference in Jer. 25:10 is particularly interesting, as it occurs in one

---

[3] Winsor, *A King Is Bound*, 22.

[4] Origen, *Comm. Cant.* 2.9; Bauer, *Johannes-Evangelium*, 159; Winandy, *Cantique*, 60 and "Cantique et le NT," 166; Cambe, "Influence du Cantique," 15–17; Winsor, *A King Is Bound*, 22–23, 25–27. See also Feuillet, "Recherche du Christ," 106–7 and *Mystère de l'amour divin*, 231; Fehribach, *Women in the Life of the Bridegroom*, 93.

[5] The word νάρδου was omitted by the original copyist of 𝔓66, as well as in D and Old Latin manuscripts. It is possible that it was added in an attempt to harmonize John 12:3 with Mark 14:3. On the other hand, external evidence clearly favors its inclusion. Its omission can be explained as an attempt to harmonize this part of the verse with its final clause, where νάρδος is not mentioned.

[6] See also Cambe, "Influence du Cantique," 16; Winsor, *A King Is Bound*, 23.

of the prophet's oracles about the bridegroom and the bride.[7] The only
time that the perfume is identified as nard, however, is in Song 1:12.[8]

These striking verbal parallels are reinforced by several instances
of circumstantial correspondence. In fact, every detail of characters,
setting, and plot in Song 1:12 – the king on the couch, the woman, her
nard (νάρδος), and its fragrance (ὀσμή) – is recapitulated in John 12:3.
The details of the woman's nard and its fragrance receive special
emphasis in John's account. The anointing story begins at John 12:1,
where a change of time (πρὸ ἓξ ἡμερῶν τοῦ πάσχα) and place (εἰς
Βηθανίαν) signal the opening of a new scene. It ends at John 12:11, as
the next episode begins in John 12:12 with a similar shift in time (τῇ
ἐπαύριον) and place (εἰς Ἱεροσόλυμα). The rhetorical unit of John
12:1–11 is composed of three distinct parts. The first part sets the scene
and describes the action that precipitates the conflict (12:1–3). The
second part involves the confrontation between Jesus and Judas
(12:4–8), and the third introduces the plot to kill Lazarus (12:9–11).

The allusion to Song 1:12 occurs in the first part, John 12:1–3. The
details of the woman's nard and the release of its fragrance are placed
at the end of this unit. They follow the reappearance of three figures
from the previous chapter: Lazarus, Martha, and Mary (11:1–44).
Verses 2–3 describe what each of these familiar characters does at the
feast. The actions of Martha and Lazarus receive a rather cursory
description: Martha serves, and Lazarus reclines. Mary's deed, however, constitutes the climax of the rhetorical unit, and rates a detailed
delineation. It takes five words to describe the perfume alone (λίτραν
μύρου νάρδου πιστικῆς πολυτίμου). Mary both anoints the feet of
Jesus and wipes them with her hair. Finally, in a clause set off by a post-
positive δὲ, John indicates that the fragrance of the perfume filled the
house.

John's stress on the fragrance of the perfume serves to exaggerate
its superfluity. This detail seems somewhat unnecessary within the
context of John's story. It certainly makes sense that an expensive
ointment would emit a strong odor. The smell, however, is never
explicitly linked to any other aspect of the account, such as Mary's
extravagance or Judas' outrage. The account would stand without the
clause that describes it. This extra detail helps to signal an allusion to
Song 1:12.

---

[7] See below, p. 117.
[8] See also Cambe, "Influence du Cantique," 16–17; Winsor, *A King Is Bound*, 26.

It is significant that this detail is not included in other versions of the same story. All three Synoptic Gospels report that Jesus was anointed by a woman (Mark 14:3–9; Matt. 26:6–13; Luke 7:36–50). John's anointing story agrees with the Synoptic accounts – and especially with Mark's version – on several points.[9] First, the anointing occurred at Bethany (Mark 14:3; John 12:1; cf. Matt. 26:6). Second, Jesus was at table (Mark 14:3; John 12:2; cf. Luke 7:36). Third, the woman used costly ointment (Mark 14:3; John 12:3; cf. Matt. 26:7; Luke 7:37). Fourth, the costly ointment was "of pure nard (μύρου νάρδου πιστικῆς")" (Mark 14:3; John 12:3). Fifth, someone present contended that the ointment should have been sold for three hundred denarii and the proceeds given to the poor (Mark 14:4–5; John 12:4–6; cf. Matt. 26:8–9). Sixth, Jesus defended the woman's action, reminding its detractors that whereas they will always have the poor, they will not always have Jesus (Mark 14:6–7; John 12:7–8; cf. Matt. 26:10–11).[10] Seventh, Jesus viewed the anointing as a preparation for his burial (Mark 14:8; John 12:7; cf. Matt. 26:12). John's account even contains a curious agreement with Luke's: the woman anoints Jesus' feet and wipes them with her hair (Luke 7:38; John 12:3).[11] Clearly, John has inherited a tradition known also to Mark, and duplicated in part by Matthew. In addition, he is cognizant of a detail known also to Luke.

None of the Synoptic accounts, however, mentions the ointment's fragrance. John has either added or retained this particular detail. When he recounts this tradition, he does so in terms of Song 1:12, making special mention of the fragrance.

Circumstantial correspondence between John 12:3 and Song 1:12 is not limited to that between the women with their fragrant nard. The men are also quite similar. For one thing, both assume the same posture. In Song 1:12, the man reclines "on his couch (ἐν ἀνακλίσει αὐτοῦ)." That Jesus also reclines on a couch is implied by John's report that "Lazarus was one of those at the table (ἐκ τῶν ἀνακειμένων)" with Jesus (v. 2). John's wording is only slightly reminiscent of that in the Song, and it is not at all clear that the couch in Song 1:12 is just

---

[9] I assume that Matthew and Luke rely heavily, if not exclusively, on Mark's version of the story.

[10] John 12:8 is missing from D as well as from certain Latin and Syriac versions. This omission is not easily explained. Indeed, its presence in the vast majority of witnesses may result from an early attempt to harmonize John's anointing story with the Matthean and Markan accounts (Bruce M. Metzger, *A Textual Commentary on the Greek New Testament* [Stuttgart: United Bible Societies, 1971], 236–37). Regardless, Jesus still defends Mary in John 12:7, just as he defends the woman in Mark 14:4 and Matt. 26:10.

[11] See also Dodd, *Historical Tradition*, 162–73; Brown, *John I–XII*, 450.

for eating dinner. Nevertheless, the resemblance between the reclining men is hard to mistake.[12]

Even subtler is the unstated correspondence between Jesus and the man in the Song. According to Song 1:12, the man on the couch is "the king (ὁ βασιλεὺς)," the royal bridegroom introduced in Song 1:1–4. That Jesus is a king is never stated in John 12:1–8, but that Jesus is the Messiah constitutes one of the major concerns of John's narrative.[13] Furthermore, John 2:1–4:42 has established that Jesus is a bridegroom. Both Jesus and the king of Song 1:12 are portrayed as royal bridegrooms.

Recognition of these unstated similarities leads to an interesting reading of John 12:1–8. John's superfluous reference to fragrance does not require interpretation; it simply helps to signal the presence of the allusion. The other corresponding elements in Song 1:12 then enhance Johannine themes in the anointing scene that foreshadows the Messiah's death. First, Jesus' role as the king on the couch once more identifies him as a bridegroom-Messiah. Second, a woman's nard on his feet becomes a harbinger of his impending burial.

The king

The circumstantial correspondence between the reclining man of Song 1:12 and the reclining Jesus in John 12:3 implies an unstated correspondence: like the man in Song 1:12, Jesus is a king.[14] This similarity is easy to recognize, since the Gospel has consistently reiterated Jesus' royal identity.[15] Indeed, Nathanael has specifically acclaimed Jesus "the King of Israel" (1:49). Jesus' messianic identity is also highlighted in the episodes immediately preceding and following the anointing scene. The centerpiece of the Lazarus story (11:1–44) is Martha's confession, "Yes, Lord, I believe that you are the Messiah, the Son of God, the one coming into the world" (11:27). Then, in John 12:13, Jesus is proclaimed "King of Israel" as he rides into Jerusalem on a donkey's colt (12:12–19).

Jesus resembles the man in Song 1:12 not only in that he is a king, but also in that he is a bridegroom. As we have seen, he has been portrayed as a bridegroom-Messiah in John 2:1–11, 3:22–30, and 4:4–42.[16] He

---

[12] See also Cambe, "Influence du Cantique," 16; Winsor, *A King Is Bound*, 22.

[13] See also Winsor, *A King Is Bound*, 22.

[14] For a discussion of the messianic significance of Song 1:12, see below, pp. 111–15.

[15] See above, pp. 38–39.

[16] See above, pp. 47–49, 57–58, 72–73.

has assumed the role of the messianic provider of abundant wine, the bridegroom of Jer. 33:10–11, and Jacob at the well. Now his similarity to the royal bridegroom of the Song of Songs reaffirms that he is a bridegroom-Messiah.

The woman's nard

Just as Jesus assumes the role of the Song's bridegroom, so Mary of Bethany is portrayed as the Song's bride. John implicitly identifies her with the (presumably female) speaker of Song 1:12. Some scholars even argue that, since the Song's bride can be understood as a symbol for the people of God, then Mary of Bethany, in the role of the bride, represents the church.[17]

This argument cannot be made with respect to John's implied author, however. Nothing in the narrative clearly indicates that John understands the Song of Songs as an allegory about Jesus and the church. In addition, nothing else about Mary of Bethany indicates that she is a representative figure for John's implied author and audience. She possesses no distinctive traits and she is not explicitly associated with any group. John's implied author is not so much interested in Mary's symbolic role as in the significance of her deed.

Like the bride in Song 1:12, Mary bears fragrant nard to a reclining royal bridegroom. John's echo, however, transposes the Song's sensuous tones into a minor key. Mary's nard does more than perfume the bower of the king. Jesus wants Mary to "keep it for the day of my burial" (v. 7). The scent that Mary has so lavishly poured on Jesus' feet will be saved for use as his embalming fluid. It serves as a shocking reminder that this royal bridegroom will die.[18]

Such a reminder is certainly in keeping with the themes of John 11–12, which more and more emphasize Jesus' impending doom. The threat to Jesus' life increases in the aftermath of Lazarus' resuscitation (11:45–57). First, Caiaphas the high priest explains to the council that Jesus must die for the people. The Evangelist further clarifies that Jesus' death will "gather into one the dispersed children of God" (11:52).

---

[17] E.g., Cambe, "Influence du Cantique," 25; Fehribach, *Women in the Life of the Bridegroom*, 93.

[18] Cf. also Hoskyns, *Fourth Gospel*, 484; Dodd, *Interpretation*, 370; Lightfoot, *St. John's Gospel*, 236–37; Brown, *John I–XII*, 454; Lindars, *Gospel of John*, 414. Some recognize John 12:1–8 as a royal anointing (see, e.g., Barrett, *Gospel According to St. John*, 341). In my view, the royal element lies not in the anointing, but rather in Jesus' role as the king on the couch.

When Jesus takes cover in Ephraim in response to the council's plan to have him executed (11:53–54), the chief priests and Pharisees order the people to report his whereabouts so that they can arrest him (11:57).

After the anointing scene, a private and subtle reminder that Jesus the king faces imminent death, comes a public acclamation of Jesus as king immediately followed by a public prophecy of his impending crucifixion. The story of Jesus' entry into Jerusalem stresses his royal identity (12:12–19). The crowd hails Jesus as "the King of Israel" (12:13). Jesus then tacitly acknowledges their claim by sitting on a donkey's colt, thus evoking a prophecy concerning a coming king (12:15; cf. Zech. 9:9). In the very next scene, the arrival of some Greeks prompts Jesus to reflect on his fate (12:20–36). He declares the arrival of the hour (12:23), implicitly likening his death to that of a grain of wheat (12:24–25). He purposefully faces this hour, affirming that his crucifixion will glorify the Father's name (12:27–28; cf. 11:4), cast out the ruler of this world (12:31), and draw all people to himself (12:32).[19]

Jesus' predictions in turn prompt an important question from the crowd: if the Messiah remains forever, why must he die (12:34)? Apparently, the death of the Messiah defies their expectations. If Jesus must die, they cannot believe that he is the Messiah. John's continued affirmations that Jesus is the Messiah who knowingly faces death address this problem for the Gospel's audience. Jesus' crucifixion is a necessary component of his messianic mission. Indeed, Jesus has already informed the crowd that the Messiah must die in order to remain forever. As a grain of wheat must fall into the earth before it bears fruit, so his death will result in eternal life (12:24–25; cf. 11:25–26).

Accordingly, John reinforces Jesus' messianic identity at his trial and crucifixion (18:33–19:22).[20] This section of John's passion narrative begins with Pilate's question, "Are you the King of the Jews?" (18:33) and ends with a dispute over Pilate's inscription, "Jesus of Nazareth, the King of the Jews" (19:19–22). The scenes surrounded by this royal *inclusio* focus on Jesus' messianic identity. First comes a discussion between Jesus and Pilate concerning Jesus' kingship (18:33–38). Next, Pilate ironically refers to Jesus as "the King of the Jews" in his address to Jesus' accusers (18:39). John follows up this reference with still more irony as soldiers array Jesus in a royal robe and a crown of thorns and then strike his face, acclaiming him "King of the Jews" (19:2–3).

---

[19] See also Culpepper, *Anatomy*, 94.

[20] See also Moloney, *Gospel of John*, 493; Winsor, *A King Is Bound*, 22.

What really frightens Pilate about Jesus is not his messianic preten-
sion but rather his claim to be the Son of God (19:4). This claim
prompts another round of interrogation, in which Jesus reminds Pilate
that all human authority comes from God (19:8–11). Not even Pilate
has power over Jesus (cf. 14:30). When Pilate tries once again to release
Jesus, Jesus' accusers remind him that Jesus' royal claims challenge the
authority of the emperor (19:12).

Since Jesus is tried as a messianic pretender, he is also condemned
and crucified as a messianic pretender. Twice more, Pilate ironically
introduces Jesus to the Jews as their "king." Even more ironically,
Jesus' accusers respond by rejecting this "king" and swearing alle-
giance to Caesar (19:14–15). The final irony is Pilate's inscription,
telling the world in three languages that the crucified man is "the King
of the Jews" (19:19–22).[21]

John thus aptly foreshadows the death of the Messiah as portrayed in
John 12:12–36; 18:33–19:22 by alluding to Song 1:12 in his anointing
story. John's association of the reclining Jesus with the Song's king
on the couch reaffirms Jesus' royal identity, while Mary's fragrant
nard heralds his impending crucifixion. Jesus, the bridegroom-Messiah,
is anointed with perfume intended for his burial.

Recognizing the risen Lord

Jesus is buried in a garden tomb near the site of his crucifixion (John
19:41–42). Early in the morning after the Sabbath, Mary Magdalene
arrives at the tomb and notices that the stone has been removed. Several
aspects of the ensuing episode have been proposed as echoes of the
Song of Songs. They include the garden (19:41), the dark setting (20:1),
Mary's search for the missing Jesus (20:2, 11–15), her looking into
the tomb (20:11; cf. 20:5), her conversation with the angels (20:12–13),
her turning (20:14, 16), her sudden encounter with Jesus (20:14–16),
their mutual recognition (20:16), and her holding him (20:17).

Some of these proposed allusions consist of just one parallel element.
For example, Schneiders notes that the word παρακύπτω appears in
John 20:5, John 20:11, and Song 2:9.[22] Apart from this word, however,

---

[21] For further discussion of royal imagery in John's passion narrative, see Wead,
Literary Devices, 55–59; Culpepper, *Anatomy*, 172; Duke, *Irony*, 126–37; Donald Senior,
The Passion of Jesus in the Gospel of John (The Passion Series 4; Collegeville: Liturgical
Press, 1991), 79–105.

[22] Schneiders, "Resurrection Narrative," I:407–8 and "Easter Jesus," 161. See also
Reinhartz, *Befriending the Beloved Disciple*, 108.

the Beloved Disciple's and Mary Magdalene's looking into the tomb
does not closely resemble a lover's looking in at the window. Schneiders also compares John 20:16, "Jesus said to her, 'Mary!' She turned
and said to him in Hebrew, 'Rabbouni!'" to Song 2:16, "My beloved is
mine and I am his." This also does not constitute a very strong allusion,
as no verbal correspondence links these two passages.

Other detected echoes are somewhat louder. It has been suggested
that Mary Magdalene's repetitive turning in John 20:14–16 signals an
allusion to Song 6:13 (7:1). Feuillet notes (as does Winsor) that John
fails to give a coherent account of Mary's orientation.[23] According to
John 20:14, Mary first turns away from the angels and towards Jesus
(ἐστράφη). Then, after Jesus addresses her by name, she turns
(στραφεῖσα) again (20:16). If Mary is already facing Jesus, why does
she make a second turn?

Since this second turn seems somewhat awkward in its Johannine
context, it could be consonant with a precursor text. According to
Feuillet and Winsor, it may refer to the request made by the daughters
of Jerusalem in Song 6:13 (7:1), "Return, return ('Επίστρεφε
ἐπίστρεφε), O Shulamite! Return, return (ἐπίστρεφε ἐπίστρεφε),
that we may look upon you."[24] Feuillet suggests an interpretation based
on the insights of André Robert. For Robert, the four-fold repetition of
the word "return" in Song 6:13 (7:1) contains a two-fold meaning: first
a physical, then a spiritual return is indicated.[25] According to Feuillet,
Mary initially seeks to re-establish her relationship with Jesus based
on sight (John 20:14) and touch (John 20:17). When her efforts fail, she
learns that she must instead return spiritually in order to establish a
new relationship with the risen Lord – one mediated by faith and
sacraments.[26]

Apart from the repetition of a variant of στρέφω, the proposed
allusion to Song 6:13 (7:1) is based on only one other similarity: the
female gender of the verb's subject. Correspondence between Song 6:13
(7:1) and John 20:1, 11–18 is thus insufficient to support the contention

[23] Feuillet, "Recherche du Christ," 106; Winsor, *A King Is Bound*, 37–38. See also
Lindars, *St. John's Gospel*, 606.
[24] Feuillet, "Recherche du Christ," 106; Winsor, *A King Is Bound*, 39. See also
Schneiders, "Resurrection Narrative," I:417–22.
[25] André Robert and Raymond Tournay, *Le Cantique des Cantiques* (*Ebib*; Paris:
Gabalda, 1963), 248–49.
[26] Feuillet, "Recherche du Christ," 99–100, 106. See also his "The Time of the Church
in St. John," in *Johannine Studies*, trans. Thomas E. Crane (Staten Island: Alba House,
1965), 153. Schneiders offers a similar interpretation ("Resurrection Narrative," I:417–22;
"Easter Jesus," 162; *Written That You May Believe*, 196).

that John alludes to this verse. Two indications that Mary Magdalene "turned (ἐστράφη)" and was "turning (στραφεῖσα)," separated by a brief dialogue, are hardly sufficient to evoke the four-fold command directed at the Shulamite woman, "'Ἐπίστρεφε ἐπίστρεφε, . . . ἐπίστρεφε ἐπίστρεφε." The dissonant detail of Mary's turning is better explained in Godfrey Nicholson's dissertation, *Death As Departure*. According to Nicholson, Mary's turning is consonant with Jesus' turning in John 1:38. Nicholson points out several parallels between John 1:38 and 20:11–18. In John 1:38, Jesus turns and sees two disciples following. He asks them, "What are you looking for?" They reply, "Rabbi, where are you staying?" In John 20:14–16, Mary turns and sees Jesus standing there. "Whom are you looking for?" he asks. She replies, "Tell me where you have laid him." Finally, she addresses him as "Rabbouni."[27] These two recognition scenes form a neat *inclusio* for the Gospel.

Cambe and Winsor note several similarities between John 20:1–18 and another passage from the Song of Songs. According to Winsor, John may have associated Mary Magdalene with the figure described in Song 8:13:

> O you who dwell in the gardens (ὁ καθήμενος ἐν κήποις),
>   my companions are listening for your voice;
>   let me hear it.

Like John's resurrection narrative, Song 8:13 mentions a "garden (κῆπος)" (John 19:41; 20:15) and a beloved voice that addresses a group of companions (John 20:18). To be sure, the LXX depicts the garden dweller as a man. In the MT, however, this individual is female (הַיּוֹשֶׁבֶת בַּגַּנִּים). For Winsor, the allusion indicates the importance of Mary's apostolic proclamation: the disciples are listening for a voice from the garden that reports, "I have seen the Lord."[28]

Cambe suggests rather that John may associate Jesus with the male garden dweller of the LXX. Mary Magdalene would then be identified with the speaker, and her companions might be understood as Peter and the Beloved Disciple.[29] In this case, corresponding details between Song 8:13 and John 20:1–18 include a man in a garden, a listening woman, the man's voice, and the woman's companions – an impressive array of parallel circumstances.

---

[27] Nicholson, *Death As Departure*, 72; cf. Raymond E. Brown, *The Gospel According to John XIII–XXI* (AB 29A; Garden City: Doubleday, 1970), 1010.

[28] Winsor, *A King Is Bound*, 43–44.

[29] Cambe, "Influence du Cantique," 19; see also Joüon, *Cantique*, 331–32.

Nevertheless, if John 20:1–18 does allude to Song 8:13, the allusion is rather weak. The circumstantial correspondence does not extend to specific details. No one in John's account listens for the voice either of Jesus or of Mary Magdalene. The absence of any other verbal correspondence save the setting in a "garden (κῆπος)" also mitigates against the plausibility of an allusion. Key words from Song 8:13, such as κάθημαι, ἀκούω, φωνή, and ἑταῖρος, although appropriate within the context of John 20:1–18, never appear. Cambe himself admits that the echo is faint, if not improbable.[30]

Possible allusions to Song 3:1–4 and 5:2–8 are more difficult to discount. Among modern interpreters who recognize such allusions are Cambe, Hanson, Schneiders, and Winsor (ancient interpreters include Hippolytus, The Venerable Bede, and St. John of the Cross).[31] In both scenes from the Song, as well as in John 20:1, 11–18, a woman searches for her beloved at night. Song of Songs 3:1–4 describes her rising from her bed to hunt all over the city, in the streets and in the squares. After inquiring of the sentinels, she immediately finds her lover. She holds him fast until she has brought him to her mother's chamber. In Song 5:2–8, the lover begs to be admitted into the woman's bedroom. When she finally gets up and opens the door, he has vanished into the night. Desperately she seeks him, enduring a beating from the sentinels. In the end, she leaves word for him with her maidens: "I am faint with love."

John 20:1–18 exhibits an interesting verbal similarity with a phrase that appears in both Song 3:1–2 and Song 5:6: "I sought him, but did not find him (ἐζήτησα αὐτὸν καὶ οὐχ εὗρον αὐτόν)." Song of Songs 3:1–2 gives this phrase strong poetic emphasis, as each verse repeats a variation of the couplet:

ἐζήτησα ὃν ἠγάπησεν ἡ ψυχή μου,
ἐζήτησα αὐτὸν καὶ οὐχ εὗρον αὐτόν.

---

[30] Cambe, "Influence du Cantique," 19.

[31] Hippolytus, Εἰς τὸ ᾆσμα, Frag. 15; The Venerable Bede, *In Cantica Canticorum*; St. John of the Cross, *Dark Night* 2.13.6; Cambe, "Influence du Cantique," 17–18; Hanson, *Prophetic Gospel*, 228; Schneiders, "Resurrection Narrative," I:413–16; Winsor, *A King Is Bound*, 40–43. See also Bauer, *Johannes-Evangelium*, 159; Feuillet, "Recherche du Christ," 103–4 and *Mystère de l'amour divin*, 231; Brown, *John XIII–XXI*, 1010; Jaubert, "Symbolique des femmes," 117; Nicholson, *Death As Departure*, 73; Baril, *Feminine Face*, 96–97; Okure, "Commission of Mary Magdalene," 181; Stibbe, *John*, 205; Lundbom, "Mary Magdalene," 172–75; Fehribach, *Women in the Life of the Bridegroom*, 159–60; D'Angelo, "(Re)Presentations of Women," 136; Reinhartz, *Befriending the Beloved Disciple*, 108.

John first echoes this couplet in v. 2, when Mary Magdalene tells Peter and the Beloved Disciple, "They have taken the Lord out of the tomb, and we do not (καὶ οὐκ) know where they have laid him (αὐτόν)." He stresses the allusion by repeating the echo in v. 13, as Mary reiterates her story to the two angels: "They have taken away my Lord, and I do not (καὶ οὐκ) know where they have laid him (αὐτόν)." He generates a final echo with Jesus' question in v. 15: "Whom are you looking for (τίνα ζητεῖς)?"[32] In John 20:1–18, as in Song 3:1–2 and Song 5:6, a woman looks (ζητέω) for her man, and she cannot (καὶ οὐκ) locate him (αὐτόν).[33]

These faint yet insistent verbal echoes are reinforced by a number of circumstantial parallels. Song of Songs 3:1–4, Song 5:2–8, and John 20:1–18 share the same basic plot: a woman seeks a missing man in the dark. The bride of Song 3:1–4 and 5:2–8 looks all over the city at night for her lover, and Mary Magdalene approaches Jesus' tomb while it is still dark.[34] No additional verbal correspondence supports these connections. Song of Songs 3:1–4 and 5:2–8 take place "at night (ἐν νυξὶν)" (Song 3:1; cf. 5:2), while John's resurrection narrative opens "early . . . while it was still dark (πρωῒ σκοτίας ἔτι οὔσης)" (John 20:1). Jesus is never named "the one whom my soul loves (ὅν ἠγάπησεν ἡ φυχή μου)," as is the missing man in Song 3:1–4, or "beloved (ἀδελφιδός)," as in Song 5:2–8. Still, the rhetorical emphasis placed on the darkness and on Mary's search for the missing Jesus lends support to the possibility of an allusion.

Song of Songs 5:2–8 alone features two additional details that have been linked to John 20:1–18. According to Hanson, the myrrh that drips from the woman's fingers (Song 5:5) may correlate with the ointment that Mary presumably brought to the tomb (John 20:1).[35] Furthermore, both Hanson and Winsor point out that the bride and Mary Magdalene each respond to a man's speech. In Song 5:6, the bride's soul fails her

---

[32] A few witnesses (including A* and D) attribute this question to the angels in v. 13.

[33] Cf. also Cambe, "Influence du Cantique," 18; Reinhartz, *Befriending the Beloved Disciple*, 108. Martin Scott argues rather that Mary's search is patterned after the search for wisdom as expressed in Prov. 8:17: "Those who seek (ζητοῦντες) me diligently find me" (*Sophia and the Johannine Jesus* [JSNTSup 71; Sheffield: JSOT Press, 1992], 232). John 20:1–18, however, is more reminiscent of the Song of Songs with its searching woman and missing man than of Prov. 8 with its beckoning woman.

[34] Cambe also remarks on this similarity with regard to Song 3:1 ("Influence du Cantique," 17–18), while Winsor adds the same observation concerning Song 5:2 (*A King Is Bound*, 41).

[35] Hanson, *Prophetic Gospel*, 228.

when her lover speaks. In John 20:16, Jesus calls Mary by name, causing Mary to turn and say, "Rabbouni!"[36]

Details that have been detected in both John 20:1–18 and Song 5:2–8 thus include a dark setting, a woman's search for a missing man, myrrh, and the woman's response to the man's speech. These corresponding details are not sufficient to establish that John alludes to all or part of Song 5:2–8, however. For one thing, the proposed connection between John 20:1 and Song 5:5 is somewhat weak. John never mentions that Mary was bringing myrrh to the tomb. Hanson acknowledges this, but suggests that an audience familiar with Synoptic tradition would have assumed that she had come to anoint Jesus' body (cf. Mark 16:1; Luke 24:1).[37] John's implied author, however, never makes this connection explicit.

Furthermore, John 20:16 does not offer a strong echo of Song 5:6. Although both involve a speaking man and a responding woman, the bride's response differs from that of Mary Magdalene. The bride evinces an emotional reaction. Her soul fails her. She is so overcome she can barely breathe. On the other hand, John makes no mention of Mary Magdalene's soul. Hanson infers that Mary's turning and exclamation indicate her astonishment, while Winsor asserts that the turning expresses a profound emotional upheaval.[38] John, however, does not explicitly describe Mary's emotional state, nor does he clearly associate it with that of the bride in Song 5:6.

A woman's nocturnal search for a missing man thus provides the only direct correspondence between John 20:1–18 and Song 5:2–8. This in itself is not enough to indicate an allusion. Significant differences in plot further decrease the likelihood that John alludes to Song 5:2–8. The Song's sleeping woman, beckoning man, intervening door, and abusive sentinels never appear in John's resurrection narrative. Most importantly, the woman in Song 5:2–8 never finds her lover. Unlike Mary's search, hers is not resolved.

Song of Songs 3:1–4 features more details that correspond more closely. Along with the nocturnal setting, the searching woman, and the missing man, three other patent similarities link it to John 20:1–18. One is the woman's encounter with a peaceable third party. The Song's bride shares her predicament with the sentinels (Song 3:3); Mary

[36] Ibid.; Winsor, *A King Is Bound*, 41.
[37] Hanson, *Prophetic Gospel*, 228.
[38] Ibid.; Winsor, *A King Is Bound*, 43.

explains to two angels that Jesus' body is missing (John 20:12–13).[39] The angels do not even bother to inform her that Jesus has risen. Like the sentinels of Song 3:3, they simply listen to Mary's complaint.

A second similarity is the woman's sudden discovery of the missing man. Immediately upon leaving the sentinels, the bride finds her beloved. "Scarcely had I passed them," she sings, "when I found him whom my soul loves" (Song 3:4). Likewise, when Mary turns away from the angels, she sees the risen Jesus.[40] John makes the sudden nature of this encounter quite explicit: "When she had said this, she turned around and saw Jesus standing there" (John 20:14).

Third, both stories refer to the woman's holding the man. In Song 3:4, the bride declares, "I held him (ἐκράτησα αὐτὸν) and would not let him go until I brought him into my mother's house, and into the chamber of her that conceived me." In John 20:17, Jesus warns Mary, "Do not hold me (μή μου ἅπτου), for I have not yet ascended to the Father."[41] This similarity lacks verbal correspondence: the Song uses the verb κρατέω, while John prefers the middle voice of ἅπτω. Still, the similar circumstances are difficult to ignore.

Dissonance draws even further attention to the parallel between John 20:17 and Song 3:4. The negative particle μή used with the present imperative prohibits either an action that is already taking place or an attempt at such action.[42] John, however, describes neither the action nor the attempt. Jesus' prohibition immediately follows Mary's cry of "Rabbouni" (v. 16), with no intervening indication that Mary is holding or trying to hold Jesus in any way.[43] The dissonance is augmented in the very next scene, when Jesus gives Thomas what seems like a contrary command: "Put your finger here and see my hands. Reach out your hand and put it in my side" (v. 27).

---

[39] See also Cambe, *Influence du Cantique*, 18; Reinhartz, *Befriending the Beloved Disciple*, 108.

[40] See also Cambe, *Influence du Cantique*, 18; Reinhartz, *Befriending the Beloved Disciple*, 108.

[41] RSV. See also Cambe, *Influence du Cantique*, 18; Reinhartz, *Befriending the Beloved Disciple*, 108; Hanson, *Prophetic Gospel*, 229; Okure, "Commission of Mary Magdalene," 181; Stibbe, *John*, 205; Lundbom, "Mary Magdalene," 174–75; Winsor, *A King Is Bound*, 40–41; Fehribach, *Women in the Life of the Bridegroom*, 160.

[42] BDF, § 336, 3.

[43] See especially Winsor, *A King Is Bound*, 37. Interestingly, a few manuscripts insert the phrase "καὶ προσέδραμεν ἅψασθαι αὐτοῦ" at the end of v. 16 – evidence that at least one copyist also found the transition from v. 16 to v. 17 awkward. Witnesses to this emendation include ℵ¹, Θ, and Ψ. Older and more reliable manuscripts such as ℵ and B omit this phrase. This suggests that it was added to ease the transition to v. 17 (Metzger, *Textual Commentary*, 255).

Many commentators discuss the difficulties raised by Jesus' prohibition in John 20:17, including Marie-Joseph Lagrange and Rudolf Schnackenburg.[44] John Bernard finds it so awkward, he suggests that μή μου ἅπτου is a corruption of μὴ πτόου.[45] Others seek a theological explanation. According to Randolph Tasker and Herman Ridderbos, the prohibition means that Mary is not to hold Jesus back.[46] Samuel Terrien and Gail O'Day understand that Mary is not to control Jesus.[47] Koester understands the prohibition as an indication that visual and tactile experience alone will not allow Mary to understand the full meaning of the resurrection, while Mary Rose D'Angelo argues that Jesus' liminal state does not permit touching.[48] Most commentators simply suggest that she must forsake a physical relationship with Jesus for a more spiritual one.[49] By contrast, Michael McGehee's "less theological reading" depends on an unusual interpretation of the conjunction γάρ.[50]

I argue here that the apparent difficulty of Jesus' prohibition can be explained, not by exploring possible variants, theological nuances, or esoteric grammar, but by comparing John 20:17 with Song 3:4. Jesus' abrupt prohibition, while creating dissonance within John's resurrection narrative, maintains consonance with Song 3:4. An audience listening to echoes of Song 3:1–4 in John 20:1–18 is not surprised to learn that Mary is holding Jesus. Furthermore, a contrast perhaps prompted by Song 3:4 can be detected in Jesus' enigmatic statement, "I have not yet ascended to the Father."[51] Whereas the Song's bride intends to carry her man off into the chamber of her mother, Mary Magdalene has no such

[44] Lagrange, *Évangile selon S. Jean*, 511; Schnackenburg, *Gospel According to St. John*, III:318.

[45] Bernard, *Critical and Exegetical Commentary*, 670–71.

[46] Randolph V. G. Tasker, *The Gospel According to St. John: An Introduction and Commentary* (TNTC; London: Tyndale, 1960), 222; Ridderbos, *Gospel According to John*, 638.

[47] Samuel Terrien, *Till the Heart Sings: A Biblical Theology of Manhood and Womanhood* (Philadelphia: Fortress, 1985), 136–37; O'Day, *Word Disclosed*, 103–5.

[48] Craig A. Koester, "Hearing, Seeing, and Believing in the Gospel of John," *Bib* 70 (1989), 345; Mary Rose D'Angelo, "A Critical Note: John 20:17 and Apocalypse of Moses 31," *JTS* 41 (1990), 532–35.

[49] Lagrange, *Évangile selon S. Jean*, 512; Bultmann, *Gospel of John*, 687; Barrett, *Gospel According to St. John*, 470; Brown, *John XIII–XXI*, 1012; Sanders, *Commentary*, 428–29; Lindars, *Gospel of John*, 607; Moloney, *Gospel of John*, 526; Dorothy A. Lee, "Partnership in Easter Faith: The Role of Mary Magdalene and Thomas in John 20," *JSNT* 58 (1995), 42.

[50] Michael McGehee, "A Less Theological Reading of John 20:17," *JBL* 105 (1986): 299–302.

[51] See also Winsor, *A King Is Bound*, 42; Reinhartz, *Befriending the Beloved Disciple*, 108.

option. She cannot even hold Jesus, because he is ascending to the Father.[52]

In addition to these three parallels, Winsor perceives a few less obvious similarities. She notes that the tomb (τὸ μνημεῖον) of John 20:1–11 resembles the chamber (τὸ ταμίειον) of Song 3:4. Both are small rooms denoted by similar Greek words.[53] In addition, Winsor submits that the bride's resolution, "I will rise now (ἀναστήσομαι)," in Song 3:2 is echoed in Mary Magdalene's complaint in John 20:13, "They have taken away my Lord, and I do not know where they have laid him." Each woman undertakes a personal search for her beloved. In an aside, Winsor suggests that the word ἀναστήσομαι imparts irony to the intertextual relationship between Song 3:1–4 and John's resurrection narrative.[54] Presumably, the reader is meant to associate the bride's arising with Jesus' resurrection.

These parallels, however, do not reflect a close correspondence between the plots of John 20:1–18 and Song 3:1–4. The tomb of John 20:1–11 is Jesus' grave that now stands empty, whereas the chamber in Song 3:4 is the private apartment of the bride's mother. The bride's resolution in Song 3:2 is not immediately reminiscent of Mary's complaint in John 20:13; indeed, the only similarity is the use of the first person singular. It is also quite different from John's use of the verb ἀνίστημι in 20:9, "They did not understand the scripture, that he must rise (ἀναστῆναι) from the dead." Nothing in John 20:1–18 except for Mary's actual search constitutes a clear parallel to Song 3:2, "I will rise now and go about the city."

To summarize the elements that correspond more closely, both John 20:1–18 and Song 3:1–4 feature a dark setting, a woman's search (ζητέω) for a missing man, her inability (καὶ οὐκ) to locate him (αὐτόν), her conversation about the problem with a third party, her sudden discovery of the man, and her holding him. It is significant that most of these elements are missing from Synoptic parallels to John 20:1–18 (Mark 16:1–8; Matt. 28:1–10; Luke 24:1–11). First of all, while all four Gospels explain that Mary Magdalene came to the tomb right around sunrise, only John explicitly mentions that it was still dark, emphasizing the detail by modifying the adverb πρωΐ with a participial phrase of three words: "σκοτίας ἔτι οὔσης" (John 20:1). In contrast, Mark describes the time as "very early (λίαν πρωΐ)"

---

[52] See also Lundbom, "Mary Magdalene," 174–75.
[53] Winsor, *A King Is Bound*, 41–42.
[54] Ibid., 42–43.

(Mark 16:2), Matthew simply tells us that the day "was dawning (τῇ ἐπιφωσκούσῃ)" (Matt. 28:1), and Luke reports that it was "early dawn (ὄρθρου βαθέως)" (Luke 24:1). Second, only John indicates that Mary Magdalene came to the tomb alone (John 20:1).[55] In Mark, Mary Magdalene is joined by another Mary and Salome (Mark 16:1); in Matthew, she is accompanied only by "the other Mary" (Matt. 28:1); in Luke, the contingent includes Mary Magdalene, Joanna, and Mary the mother of James, among others (Luke 24:10). Third, only John details Mary Magdalene's extended search for the body of Jesus, a search that takes her from the tomb to the disciples (John 20:1–2) and then back to the tomb again, where she looks both inside (John 20:11–13) and out (John 20:14–15). The women in the Synoptic accounts are not kept in suspense; when they arrive at the tomb, they are immediately informed that Jesus has risen (cf. Mark 16:6; Matt. 28:5; Luke 24:5–6). Fourth, only John describes a dialogue between Mary and the angels (John 20:13). In the Synoptic accounts, the messengers at the tomb simply share the good news of Jesus' resurrection while the women remain silent (Mark 16:6–7; Matt. 28:5–7; Luke 24:5–7). Finally, only John includes a vision of angels followed by an abrupt encounter with Jesus (John 20:13–14). Indeed, neither Mark nor Luke reports that the women meet the risen Jesus at all. In Matt. 28:9, they are on their way to convey an angel's message when they run into him. Still, Matthew's account does not impart the sense of immediacy found in John. Matthew's angel commands the women to report to the disciples (Matt. 28:7), so that they are hastening away from the tomb (Matt. 28:8) when they meet Jesus. In contrast, John's Mary Magdalene just turns around and there he is.

Interestingly, Matthew contains a second detail missing from Mark but common to both John 20:11–18 and Song 3:1–4. According to Matthew, the women hold Jesus when they meet him (Matt. 28:9; John 20:17).[56] Matthew even agrees with the Song in using the verb κρατέω

---

[55] This seems to be contradicted in v. 2: "We do not know where they have laid him." Many scholars suggest that the plural "we" recalls an inherited tradition in which several women went to the tomb (see, e.g., Brown, *John XIII–XXI*, 984, 1000). Koester contends that here, as elsewhere in the Gospel, an incongruous plural indicates representative significance (Koester, *Symbolism*, 69; see also Edward L. Bode, *The First Easter Morning: The Gospel Accounts of the Women's Visit to the Tomb of Jesus* [AnBib 45; Rome: Biblical Institute, 1970], 73–75; Collins, "Representative Figures," 122–24).

[56] For a detailed comparison of John's resurrection story with its Synoptic parallels, see Barnabas Lindars, "The Composition of John xx," *NTS* 7 (1960–61): 142–47. Dodd contends that both John and Matthew are aware of the tradition that women held the risen Jesus (*Historical Tradition*, 147–48).

(cf. Song 3:4). Perhaps Matthew also alludes to Song 3:1–4. If so, the allusion is relatively weak. It consists of one word and two instances of circumstantial correspondence. It should be noted that the holding of Jesus, like the encounter with Jesus, takes place under slightly different circumstances in Matthew than in John. Matthew's women are holding Jesus' feet in an attitude of worship (cf. Matt. 28:17). Jesus then tells them not to be afraid (Matt. 28:10; cf. Matt. 28:5) before commissioning them with a message for the disciples. In contrast, John never describes the holding, and prefixes Jesus' commission with a prohibition.

As with the anointing story, then, John seems to customize the tradition about Mary Magdalene so that it agrees with Song 3:1–4. John relates the episode in terms of the evoked text: Mary Magdalene looks for Jesus alone and in the dark, she suddenly finds him after conversing with a third party, and she holds him.

Three of these elements – the dark setting, the futile search, and the sudden discovery – make a strong contribution to the complex ironies of John's resurrection story.[57] They provide a plot sequence for Mary Magdalene to realize what John's audience already knows: that Jesus has been raised from the dead. John evokes the Song's vain search in the dark to depict Jesus' absence from the tomb and Mary's ignorance as to his whereabouts, and refers to the Song's abrupt encounter to illustrate her recognition of the risen Lord. The holding then describes the necessary response to Jesus' ascension. Jesus' followers must not emulate the Song's bride, who holds her lover, intending to bring him to her mother's chamber. Mary Magdalene must not hold Jesus because he is ascending to his Father.

The dark setting

The scene in Song 3:1–4 takes place "at night (ἐν νυξὶν)" (v. 1). Similarly, Mary Magdalene comes to the tomb early, "while it was still dark (πρωῒ σκοτίας ἔτι οὔσης)" (John 20:1). John uses this aspect of Song 3:1 to reprise one of his favorite symbolic motifs: darkness.[58] In the Fourth Gospel, darkness and night often signify Jesus' absence or imminent departure, just as light and day symbolize his presence. For example, Jesus heals the man born blind after stating, "We must work the works of him who sent me while it is day; night is coming when no

---

[57] For a discussion of irony in John 20:11–18, see Duke, *Irony*, 104–5.
[58] For a discussion of light and darkness symbolism in John's Gospel, see Koester, *Symbolism*, 123–52.

one can work. As long as I am in the world, I am the light of the world"
(9:4–5). Jesus' presence in the world is like the light of day; in his
absence, night will fall. Jesus makes a similar comparison before
journeying to Lazarus' tomb: "Are there not twelve hours of daylight?
Those who walk during the day do not stumble, because they see the
light of this world. But those who walk at night stumble, because the
light is not in them" (11:9–10). Jesus' presence illuminates his followers, but those without Jesus live like people who blunder about at night.
This imagery appears yet again when, after entering Jerusalem, Jesus
reflects on his impending crucifixion: "The light is with you for a little
longer. Walk while you have the light, so that the darkness (σκοτία)
may not overtake you. If you walk in the darkness (ἐν τῇ σκοτίᾳ), you
do not know where you are going. While you have the light, believe in
the light, so that you may become children of light" (12:35–36). When
Jesus departs, the light will disappear and darkness will descend. Only
believers will remain in the light.

Not only do darkness and night illustrate Jesus' absence or departure;
they also symbolize various levels of human disbelief, ranging from
ignorance to defiance.[59] This becomes especially apparent in two stories about the disciples. One takes place after the feeding of the five
thousand. The disciples are rowing across the Sea of Galilee in the
darkness (σκοτία ἤδη ἐγεγόνει) when Jesus appears, walking on the
water. At first, the disciples are terrified. After he identifies himself,
however, they take him into the boat (6:16–21). The other story occurs
after the resurrection, when some of the disciples go fishing at night (τῇ
νυκτὶ). As dawn is breaking (πρωΐας δὲ ἤδη γενομένης), Jesus
appears on the beach. Again, the disciples do not recognize him until
he helps them fill their net with fish (21:1–8).[60] Each story begins with
Jesus' absence. When Jesus finally appears, the disciples initially fail to
recognize him. Darkness and night provide an appropriate symbolic
setting for both his absence and their misunderstanding.

Likewise, John 20:1 alludes to the darkness of Song 3:1 to signify
both that Jesus is missing from the tomb and that Mary Magdalene
neither understands his absence nor recognizes his presence. As he has
prophesied in John 9:4–5, he is no longer in the world. He has been

---

[59] See also Duke, *Irony*, 108; Koester, *Symbolism*, 152; Robert Gordon Maccini, *Her
Testimony Is True: Women As Witnesses According to John* (JSNTSup 125; Sheffield:
Sheffield Academic Press, 1996), 207–8.
[60] Bernard and Lightfoot also make a connection between John 20:1–18 and 21:1–8
(Bernard, *Critical and Exegetical Commentary*, 665; Lightfoot, *St. John's Gospel*, 330).

crucified, buried, and raised, and he is about to ascend to the Father. The light of the world has vanished, and it is still dark.[61] Moreover, the darkness seems to have dulled Mary's perception. She has no idea where Jesus is, and, when she finally finds him, she does not realize who he is. Ironically, the Gospel's audience knows exactly what has happened. John 20:9 contains an explicit reminder that Jesus has risen from the dead, and John 20:14 reveals the identity of the supposed gardener. Mary, however, remains in the dark.

The woman's futile search

John adds to the irony with his description of Mary Magdalene's futile search for the body of Jesus. This can be seen first of all in the intertextual association of John 20:1–18 with Song 3:1–4. The Song of Songs depicts the distressed bride roaming the city in search of her lover. Similarly, Mary Magdalene runs from the tomb to the disciples and back again, looking for the body of Jesus. The bride inquires of the city sentinels; likewise, Mary tearfully explains her loss to two angels. As does the bride, Mary Magdalene then immediately encounters her missing man. Here, however, the similarities end. Whereas the bride immediately recognizes her lover, Mary supposes that Jesus is the gardener. She is unable to recognize him because she is not looking for a risen Lord. She is looking for a corpse. The bride's search is futile simply because her missing lover cannot be found; Mary's search is futile because she seeks the wrong thing.

Echoes of a previous scene near Lazarus' tomb add still more irony. When Lazarus' sister Mary goes out to meet Jesus, she and her companions weep (κλαίουσαν . . . κλαίοντας) for the dead man (John 11:33). Jesus then asks, "Where have you laid him (ποῦ τεθείκατε αὐτόν)?" (John 11:34). Mary Magdalene also weeps and wonders where the body has been laid. "They have taken the Lord out of the tomb," she tells Peter and the Beloved Disciple, "and we do not know where they have laid him (ποῦ ἔθηκαν αὐτόν)" (John 20:2). She returns to the tomb and weeps (κλαίουσα . . . ἔκλαιεν) there, so that the angels sitting inside ask her, "Woman, why are you weeping (τί κλαίεις)?" She replies, "They have taken away my Lord, and I do not know where they have laid him (ποῦ ἔθηκαν αὐτόν)" (John 20:11–13). When the risen Jesus repeats the question, "Woman, why are you weeping

---

[61] See also Feuillet, *Mystère de l'amour divin*, 231.

(τί κλαίεις)?" she responds like a broken record: "Sir, if you have carried him away, tell me where you have laid him (ποῦ ἔθηκας αὐτόν), and I will take him away" (John 20:15). Weeping and inquiring where the body has been laid are perfectly appropriate behaviors for the friends and relatives of a dead man like Lazarus. Unlike Lazarus, however, Jesus has already been raised. Mary Magdalene's constant weeping and searching for Jesus' body are entirely unnecessary. She unwittingly weeps for someone who is no longer dead. Her constant complaint, "I do not know where they have laid him," seems out of place when applied to the risen Jesus.

However ironic, Mary's search is not without precedent. John's Gospel begins with disciples seeking Jesus. Jesus' question to Mary in John 20:15, "Whom are you looking for (τίνα ζητεῖς)?" echoes not only the four-fold variation of ἐζήτησα αὐτὸν in Song 3:1–2, but also his question to John the Baptist's disciples in John 1:38. When he sees Andrew and another disciple following him, he asks, "What are you looking for (τί ζητεῖτε)?" Mary Magdalene seeks Jesus, as have other disciples before her.[62]

In addition, Mary's tearful search fulfills a prophecy from Jesus' Farewell Discourse. After the departure of Judas in John 13:30, Jesus announces the hour of his glorification and then declares, "Little children, I am with you only a little longer. You will look for me (ζητήσετέ με); and as I said to the Jews so now I say to you, 'Where I am going you cannot come'" (13:33; cf. 7:33–34; 8:21). Later in the discourse, Jesus supplements this statement. He will come to his disciples (14:3, 18, 28). The world will not be able to see him, but the disciples will see him again (14:19; 16:16). When the disciples wonder what he means (16:17–19), Jesus explains:

> Very truly, I tell you, you will weep (κλαύσετε) and mourn, but the world will rejoice; you will have pain, but your pain will turn into joy. When a woman is in labor, she has pain, because her hour has come. But when her child is born, she no longer remembers the anguish because of the joy of having brought a human being into the world. So you have pain now, but I will see you again, and your hearts will rejoice, and no one will take your joy from you. (16:20–22)

---

[62] See also Feuillet, "Recherche du Christ," 96; Brown, *John XIII–XXI*, 1010; Nicholson, *Death As Departure*, 72; O'Day, *Word Disclosed*, 101 and "John," 301; Stibbe, *John*, 199.

John alludes to Song 3:1–4 to show how Mary's futile search fulfills Jesus' prophecies. He depicts her running back and forth from the tomb, looking for Jesus (20:15; cf. 13:33) and weeping (20:11, 13, 15; cf. 16:20) – just like the anguished bride in Song 3:1–4. He also uses the allusion, as well as Jesus' prophecy, to foreshadow the outcome of her search. Jesus' prophecy indicates that the disciples will see him again (14:19; 16:16–22), while the allusion raises the expectation that Mary will eventually find her missing man. Her weeping will turn into joy (cf. 20:20).[63]

The sudden discovery

So far, John's allusion to the Song of Songs has enhanced the irony of Mary Magdalene's search for Jesus. She approaches the tomb in the dark, symbolizing his absence and her ignorance. She then runs back and forth from the tomb, weeping and wondering where his corpse has been laid. Now, however, the plot sequence echoed from Song 3:1–4 brings some resolution to her predicament. Like the bride (Song 3:3), she sees her missing beloved immediately following an exchange with a third party (John 20:14). To be sure, she does not recognize him at first – she is still looking for a corpse (20:15). She knows him only after he pronounces her name (20:16). Mary's sudden discovery of her missing man involves a move from ignorance to recognition.

Darkness, initial ignorance, eventual recognition – this sequence also occurs in John 6:16–21 and 21:4–8, the two other scenes where the disciples meet Jesus at night.[64] In John 6:16–21, Jesus makes a supernatural appearance, walking on the water. The disciples fail to recognize him until Jesus identifies himself: "It is I" (6:20). In John 21, the risen Jesus makes a supernatural appearance on the beach. The disciples fail to recognize him until he orchestrates a miraculous catch of fish, prompting the Beloved Disciple to exclaim, "It is the Lord!" (21:7).[65]

---

[63] Feuillet and Paul S. Minear also make the connection between John 7:33–34; 8:21; 16:17–19 and 20:11–18 (Feuillet, "Recherche du Christ," 97; Minear, "'We Don't Know Where . . .': John 20:2," *Int* 30 [1976], 131–33). According to Nicholson, John believes that it is inappropriate for Mary and the disciples to seek Jesus, as their doing so robs God of the initiative Jesus so obviously values in John 6:44–45; 12:32; 15:16, 19 (*Death As Departure*, 72). On the basis of John 6:44, however, it is possible to argue that Mary and the disciples seek Jesus because God is already drawing them. John does not condemn Mary for seeking Jesus. He only shows that she is looking in the wrong place.

[64] See above, p. 99.

[65] Lindars also notices the similarities between John 21:4–8 and 20:11–18 (*The Gospel of John*, 605).

For both Mary and the disciples, the stimulus for recognition is the voice of Jesus. The disciples know Jesus when he declares himself (6:20) or when he instructs them (21:5–7); Mary realizes her mistake when Jesus speaks her name (20:16). This kind of recognition is described by Jesus in John 10:3–4: "The sheep hear [the shepherd's] voice, and he calls his own sheep by name and leads them out. When he has brought out all his own, he goes before them, and the sheep follow him, for they know his voice."[66] It is not as easy for Mary Magdalene to recognize the risen Jesus as it is for the Song's bride to recognize her missing man. Jesus' supernatural appearance often causes confusion among his disciples. Once he calls them by name and leads them out, however, the confusion abates. They know him and follow him. When Jesus says "Mary," she recognizes the risen Lord. The irony and frustration of her search have been resolved.

The holding

In Song 3:4, the bride finishes her story: "I held him (ἐκράτησα αὐτὸν) and would not let him go until I brought him into my mother's house (εἰς οἶκον μητρός μου), and into the chamber of her that conceived me." The ending of John 20:1–18 is slightly different. Rather than show that Mary is holding Jesus, John reports Jesus' prohibition: "Do not hold me (μή μου ἅπτου), for I have not yet ascended to the Father."[67] Instead, she is to tell the disciples, "I am ascending to my Father and your Father, to my God and your God" (John 20:17).

It is not at all clear why John uses the middle voice of ἅπτω instead of duplicating the Song's verb κρατέω. The most that can be said is that, for some reason, John chooses the verb ἅπτομαι. This imparts a slightly different meaning to his recognition scene. Whereas both words can be translated "hold," κρατέω can also mean "apprehend," while ἅπτομαι denotes "touch."[68] Mary Magdalene is not necessarily grabbing Jesus in an attempt to capture him or to prevent him from leaving her again. She is simply touching him.

This action both illustrates the nature of Jesus' ascension and dictates his followers' response. Jesus' return to his Father should come as no surprise. In fact, it constitutes the premise of the Farewell Discourse:

---

[66] Most commentators also recognize a connection between John 10:3–4 and 20:16 (see, e.g., Plummer, *Gospel According to S. John*, 359; Bultmann, *Gospel of John*, 686; Brown, *John XIII–XXI*, 1009–10).

[67] RSV.

[68] BDAG, 564–65, 126.

"Jesus knew that his hour had come to depart from this world and go to the Father . . . and that he had come from God and was going to God" (John 13:1). Throughout the discourse, he reminds his disciples that he will be leaving. He tells them, "I am going to the Father" (John 14:28), and, "I am going to him who sent me" (John 16:5). In his final prayer, he twice tells the Father, "I am coming to you" (John 17:11, 13).

These words are not a euphemism for his death, but a prophecy of his ascension. In John's Gospel, Jesus' ascension is not a sequential event following the crucifixion and resurrection. Rather, Jesus' crucifixion and resurrection constitute an integral part of the process of his glorification – his departure from the world and his return to the Father.[69] In his statement, "I have not yet ascended (οὔπω γὰρ ἀναβέβηκα) to the Father," a verb in the perfect tense is modified by a negative adverb, indicating that the process is not yet complete. The message in John 20:17, "I am ascending (ἀναβαίνω) to my Father," likewise connotes an ongoing activity.

In order to complete the allusion to Song 3:1–4, Mary Magdalene must hold Jesus. John adapts the allusion, however, in order to account for the fact that when Mary reaches for Jesus, he is in the process of ascending to the Father. As he has prayed in John 17:11, he is no longer in the world. The disciples are in the world, but he is going to the Father. As he has prophesied in John 13:33, 38, the disciples cannot yet follow him. This is the situation experienced by Mary Magdalene. Like the disciples, she remains in the world while Jesus ascends to the Father. John therefore continues his recognition scene with the prohibition, "Do not hold me."[70]

Since Mary Magdalene, like Mary of Bethany, assumes the role of the Song's bride, it is argued that she, too, represents the church.[71]

---

[69] Lagrange, *Évangile selon S. Jean*, 511–12; Hoskyns, *Fourth Gospel*, 542–43; Brown, *John XIII–XXI*, 1012–13; Wayne A. Meeks, "The Man from Heaven in Johannine Sectarianism," *JBL* 91 (1972): 44–72; Nicholson, *Death As Departure*; Pheme Perkins, *Resurrection: New Testament Witness and Contemporary Reflection* (New York: Doubleday, 1984), 176; John Ashton, *Understanding the Fourth Gospel* (Oxford: Clarendon, 1991), 448–59; Martinus de Boer, *Johannine Perspectives on the Death of Jesus* (CBET 17; Kampen: Pharos, 1996), 118–24; Maccini, *Her Testimony is True*, 214–16; Moloney, *Gospel of John*, 529; Harold W. Attridge, "'Don't Be Touching Me': Recent Feminist Scholarship on Mary Magdalene," in *A Feminist Companion to John*, II:166.

[70] RSV. See also Nicholson, *Death As Departure*, 73.

[71] Cambe, "Influence du Cantique," 25; Feuillet, "Recherche du Christ," 103–7 and *Mystère de l'amour divin*, 231; Schneiders, "Resurrection Narrative," I:338; "Easter Jesus," 161; and *Written That You May Believe*, 35; Baril, *Feminine Face*, 97; Fehribach, *Women in the Life of the Bridegroom*, 161–62.

Because this argument depends on allegorical interpretation of the Song of Songs, it cannot be applied to John's implied author or audience.[72] There is no indication that they would have recognized the resemblance. Nonetheless, it is apparent that John associates Mary Magdalene with the disciples. Like the disciples in John 6:16–21 and John 21:1–8, she moves from mistaking Jesus in the dark to recognizing him when he speaks. Like the disciples in John 1:38, Mary seeks Jesus, is asked by him what she is looking for, demands his whereabouts, and calls him "Teacher." Like the disciples as described in John 16:20–22, she weeps and mourns until she sees Jesus. Like the disciples as described in John 13:33, 38 and John 17:11, she must remain in the world while Jesus ascends to the Father. Even though Mary Magdalene does not necessarily symbolize the church for John's implied author and audience, she at least exemplifies the disciples.[73] Perhaps this is why she refers to herself using a plural pronoun (John 20:2).[74]

Jesus leaves Mary with two promises. He alludes to one of them in his commission: "I am ascending to my Father and your Father, to my God and your God." This is the first and only time in John's Gospel where Jesus indicates that his Father is also the Father of believers. The agenda set in John 1:12–13 has been accomplished.[75] Those who believe in Jesus have become children of God.[76]

John alludes to the second promise in his echo of the Song of Songs. The bride in Song 3:4 declares, "I held him, and would not let him go until I brought him into my mother's house." The phrase "mother's house (οἶκον μητρός μου)" is reminiscent of the promise given in John 14:2: "In my Father's house (οἰκίᾳ τοῦ πατρός μου) there are many dwelling places." The Song's bride wishes to bring her man to her mother's house, but Jesus is on his way to his Father's house.[77] Mary must wait for the fulfillment of his promise: "I will come again and will take you to myself, so that where I am, there you may be also" (John 14:3).

---

[72] See above, p. 86.
[73] See also Bode, *First Easter Morning*, 73–75.
[74] Koester, *Symbolism*, 69.
[75] See above, p. 46.
[76] See also Schneiders, *Written That You May Believe*, 200.
[77] See also Lundbom, "Mary Magdalene," 174–75; Winsor, *A King Is Bound*, 42.

5

THE BRIDEGROOM-MESSIAH OF PSALM 45 IN THE SONG OF SONGS, JEREMIAH 33:10–11, AND GENESIS 29:1–20

Thus far, the evidence supports the probability that John echoes Jer. 33:10–11, Gen. 29:1–20, Song 1:12, and Song 3:1–4. For each proposed allusion, several instances of verbal correspondence are reinforced by significant parallel circumstances. Each is marked by dissonance or rhetorical emphasis (or both). What is more, each helps to illustrate the revelation and glorification of the Messiah. In John 3:22–30, Jeremiah's prophecy helps to portray Jesus as the bridegroom-Messiah whose voice, heard by his friend John the Baptist, causes him to rejoice. John 4:4–42 echoes Jacob's betrothal narrative to depict Jesus as the bridegroom-Messiah who offers eternal life and, together with the Samaritan woman, establishes a family of faith. In John 12:1–8, an allusion to the Song's reclining king helps to foreshadow the impending death of Jesus, the bridegroom-Messiah. Finally, John 20:1–18 echoes the search of the Song's bride to describe Mary Magdalene's recognition of Jesus, the risen and ascending Lord.

As yet, however, it is not at all clear why the Fourth Evangelist echoes these particular passages. What attracts him to a marriage metaphor? Why does he liken Jesus to Jeremiah's bridegroom? Why does he allude to a betrothal narrative and an erotic poem? In short, how were Jer. 33:10–11, Gen. 29:1–20, Song 1:12, and Song 3:1–4 prominent for the Fourth Gospel's implied author?

I think the answers to these questions lie in a messianic interpretation of the evoked texts. This supposition is warranted by John's stated purpose: "that you may come to believe that Jesus is the Messiah" (20:31). It makes sense that John would allude to messianic prophecy. Indeed, three of the four allusions can be related to Jesus' messianic identity. In John 3:28–29, John the Baptist carefully differentiates himself from the Messiah before likening Jesus to a bridegroom. Jesus' revelation of his messianic identity in John 4:26 constitutes the climax of the Samaritan story. The allusion to Song 1:12 in John 12:3 can also be understood as a reference to the Messiah, since the evoked text mentions a king.

It does not, however, explicitly state that the reclining king is the Messiah. Similarly, Jeremiah's bridegroom prophecy, Jacob's betrothal story, and the Song's lines about a missing lover never mention the Lord's anointed one. How, then, did John come to impart messianic significance to these passages? The key lies with Ps. 45, a royal psalm that celebrates the marriage of God's anointed king. Jeremiah 33:10–11, Gen. 29:1–20, Song 1:12, and Song 3:1–4 can be interpreted as messianic prophecies because they can be linked by means of shared vocabulary to Ps. 45.

The process begins with a comparison of Ps. 45 to the Song of Songs. They are both love songs about a handsome king. Both feature a beautiful bride, mighty men with swords at their thighs, myrrh and aloes, a woman at her lover's right hand, daughters, and a joyful procession to the king's quarters. In light of these similarities, the bridegroom of the Song of Songs can be identified as the Messiah of Ps. 45. He can also be recognized as Jesus, who was perfumed with nard (Song 1:12 in John 12:3) and sought, found, and held by a devoted woman (Song 3:1–4 in John 20:1–18).

A connection between Ps. 45 and the Song of Songs leads to further links with Jer. 33:10–11 and Gen. 29:1–20. Jeremiah 33:11 features a wedding procession like those depicted in Ps. 45:15 and Song 1:4. Similar details include joy, an entrance into the king's residence, and an expression of praise. Therefore, the bridegroom-Messiah of Ps. 45 and the Song of Songs can be found in Jer. 33:11. He can also be identified with Jesus, who inspires joy in John the Baptist (Jer. 33:10–11 in John 3:22–30).

Finally, Gen. 29:1–20 contains several verbal parallels to the Song of Songs. Both mention flocks, sheep, and pasturing, and both portray the bridegroom as a shepherd. The bride featured in each is a daughter, beautiful and lovely in appearance. Jacob and Rachel share the love described in the Song of Songs, and they meet at a well like the well of Song 4:15. Thus Jacob, too, can represent the bridegroom-Messiah of Ps. 45 and the Song of Songs. Jacob can also be compared to Jesus, who offers living water and becomes the father of a family of faith (Gen. 29:1–20 in John 4:4–42).

Psalm 45 as a messianic psalm

Psalm 45 celebrates a royal wedding. Anyone interested in messianic prophecy would find it difficult to disregard Ps. 45, since it is one of only two psalms that actually describe a royal anointing:

> Your throne, O God, endures forever and ever.
> Your royal scepter is a scepter of equity;
>   you love righteousness and hate wickedness.
> Therefore God, your God, has anointed you (מְשָׁחֲךָ; ἔχρισεν σε)
>   with the oil of gladness beyond your companions.
>
> (Ps. 45:6–7)[1]

Accordingly, both Jewish and Christian traditions include messianic interpretations of Ps. 45. The Letter to the Hebrews certainly assumes that Ps. 45 refers to the Messiah. Its author relies heavily on Israel's Scriptures to demonstrate who Jesus is and why believers should remain faithful to Jesus. At the very beginning of the argument (Heb. 1:8–9), the author incorporates Ps. 45:6–7 into a series of royal prophecies that demonstrates the superiority of God's Son to angels. Psalm 2:7 and 2 Sam. 7:14 first show that God has acknowledged the Son (Heb. 1:5). Psalm 45:6–7 then describes the Son's eternal, righteous rule and states that God has anointed him (Heb. 1:8–9). Finally, Ps. 110:1 indicates that the victorious Son sits at God's right hand (Heb. 1:13).[2] This collection of verses, which mentions the Son of God, his kingdom, his anointing, and his position at God's right hand, constitutes a clear reference to the Messiah. The writer of Hebrews considers Ps. 45 to be a messianic prophecy just like 2 Sam. 7:14, Ps. 2, and Ps. 110. All four passages are applied to Jesus, the exalted and eternal Son of God.[3]

Justin Martyr (ca. 100–165) also understands Ps. 45 as a messianic prophecy. What is more, he assumes that his conversation partner, Trypho the rabbi, agrees. Each time Justin cites Ps. 45 in his *Dialogue with Trypho*, he operates from the premise that Ps. 45 is about the Messiah. In *Dial.* 38:3, he introduces a recitation of the entire psalm with the simple observation that these things were said concerning the Messiah. *Dialogue with Trypho* 86:3 relies on shared vocabulary to

---

[1]   A royal anointing is also described in Ps. 89:20. The verses reckoned as Pss 45:6–7; 89:20 in the NRSV are reckoned as Pss 45:7–8; 89:21 in the MT and Pss 44:7–8; 88:21 in the LXX. Unless otherwise noted, I refer to the standard reckoning used in English translations.

[2]   For messianic interpretation of 2 Sam. 7:10–14 and Ps. 2, see above, pp. 39, 42. Messianic interpretation of Ps. 110 is assumed in Mark 12:36 and par., Acts 2:34–35, and 1 Cor. 15:25–27, as well as in Hebrews.

[3]   Juel, *Messianic Exegesis*, 77–79. See also Donald Guthrie, *The Letter to the Hebrews: An Introduction and Commentary* (TNTC; Grand Rapids: Eerdmans, 1983), 76–77; L. D. Hurst, "The Christology of Hebrews 1 and 2," in *The Glory of Christ in the New Testament: Studies in Christology* (ed. L. D. Hurst and N. T. Wright; Oxford: Clarendon, 1987), 159; F. F. Bruce, *The Epistle to the Hebrews* (rev. edn; NICNT; Grand Rapids: Eerdmans, 1990), 51–65.

demonstrate that the rock of Gen. 28:18, anointed by Jacob, is the
Messiah of Ps. 45:7, anointed by God. Twice Justin uses Ps. 45:6 to
demonstrate the divinity of the Messiah. He argues that David addresses
the Messiah as "God" because the Messiah shares in God's nature
(*Dial.* 56:14; 63:4–5).[4]

The Aramaic Targums confirm Justin's assumption that at least
some Jews would have no difficulty understanding Ps. 45 as a messianic
prophecy. *Targum Ketuvim* Ps. 45:3 offers an interpretation of Ps. 45:2,
"You are the most handsome of men." It reads, "Your beauty, O King
Messiah, surpasses that of ordinary men."[5] This exegetical tradition
explicitly identifies the king of Ps. 45 as the Messiah. It cannot confi-
dently be dated to the first century, although the fact that messianic
interpretation of Ps. 45 survives in both Jewish and Christian documents
indicates that it probably predates Jesus. Regardless of its date, messianic interpretation of Ps. 45 in the Aramaic Targum at least demonstrates that it is not out of the question for Jews to read Ps. 45 as a
messianic psalm.

Additional confirmation of messianic interpretation of Ps. 45 is
offered by the *Testament of Judah*, a document that reflects both Jewish
and Christian influence. Again, the document's date renders it useless
as evidence of a first-century exegetical tradition.[6] It does, however,
indicate the ease with which Ps. 45 is read as a messianic prophecy.
Like Hebrews, it refers to Ps. 45 along with several other messianic
prophecies to describe a coming king. The relevant allusion appears in
T. Jud. 24:1:

> And after this there shall arise for you a Star from Jacob in
> peace: And a man shall arise from my posterity like the Sun of
> righteousness, walking with the sons of men in gentleness and

---

[4] Justin's references to Ps. 45 are cited by Günter Reim ("Paralleltraditionen zum
Johannesevangelium aus Justins Werken," in *Jochanan: Erweitere Studien zum alttestamentliche Hintergrund des Johannesevangeliums* [Erlangen: Ev.-Luth. Mission, 1995],
526). The Greek text of Justin's *Dialogue with Trypho* is available in *Die ältesten Apologeten: Texte mit kurzen Einleitungen* (ed. Edgar J. Goodspeed; Göttingen: Vandenhoeck &
Ruprecht, 1941), 26–265.

[5] Trans. Samson H. Levey (*The Messiah: An Aramaic Interpretation* [HUCM 2;
Cincinnati: Hebrew Union College Press, 1977], 109).

[6] The original work predates the first century. According to Howard Clark Kee, the
Testaments of the Twelve Patriarchs is a product of the Maccabean period ("Testaments
of the Twelve Patriarchs," *OTP* I:778). Doron Mendels concurs, suggesting a date of ca.
108/7 BCE (*The Land of Israel as a Political Concept in Hasmonean Literature* [TSAJ 15;
Tübingen: Mohr Siebeck, 1987], 89–91). Christian interpolations have been dated to the
second century (Kee, *OTP* I:777).

righteousness (πραότητι καὶ δικαιοσύνη), and in him will be
found no sin.   (*T. Jud.* 24:1)[7]

The evoked text is Ps. 45:4:

> In your majesty ride forth victoriously
>   in behalf of truth, humility, and righteousness (πραΰτητος
>   καὶ δικαιοσύνης).[8]

Testament of Judah 24 identifies the expected descendant of Judah
with the subject of several other messianic prophecies. He is the Star of
Jacob from Num. 24:17 (v. 1), the Sun of righteousness from Mal. 4:2
(v. 1), the Shoot from Isa. 11:1 and Zech. 6:12 (vv. 4, 6), and the gentle
and righteous king from Ps. 45:4.[9] The author of this passage assumes
the messianic import of all these prophecies – including Ps. 45:4.

Psalm 45 in the Fourth Gospel

Since Ps. 45 describes a royal anointing, and since other Jewish and
Christian exegetes read it as a messianic prophecy, it is not unreasonable to assume that a messianic interpretation of Ps. 45 might influence
John's understanding of Jesus. Unfortunately, John provides no quotation of Ps. 45 to support this assumption. Lack of an explicit citation
does not imply lack of importance, however. For example, Ps. 89 plays
an important role in the development of Johannine Christology. We
have seen that messianic exegesis of Pss 22 and 69 probably depends on
verbal similarities between these texts and Ps. 89. John clearly interprets Pss 22 and 69 as messianic prophecies, claiming that they are
fulfilled by Jesus (John 2:17; 15:25; 19:24, 29– 30).[10] Nevertheless, the
Gospel contains no explicit citation of Ps. 89. There is only a brief
allusion: Ps. 89:36 in John 12:34.[11]

Like Ps. 89, Ps. 45 remains in the background.[12] Indeed, how could
John have profitably quoted this royal wedding song? His crucified

---

[7] Kee, *OTP* I:801; Marinus de Jonge, *The Testaments of the Twelve Patriarchs:
A Critical Edition of the Greek Text* (Leiden: Brill, 1978), 75.

[8] The English translation of Ps. 45:4 is taken from the New International Version
(NIV). The NRSV and RSV correct the Hebrew text in order to approximate a hypothetical original. The author of the *Testament of Judah*, however, seems to refer to the LXX
(see Kee, *OTP* I:777), which more closely resembles the text translated by the NIV.

[9] Kee notes each of these allusions (*OTP* I:801).

[10] See above, pp. 43–44.

[11] See above, p. 42.

[12] For possible echoes of Ps. 45 in the Fourth Gospel, see below, pp. 121–22.

Messiah bears little resemblance to the psalm's handsome king who
rides with his sword on his thigh and waits for the royal princess. There
is little doubt, however, that the first believers accepted Ps. 45 as a
messianic prophecy. Like Ps. 89, it depicts a royal anointing. It is
regarded as a messianic prophecy in the Letter to the Hebrews, as well
as later in Justin's *Dialogue with Trypho*, an Aramaic Targum, and the
Testament of Judah. Messianic interpretation of Ps. 45, together with
the Gospel's allusions to biblical texts about marriage and use of first-
century exegetical techniques, forms the foundation for reconstructing
Johannine messianic exegesis of Jer. 33:10–11, Gen. 29:1–20, Song
1:12, and Song 3:1–4.[13] The process begins with recognizing the
similar vocabulary in Ps. 45 and the Song of Songs.

The beloved king and his beautiful bride

No fewer than nine identical words and phrases can be used to link
Ps. 45 with the Song of Songs. First, each work is described as a
song. Psalm 45 is entitled, "A love song (שִׁיר יְדִידֹת; ᾠδὴ ὑπὲρ τοῦ
ἀγαπητοῦ)."[14] Likewise, the Song of Songs begins with its title, "The
Song of Songs (שִׁיר הַשִּׁירִים; 'Αισμα ᾀσμάτων)" (1:1). The Hebrew
word שִׁיר provides a direct connection. Both Ps. 45 and the Song of
Songs are songs.[15]

Moreover, the subject of each song is the same. According to the MT,
Ps. 45 is "A love (יְדִידֹת) song." As it turns out, the Song of Songs is all
about "love." Its opening verses celebrate a "love (דֹּדֶיךָ)" that is better
than wine (1:2, 4). "Love (דֹּוד)" is mentioned again in Song 5:1; 7:12
(13) and the "beloved (דֹּוד)" appears in Song 1:13–16; 2:3, 8–10, 16–17;
4:16; 5:2–10, 16; 6:1–3; 7:10–11 (11–12); and 8:5, 14.

The subject of Ps. 45 in the LXX is only slightly different. Its Greek
title reads, "A song concerning the beloved (ὑπὲρ τοῦ ἀγαπητοῦ)." The
Greek Song of Songs also features a beloved man. Song of Songs 1:3–4
declares that the maidens "love (ἠγάπησάν)" him. In addition, Song
1:7 and 3:1–4 feature "him whom my soul loves (ὅν ἠγάπησεν
ἡ ψυχή μου)."

---

[13] John's familiarity with first-century exegetical techniques is discussed above,
pp. 40–41.

[14] Since John's implied author may be familiar with a Hebrew as well as a Greek Bible
(see above, pp. 23–25), both Hebrew and Greek are considered as potential resources for
Johannine exegesis. Unless otherwise noted, however, my argument depends only on
exegesis of the LXX.

[15] This point is valid only for messianic exegesis of the MT.

Psalm 45 and the Song of Songs are not only both about love or the beloved, they are also both about a king. Psalm 45:1 declares, "I address my verses to the king (לְמֶלֶךְ; τῷ βασιλεῖ)." This king appears three more times in the psalm. He conquers his enemies (v. 5), he desires the beauty of the princess (v. 11), and the princess is led to him (v. 14). The "king (מֶלֶךְ; βασιλεύς)" also appears in the Song of Songs. He brings the bride into his chambers (1:4), he reclines on a couch (1:12), he is identified as Solomon (3:9, 11), and he is held captive in his lover's tresses (7:5 [6]).[16]

A fourth connection between Ps. 45 and the Song of Songs involves the physical appearance of the protagonists. The king of Ps. 45:2 is "the most handsome (יָפְיָפִיתָ; ὡραῖος κάλλει) of men."[17] According to Ps. 45:11, he desires the beauty "(יָפְיֵךְ; τοῦ κάλλους σου)" of the equally attractive princess. The same is said of the bridegroom and bride in the Song of Songs. Song of Songs 1:16 describes the bridegroom: "Ah, you are beautiful (יָפֶה; καλός), my beloved, truly lovely (נָעִים; ὡραῖος)." The bride is also termed "beautiful (יָפָה; καλή)" throughout the Song (1:5, 8, 15; 2:10, 13; 4:1, 7; 5:9; 6:1, 4, 10).[18]

Fifth, both Ps. 45 and the Song of Songs describe mighty men with swords on their thighs. In Ps. 45:3, the king is addressed as "mighty one (גִּבּוֹר; δυνατέ)" and enjoined, "Gird your sword on your thigh (חֲרָבְּךָ עַל־יָרֵךְ; τὴν ῥομφαίαν σου ἐπὶ τὸν μηρόν σου)."[19] This phrase appears elsewhere in Israel's Scripture only at Song 3:7–8, where the litter of Solomon is guarded by "sixty mighty men (גִּבֹּרִים; δυνατοί)." Each of them wears "his sword at his thigh (חַרְבּוֹ עַל־יְרֵכוֹ; ῥομφαία αὐτοῦ ἐπὶ μηρὸν αὐτοῦ)."[20]

---

[16] See also Dijkema, "Zu Psalm 45," 27. He mentions the similar situations of Ps. 45:11 and Song 1:1–7, but does not mark the shared vocabulary.

[17] A variation of the same phrase is repeated in v. 4 of the LXX.

[18] See also Dijkema, "Zu Psalm 45," 27; Mulder, *Studies on Psalm 45*, 102, n. 83; Tournay, "Affinités du Ps. xlv avec le Cantique," 176–77. Dijkema mentions the similar situations of Ps. 45:11 and Song 1:13–14, but does not mark any shared vocabulary. Both Mulder and Tournay note the similar Hebrew vocabulary of Ps. 45:2 and Song 1:16.

[19] The title δυνατός is repeated in v. 6 of the LXX.

[20] See also Dijkema, "Zu Psalm 45," 27; Tournay, "Affinités du Ps. xlv avec le Cantique," 179–80. Dijkema mentions the similar situations of Ps. 45:3 and Song 3:7–8, but does not mark any shared vocabulary. Tournay notes the similar Hebrew vocabulary of Ps. 45:3 and Song 3:7–8. A slightly different phrase does occur in Judg. 3, where Ehud assassinates Eglon. In verse 16, Ehud first fashions a "sword (חֶרֶב; μάχαιραν)" and fastens it "on his right thigh (עַל יֶרֶךְ יְמִינוֹ; ἐπι τὸν μηρὸν τὸν δεξιὸν αὐτοῦ)." In verse 21, he then takes "the sword from his right thigh (אֶת־הַחֶרֶב מֵעַל יֶרֶךְ; τὴν μάχαιραν ἀπο τοῦ μηροῦ τοῦ δεξιοῦ αὐτοῦ)." The differences between Judg. 3:16, 21 and Ps. 45:3 are more pronounced in Greek than in Hebrew.

The sixth parallel derives from the phrase "myrrh and aloes." Psalm 45:8 describes the king's robes, fragrant with "myrrh and aloes (מֹר־וַאֲהָלוֹת; σμύρνα καὶ στακτή)." Myrrh (מֹר; σμύρνα; στακτή) appears in Song 1:13; 3:6; 4:6, and 5:1, 5, 13.[21] Additionally, Song 4:14 depicts a garden that produces "myrrh and aloes (מֹר־וַאֲהָלוֹת; σμύρνα ἀλώθ)."[22] The Greek varies slightly from Ps. 45:8 to Song 4:14, but the Hebrew is exactly the same.[23]

A seventh similarity involves the relative positions of the king and his consort. According to Ps. 45:9, the queen stands at the king's "right hand (לִימִינְךָ; ἐκ δεξιῶν σου)." In Song 2:6 and 8:3, the bride expresses her wish to be embraced with her lover's "right hand (וִימִינוֹ; ἡ δεξιὰ αὐτοῦ)." Both texts place the woman at the right hand of the man.[24]

The eighth significant parallel concerns the name given to the bride and the attendant maidens. Psalm 45:9, 12 calls the king's ladies "daughters (בְּנוֹת; θυγατέρες)," and Ps. 45:10 addresses the princess as "daughter (בַּת; θυγάτηρ)."[25] The same terms are used to describe the maiden in Song 7:1 (2), as well as the other attendant maidens in Song 2:2 and Song 6:9.[26]

Finally, both Ps. 45 and the Song of Songs use the same words to depict the bride's festive procession into the king's quarters. Psalm 45:15 describes the princess and her virgin companions. It reads, "With joy and gladness (בְּשִׂמְחֹת וָגִיל; εὐφροσύνη καὶ ἀγαλλιάσει) they are led along (ἀπενεχθήσονται) as they enter (תְּבֹאֶינָה) the palace of the king (מֶלֶךְ; βασιλέως)." Song of Songs 1:4 describes a similar scene: "The king (הַמֶּלֶךְ; ὁ βασιλεὺς) has brought me (הֱבִיאַנִי; εἰσήνεγκέν με) into his chambers. We will exult and rejoice (נָגִילָה וְנִשְׂמְחָה; ἀγαλλιασώμεθα καὶ εὐφρανθῶμεν) in you." The four parallels in Hebrew and Greek vocabulary are quite remarkable.[27]

---

[21] See also Dijkema, "Zu Psalm 45," 27. He notes the presence of myrrh and the king in both Ps. 45:8 and Song 3:6, but does not mark any shared vocabulary.

[22] See also Mulder, *Studies on Psalm 45*, 125, 155, n. 232; Tournay, "Affinités du Ps. xlv avec le Cantique," 190–91. Mulder notes the similar Hebrew vocabulary of Ps. 45:8 and Song 1:13; 3:6; 4:6, 14; 6:1, 5, 13. Tournay emphasizes parallels between Ps. 45:8 and Song 3:6–7; 4:14.

[23] Although there is more shared vocabulary in Hebrew, this point is valid for messianic exegesis of both the MT and the LXX.

[24] Tournay also recognizes that both Ps. 45:9 and Song 2:6; 8:3 refer to the bridegroom's "right hand" ("Affinités du Ps. xlv avec le Cantique," 196).

[25] In Ps. 45:12, the NRSV translates this word "people."

[26] See also Dijkema, "Zu Psalm 45," 27. He notes that king's daughters act as bridesmaids in both Ps. 45:9, 13 and Song 6:9; 7:1 (2), but does not mark any shared vocabulary.

[27] See also Dijkema, "Zu Psalm 45," 27; Mulder, *Studies on Psalm 45*, 136–37, 155, n. 232; Tournay, "Affinités du Ps. xlv avec le Cantique," 204. Dijkema mentions the similar

On the basis of shared vocabulary, then, it is possible to associate the bridegroom in the Song of Songs with the Messiah in Ps. 45. Like the Messiah of Ps. 45, the bridegroom of the Song of Songs is the subject of a love song, and he is called a king. He is extraordinarily handsome, and his consort is also quite beautiful. His retinue of mighty men all wear swords on their thighs. The fragrance of myrrh and aloes surrounds him, and his consort is at his right hand. The bride (along with the other female attendants) is called a daughter, and she is led to the king's quarters with joy and gladness.[28] Like Ps. 45, the Song of Songs can be understood as a description of the Messiah's marriage celebration.

The Fourth Evangelist never explicitly makes any of these nine connections between Ps. 45 and the Song of Songs. Nevertheless it is not unreasonable to conclude that he might have initiated or inherited them, since other exegetes do in fact recognize the same connections. At least five of them receive attention in third-century commentaries. Hippolytus specifically mentions two in his *Commentary on the Song of Songs*. He apparently links the adjective καλή in Song 1:8 with the noun κάλλος in Ps. 45:2, explaining that since Christ is more beautiful than the sons of men (Ps. 45:2), his follower has become beautiful among women (Song 1:8).[29] In addition, Hippolytus uses the description of the warrior king in Ps. 45:3–5 to interpret the significance of the armed guard in Song 3:7. He notes that sixty ancestors of Christ (Song 3:7) bore the sword of the Word on their thighs, going forth for the sake of truth (Ps. 45:4).[30]

Origen engages in a similar method of exegesis, achieving similar results. His *Commentary on the Song of Songs* contains an extensive discussion of Song 1:4: "The king has brought me into his chambers. We will exult and rejoice in you." According to Origen, the bride of Song 1:4 is accompanied by virgins as described in Ps. 45:14–15: "Behind her the virgins, her companions, follow. With joy and gladness

---

situations of Ps. 45:15 and Song 1:4, but does not mark any shared vocabulary. Both Mulder and Tournay note the similar situations as well as the shared Hebrew vocabulary.

[28] Scholars have also noted other, less remarkable parallels. Mulder (*Studies on Psalm 45*, 123) and Tournay ("Affinités du Ps. xlv avec le Cantique," 190) point out that Ps. 45:7 and Song 1:7 both mention "companions." Mulder notes shared Hebrew vocabulary in Ps. 45:17, which celebrates the king's name, and Song 1:4, which extols the couple's love (*Studies on Psalm 45*, 140). Tournay draws attention to the "lilies" in the superscription of Ps. 45 and in Song 2:1–2, 16; 4:5; 6:2–3; 7:2 (3) ("Affinités du Ps. xlv avec le Cantique," 173, 177). Lorentz observes that Ps. 45 is a love song about a king waiting for the bridal procession, as in Song 3:6–10 (*Das althebräische Liebeslied*, 67).

[29] Hippolytus, Εἰς τὸ ᾆσμα, Frag. 5. The commentary reckons Song 1:8 as 1:7b.

[30] Ibid., Frag. 17.

they are led along as they enter the palace of the king."[31] Origen presumably quotes Ps. 45:14–15 here because of its likeness to Song 1:4.[32] He then cites Ps. 45:8, "Your robes are all fragrant with myrrh and aloes and cassia," in a discussion about the bag of myrrh in Song 1:13. He points out that the unguent worn by the Song's bride also perfumes the garments of the Psalm's king. At the same time, he makes an implicit connection between the "beloved" of Ps. 45 (LXX Ps. 44) and the "beloved" of the Song of Songs. He notes that Ps. 45:8, along with the rest of the Psalm, is "also" addressed to the "beloved." In other words, Ps. 45 is addressed to the "beloved," as is the Song of Songs.[33]

This does not necessarily mean that Hippolytus and Origen have inherited a first-century tradition of using shared vocabulary to connect the Song of Songs to Ps. 45. They could just as easily have made these connections on their own. The important point is that this kind of interpretation is more than just possible. Christians actually did engage in messianic exegesis, using Ps. 45 and the Song of Songs.

Messianic interpretation of the Song of Songs in light of Ps. 45 lends strong support to the notion that John alludes to Song 1:12 and 3:1–4. John's portrayal of Jesus, the Messiah reclining at table and surrounded by the fragrance of a woman's nard, is compatible with a messianic interpretation of Song 1:12. The king (הַמֶּלֶךְ; βασιλεύς) on the couch in Song 1:12 is none other than the King (הַמֶּלֶךְ; βασιλεύς) Messiah of Ps. 45:1, 5, 11, and 14. As John sees it, the nard foreshadows the king's imminent death. In the same way, John's description of a woman's search for the missing Jesus is based on a messianic interpretation of Song 3:1–4. He identifies the Song's missing man, the one "whom my soul loves (ὃν ἠγάπησεν ἡ ψυχή μου)," as the Messiah, the subject of Ps. 45, "A song concerning the beloved (ὑπὲρ τοῦ ἀγαπητοῦ)." For John, the searching woman cannot find the risen Messiah because she is looking for a corpse. When she finally recognizes him, she cannot hold him because he is ascending to God.

A joyful wedding procession

For readers of the MT, Jer. 33:10–11 is a rather obvious candidate for some kind of messianic interpretation. The prophecy that the voice of

---

[31] Origen, *Comm. Cant.* 1.5.
[32] See above, p. 113.
[33] Origen, *Comm. Cant.* 2.10; cf. *Hom. Cant.* 2 3.

the bridegroom and the voice of the bride will once more be heard is immediately followed by a promise about a Davidic king:

> In those days and at that time I will cause a righteous Branch to spring up for David; and he shall execute justice and righteousness in the land. In those days Judah will be saved and Jerusalem will live in safety. And this is the name by which it will be called: "The LORD is our righteousness."   (Jer. 33:15–16)

This passage, together with similar references to "a branch" from Jesse's roots in Isa. 11:1–5 and "the Branch" in Zech. 6:12, was undoubtedly accepted as a messianic prophecy.[34]

Jeremiah never explicitly identifies "the bridegroom" of Jer. 33:11 with the "Branch" of Jer. 33:15. Messianic significance can be attributed to the bridegroom, however, by virtue of association with Ps. 45 and the Song of Songs. We have seen that both Ps. 45 and the Song of Songs describe a joyful wedding procession using the words "joy (εὐφροσύνη)," "gladness (שִׂמְחָה)," and "lead/enter/bring (בּוֹא; εἰσφέρω)." Jeremiah also uses these terms to describe a similar scene. In Jer. 33:11, the voice of the bridegroom and the voice of the bride are accompanied by "the voice of mirth and the voice of gladness (קוֹל שָׂשׂוֹן וְקוֹל שִׂמְחָה; φωνὴ εὐφροσύνης καὶ φωνὴ χαρμοσύνης)."[35] These voices sing "as they bring (מְבִאִים; εἰσοίσουσιν) thank offerings to the house of the Lord." In Ps. 45:15 and Song 1:4, the bride is brought into the king's quarters with joy. In the same way, the voice of joy accompanies the bride and bridegroom of Jer. 33:11 as they bring offerings into the temple.[36]

The similarities do not end here. The same note of praise is sounded at the end of both Ps. 45 and Jer. 33:11. Psalm 45:17 reads, "Therefore the peoples will praise you (יְהוֹדֻךָ; ἐξομολογήσεταί σοι) forever and ever (עַד וָעֶד לְעֹלָם; εἰς τὸν αἰῶνα καὶ εἰς τὸν αἰῶνα τοῦ αἰῶνος)."

---

[34] First-century messianic interpretation of Jer. 33:15–16 would not have been possible for exegetes using a Greek Bible. The text reckoned as Jer. 33:14–26 in the MT does not appear in the best LXX manuscripts, including A, B, ℵ, and translations by Aquila and Symmachus.

[35] The variant εισουσιν appears in B and ℵ. It is not at all likely that this reflects the original translation, as it can be easily explained as an instance of haplography. The verb εισοισουσιν is attested by both A and ℵᶜ (Bᶜ amends εισουσιν to οισουσιν) and more accurately translates the Hebrew. If a Johannine exegete sought to establish the strongest possible link between Greek versions of Jer. 33:11, Song 1:4, and Ps. 45:15, it would have been necessary for him to have had access to a text containing this reading.

[36] Mulder also recognizes the shared Hebrew vocabulary of Ps. 45:15; Song 1:4; and Jer. 33:11 (*Studies on Psalm 45*, 137, 155, n. 232).

Likewise, the voices of Jer. 33:11 sing, "Give thanks (הוֹדוּ;
Ἐξομολογεῖσθε) to the Lord of hosts, for the Lord is good, for his
steadfast love endures forever (לְעוֹלָם; εἰς τὸν αἰῶνα)!" The bridegroom-
Messiah of Ps. 45 is praised forever, and the Lord of Jer. 33:11 is praised
because his steadfast love endures forever.

Because of similar vocabulary, then, the Messiah of Ps. 45:15–17 can
be associated not only with the bridegroom of Song 1:4 but also with
the bridegroom of Jer. 33:10–11. In Ps. 45 and Song 1, the princess is
brought into his palace with joy, and in Ps. 45 he receives praise
forever. Similarly, in Jer. 33, he joins the bride in a joyful procession
to the temple, where the Lord is praised because his steadfast love
endures forever. In both passages, the advent of the Messiah becomes
the occasion for a festive gathering with joyful praise. This image in
turn may inspire John 3:22–30. The voice of the bridegroom-Messiah
in the joyful wedding procession becomes the voice of Jesus, the
bridegroom-Messiah, heard by his rejoicing friend John the Baptist.[37]

It is interesting to note that identification of the bridegroom in Jer.
33:10–11 as the Messiah enables messianic interpretation of similar
prophecies in Jer. 7:32–34, 16:9, and 25:10. This may account for
the presence of the phrase ὀσμὴ μύρου in both Jer. 25:10 and John
12:3. The fragrance of the perfume that vanishes with the bridegroom-
Messiah (Jer. 25:10) now fills the house where Jesus reclines at table
(John 12:3).

Israel's forbears at a well of living water

The story of Jacob and Rachel in Gen. 29:1–20 displays some remarkable similarities to the Song of Songs. For instance, each takes place in
a pastoral setting and portrays its protagonist as a shepherd. Genesis
29 features flocks of sheep (עֶדְרֵי־צֹאן; ποίμνια προβάτων) and the act
of pasturing (רָעָה; ποιμαίνω) them (vv. 2–3, 6–10). Jacob himself
assumes the role of a shepherd by watering "the flock (אֶת־צֹאן; τὰ
πρόβατα) of his mother's brother Laban" (v. 10). The Song of Songs
also mentions flocks (עֶדְרֵי; ποίμνια), sheep (צֹאן), and pasturing (רָעָה;
ποιμαίνω) (Song 1:7–8).[38] Like Jacob, the bridegroom in the Song of
Songs assumes the role of a shepherd. He "pastures his flock (רָעָה;
ποιμαίνω)" among the lilies and in the gardens (Song 2:16; 6:2).

---

[37] See above, p. 58.
[38] The only similar Greek words are ποίμνια and ποιμαίνω.

Both Gen. 29 and the Song of Songs also refer to a beautiful daughter who is loved by her bridegroom. Genesis 29:17–18 reads, "Rachel was graceful and beautiful (יְפַת־תֹּאַר וִיפַת מַרְאֶה; καλὴ τῷ εἴδει καὶ ὡραία τῇ ὄψει). Jacob loved (וַיֶּאֱהַב; ἠγάπησεν) Rachel; so he said, 'I will serve you seven years for your younger daughter (בִּתְּךָ; τῆς θυγατρός σου) Rachel.'" (Rachel is also called a "daughter" in vv. 6 and 10.) According to Gen. 29:20, the seven years "seemed to him but a few days because of the love (בְּאַהֲבָתוֹ; τὸ ἀγαπᾶν) he had for her."

Rachel's appearance matches that of the bride in the Song of Songs. As we have seen, this bride is also "beautiful (יָפָה; καλή)" (Song 1:5, 8, 15; 2:10, 13; 4:1, 7; 5:9; 6:1, 4, 10). Her "face is lovely (וּמַרְאֵיךְ נָאוֶה; ἡ ὄψις σου ὡραία)," and she is "comely (נָאוֶה; ὡραία)" as Jerusalem (2:14; 4:3; 6:4). She and the bridegroom share a "love (אַהֲבָה; ἀγάπη)" that is stronger than death and more precious than all of a person's worldly goods (8:6–7). Finally, like Rachel, she is called "daughter (בַּת; θυγάτηρ)" (7:1 [2]).

It should be noted that Rachel's appearance and identity as a daughter further link Gen. 29:17–18 with Ps. 45. As we have seen, Ps. 45:11 also describes the "beauty (יָפְיֵךְ; τοῦ κάλλους σου)" of the princess. In Ps. 45:10, she is said to be a "daughter (בַּת; θυγάτηρ)." Thus two of the connections between Gen. 29 and the Song of Songs derive directly from fundamental links between the Song of Songs and Ps. 45.

Finally, both Gen. 29 and the Song of Songs mention a well. Song of Songs 4:15 features "a garden fountain, a well of living water (בְּאֵר מַיִם חַיִּים; φρέαρ ὕδατος ζῶντος)." The word "well" provides the necessary connection to Gen. 29:1–12, in which Jacob encounters Rachel at a "well (בְּאֵר; φρέαρ)" (Gen. 29:2–3, 8, 10).

This link can be further related to a previously noted parallel between Song 4 and Ps. 45. According to Ps. 45:8, the robes of the king are fragrant with "myrrh and aloes." As noted above, messianic exegesis of the Song of Songs connects this phrase to Song 4:14, which mentions "myrrh and aloes."[39] The very next verse, Song 4:15, refers to the well.

Both the well and the myrrh and aloes can be understood to belong to the Song's bridegroom. The phrase "myrrh and aloes" describes the garden comprising "your shoots (שְׁלָחַיִךְ; ἀποστολαὶ σου)" (v. 13). In Hebrew, the second-person possessive feminine ending refers to the antecedent אֲחֹתִי כַלָּה, the sister-bride of the previous verse (Song 4:12). In the LXX, however, the possessive pronoun σου does not specify gender. The one whose garden contains myrrh and aloes could just as

---

[39] See above, p. 113.

easily be a man. Indeed, according to Song 4:16–5:1 (LXX), the garden with the shoots of myrrh and aloes belongs to the beloved (ἀδελφιδός). Thus the garden described in Song 4:12–15 (LXX), with its myrrh and aloes and its well of living water, belongs to the bridegroom. He can then be associated both with the bridegroom of Ps. 45, whose robes are fragrant with myrrh and aloes, and also with Jacob, who encounters Rachel at a well.

Messianic exegesis of the Song of Songs can thus lead to messianic exegesis of Gen. 29:1–20. The bridegroom-Messiah in the Song of Songs, who acts as a shepherd (Song 2:16; 6:2) and whose garden contains a well of living water (Song 4:14–15), is like Jacob, who waters sheep (Gen. 29:10) at a well (Gen. 29:2–3, 8, 10). His bride, a daughter (Song 7:1 [2]) beautiful (Song 1:5, 8, 15; 2:10, 13; 4:1, 7; 5:9; 6:1, 4, 10) and lovely in appearance (Song 2:14; 4:3; 6:4), is like Rachel, the beautiful and lovely (Gen. 29:17) daughter (Gen. 29:6, 10, 18) of Laban. Finally, the love shared by the bridegroom-Messiah and his bride (Song 8:6–7) is like the love of Jacob for Rachel (Gen. 29:18, 20). Jacob, therefore, can be associated with the bridegroom-Messiah of the Song of Songs.

This unusual interpretation seems somewhat improbable. Nevertheless, at least one early Christian does indeed recognize verbal parallels between Gen. 29 and the Song of Songs. In the prologue to his *Commentary on the Song of Songs*, Origen discusses the Song's theme of love. To show that the theme of love appears elsewhere in Scripture, Origen quotes Gen. 29:17–18: "Rachel was graceful and beautiful. Jacob loved Rachel; so he said, 'I will serve you seven years for your younger daughter Rachel.'"[40] Using shared vocabulary to link Jacob's love for Rachel with the love extolled in the Song of Songs is therefore not just a possibility. That one exegete explicitly does so increases the probability that John relies implicitly on the same connection.

So does an additional allusion in John 4:4–42 – an allusion to Song 4:13–16. When Jesus meets the Samaritan woman at Jacob's well (φρέαρ), he offers her "living water (ὕδωρ ζῶν)" (John 4:10–11) – just like the "living water (ὕδωρ ζῶν)" that flows from the well (φρέαρ) of Song 4:15.[41] The Jesus of John 4 thus resembles not only Jacob at the well in Gen. 29, but also the owner of the well of living water from Song 4. John apparently associates Gen. 29:1–20 with Song 4:13–16,

---

[40] Origen, *Comm. Cant.*, Prologue.
[41] See also Jonathan Grothe, "Seventh Sunday after Pentecost: John 4:5–15," *Concordia Journal* 11 (1985), 109.

and applies both texts to Jesus. John's Jesus, the Messiah prophesied in the Song of Songs, is like Jacob, the progenitor of a family of faith.[42]

Messianic exegesis of the Song of Songs, Jer. 33:10–11, and Gen. 29:1–20 thus provides a plausible explanation for the allusions in John 3:22–30, 4:4–42, 12:1–8, and 20:1, 11–18. These biblical texts about marriage are prominent for John because he interprets them as messianic prophecies. They can be understood as references to the Messiah in light of Ps. 45. They also help him to describe the life and death of his Messiah, Jesus. John borrows details from Jeremiah's bridegroom prophecy to describe Jesus' success in Judea and to delineate Jesus' relationship with John the Baptist. He tells the story about Jesus in Samaria after a pattern established by the account of Jacob's betrothal to Rachel. He crafts his accounts of a woman anointing Jesus and of Mary Magdalene at the empty tomb according to a structure adopted from similar scenes in the Song of Songs. Alluding to a bridegroom prophecy, a betrothal narrative, and erotic poetry thus enables John to create a portrait of Jesus as a bridegroom-Messiah: the epitome of the bridegroom in Jer. 33:10–11, of the patriarch Jacob in Gen. 29:1–20, of the beloved king in the Song of Songs – and of the royal bridegroom in Ps. 45.

Excursus: more evidence from the Fourth Gospel for messianic exegesis based on Psalm 45

John's final chapters resonate with other, fainter, echoes of biblical texts that may reflect further messianic exegesis based on Ps. 45. The strongest occurs in John's burial scene. As Joseph of Arimathea and Nicodemus prepare the body of Jesus for interment, they wrap it in linen cloths together with a "mixture of myrrh and aloes (μίγμα σμύρνης καὶ ἀλόης)" (John 19:39). A similar phrase occurs in Song 4:14, in which "myrrh and aloes (מֹר־וַאֲהָלוֹת; σμύρνα ἀλώθ)" are listed among the plants in a flourishing orchard.[43]

Yet another word links Jesus' burial to the Song's orchard: the noun "garden (κῆπος)" (John 19:41; Song 4:12, 15, 16).[44] These instances

---

[42] Hanson also notes the parallel between Song 4:15 and John 4, but cannot determine why John might have considered the Song as a prophecy of the Samaritan encounter (*Prophetic Gospel*, 58). Messianic exegesis of Gen. 29 and Song 4:14–15 in light of Ps. 45 provides the necessary warrant.

[43] John's phrase "σμύρνης καὶ ἀλόης" also closely resembles the wording of Song 4:14 as attested by א: "σμυρνα αλοη."

[44] Cf. Feuillet, "Recherche du Christ," 106; Schneiders, "Resurrection Narrative," I:394 and "Easter Jesus," 161; Winsor, *A King Is Bound*, 42.

of verbal correspondence are supported by the recurrence of an allusion to the "well (φρέαρ)" and the "living water (ὕδωρ ζῶν)" of Song 4:15 in John 4:10–11.[45] Like John's allusions to Song 1:12 and 3:1–4, these faint echoes may indicate that Jesus is the Messiah portrayed in the Song of Songs. Not only does he offer living water from a well, he also is buried with myrrh and aloes in a garden.

The phrase "myrrh and aloes" may also constitute an allusion to Ps. 45:8. This verse, which describes the robes of the king, fragrant with "myrrh and aloes (מֹר־וַאֲהָלוֹת; σμύρνα καὶ στακτὴ)," contains the only other biblical occurrence of this phrase. A possible allusion to Ps. 45:8 in John 19:39 is strengthened by circumstantial correspondence between the king's robe and Jesus' linen cloths. This imparts a touch of poignant irony to the interment scene. In Ps. 45, the myrrh and aloes lend a rich aroma to the wedding garments of God's anointed. For John, this mixture imparts its fragrance to the burial garment of Jesus, the crucified Messiah.[46]

A second echo can be detected in John's account of Jesus' arrest. John 18:6 reads, "When Jesus said to them, 'I am he,' they stepped back and fell to the ground (ἀπῆλθον εἰς τὰ ὀπίσω καὶ ἔπεσαν χαμαί)." Barrett points out parallels between John 18:6 and Ps. 27:2, "My adversaries and foes (οἱ ἐχθροί μου) . . . shall stumble and fall (ἔπεσαν)," along with Ps. 56:9, "Then my enemies will retreat (ἐπιστρέψουσιν οἱ ἐχθροί μου εἰς τὰ ὀπίσω) in the day when I call."[47] In addition, Reim proposes an allusion to Ps. 45:5:

> Your arrows are sharp
>   in the heart of the king's enemies (τῶν ἐχθρῶν τοῦ
>   βασιλέως);
> the peoples fall under you (λαοὶ ὑποκάτω σου πεσοῦνται).[48]

---

[45] See above, p. 119.

[46] The similarity between John 19:39 and Ps. 45:8 is also noted by Westcott (*Gospel According to St. John*, 281), Barrett (*Gospel According to St. John*), 465), and Hanson (*Prophetic Gospel*, 225). Brown includes a similar note about John 19:39 and Song 4:14 (*John XIII–XXI*, 940), while Adolf Schlatter briefly notes the parallel between John 19:39, Ps. 45:8, and Song 4:14 (*Der Evangelist Johannes* [Stuttgart: Calwer, 1948], 355). Hanson alone suggests a reason for the similarity: John demonstrates that Jesus is a king, like the king of Ps. 45:8. He then suggests that John 19:39 represents Jesus' body as the future church, anointed with myrrh and aloes and risen as a well of living water, as prophesied in Song 4:14–15. I suspect rather that if John indeed alludes to Song 4:14–15, he regards it as a prophecy about the Messiah.

[47] Barrett, *Gospel According to St. John*, 434; cf. Hanson, *Prophetic Gospel*, 201.

[48] Günter Reim, "Jesus As God in the Fourth Gospel: The Old Testament Background," *NTS* 30 (1984), 158–59; *Zugänge zum Evangelium des Johannes* (Erlangen: Ev.-Luth. Mission, 1994), 119. Reim also discusses other, even fainter, echoes of Ps. 45.

Both Barrett and Reim may be correct, since Pss 27:2 and 56:9 can be linked to Ps. 45:5 on the basis of shared vocabulary. All three verses refer to "enemies (אֹיְבִים; ἐχθροί)"; in both Ps. 45:5 and Ps. 27:2, those enemies "fall (נָפַל; πίπτω)." It is entirely possible that John understood Pss 27:2 and 56:9 as messianic prophecies in light of Ps. 45:5, and then alluded to this complex of messianic texts in his account of Jesus' arrest.

Two other factors add support to this notion. One is the dissonance of the falling incident. It fits neither the scene in John 18 nor the thematic structure of the Gospel as a whole. John never explains why Jesus' enemies retreat and fall to the ground, nor does he describe how they get up again before taking Jesus into custody. The event has no apparent significance. Jesus' opponents' retreating and falling down harmonizes better with Pss 27:2, 56:9, and 45:5 than with John's story.

Second, the echo is subject to an interpretation that lends it some significance. In both John 18:6 and Ps. 45:5 (as well as in Pss 27:2 and 56:9, interpreted as messianic prophecies), enemies fall to the ground before the Lord's anointed. According to Ps. 45, the nation's enemies surrender to the mighty Messiah. John, however, identifies these enemies as a Roman cohort joined by the armed representatives of the chief priests and Pharisees, who fall before Jesus as he surrenders to them. For John, the Messiah ironically topples not only the Romans but also the leaders of Israel who oppose him.

An argument can thus be made that John relies on messianic exegesis of Song 4:14, Ps. 27:2, and Ps. 56:9 in light of Ps. 45 to describe the fate of his Messiah, Jesus. It is interesting to observe the difference between possible echoes of Ps. 45 and related texts in John and the quotation of Ps. 45:6–7 in Hebrews. Hebrews 1:8–9 refers to the risen and exalted Jesus, the righteous Messiah whose kingdom lasts forever. In contrast, John seems to apply Ps. 45 to Jesus in the context of his crucifixion. The falling enemies, sent by Jewish authorities, eventually arrest John's Messiah, and the fragrant robes are his burial cloths. As we have seen, John uses messianic prophecies elsewhere to show how a crucified Christ confounds the people's expectations.[49] Here his possible echoes of messianic prophecies illustrate his portrayal of the crucified Jesus.

---

[49] See above, p. 42.

6

HEARING THE ECHOES

If a tree falls in the forest and no one is there, does it make a sound? If an implied author transmits echoes of Scripture for the benefit of an implied audience, do those echoes ever reach the ears of real audiences? If so, how do those real audiences respond? Do they disregard the noise? Do they stop up their ears? Do they listen attentively?

So far, our discussion of the Fourth Gospel's allusions to marriage texts has ignored real authors and audiences. It has stayed within parameters established by the Gospel itself. Text-related criteria such as availability, correspondence, rhetorical emphasis, recurrence, and thematic coherence have been used to show how the Gospel's implied author alludes to Jer. 33:10–11, Gen. 29:1–20, Song 1:12, and Song 3:1–4. The implied author's overriding concern with Jesus' messianic identity suggests that he and his audience attribute messianic significance to these passages. The fact that they can be interpreted as messianic prophecies in light of Ps. 45 lends strong support to this notion. There is also some indication that, for the implied author and audience, the Samaritan woman and Mary Magdalene – and perhaps the anonymous bride of John 3:29 – exemplify believers in some way. The Gospel text yields enough evidence to identify the allusions, to interpret them, and to explain their presence.

Nevertheless, one wonders how they might have been produced and perceived by real people. Might the person or persons who composed the Fourth Gospel have intended these allusions? Would the Gospel's original audience have been able to discern them? Would that audience have recognized their messianic import? Would they have understood the female characters as paradigmatic believers or representative figures? How might contemporary faith communities appreciate and appropriate John's allusions to marriage texts?

These questions cannot be definitively answered. For one thing, John's original author and audience are not strictly "real people." Because they no longer exist, they must be imagined. Contemporary audiences do exist, but their sheer number and variety makes it impossible to measure the impact of John's echoes on each one.[1] Nevertheless, we can speculate as to how well believers with a certain predisposition might hear them. In other words, the response of both the Johannine community and the church today to the Fourth Gospel's allusions to marriage texts can be constructed on the basis of the familiarity of those hypothetical audiences with the allusions' component parts. How well can they be expected to know the evoked texts? Do they – or could they – understand those texts as messianic prophecies? Are they aware of conventions, associations, and aspects of resemblance that would establish the female characters as representative figures? In this way, we can discern whether John's echoes of Jer. 33:10–11, Gen. 29:1–20, Song 1:12, and Song 3:1–4 might make a sound. We can then evaluate whether any sound they might make is worth listening to.

Hearing the echoes in the first century

Although John's original author and audience cannot be identified with any certainty, several of their traits can be posited with a high degree of probability. Extensive investigations within the past four decades into the nature of that audience have resulted in a remarkable scholarly consensus. Until the 1960s, critics had espoused various theories. Many ruled out Palestinian Jewish influence, since the Gospel's prominent dualism and λόγος-concept lack parallels in the Old Testament and Rabbinic writings. Among major commentators, C. H. Dodd and C. K. Barrett traced Johannine thought to Greek philosophy and Hellenistic Judaism.[2] Rudolf Bultmann insisted on a Gnostic background.[3] Raymond Brown, noting similarities between John's Gospel and some of the recently published Dead Sea Scrolls, argued for an eclectic setting within Palestinian Judaism.[4] Rudolf Schnackenburg posited a similar setting in Asia Minor, one that retained Syrian and Palestinian influences.[5]

During the 1960s, new discoveries and fresh realizations eroded the foundations for several of these theories. Scholars were gaining

---

[1] If this monograph is still being read fifty years from now, today's faith communities will also no longer exist.

[2] Dodd, *Interpretation*, 73; Barrett, *Gospel According to St. John*, 22–23.

[3] Bultmann, *Gospel of John*, 7–9.

[4] Brown, *John I–XII*, lii–lxiv.

[5] Schnackenburg, *Gospel According to St. John*, I:119–52.

familiarity with the Dead Sea Scrolls as well as recognizing that Palestinian Judaism was subject to greater Hellenistic influence than had been previously suspected.[6] Research on the Johannine community soon focused on the issues raised in J. Louis Martyn's *History and Theology in the Fourth Gospel*, published in 1968. Based on his interpretation of John 9, Martyn offers a reconstruction of the relationship between Jewish messianists in the Johannine community and Pharisaic Jews following the destruction of the temple in 70 CE. Because Johannine believers insisted that Jesus is the Messiah, they were put out of local synagogues.[7]

Brown and others had already argued that John's original author and audience were involved in conflict with a Jewish group.[8] In 1977, Brown published an article on the origins of the Johannine community.[9] This article was followed in 1979 by his book *The Community of the Beloved Disciple*, which presents another reconstruction of the Johannine group's development and relationship to the synagogue.[10] Brown's work manifested the growing consensus: the Fourth Gospel reflects the late first-century emergence and mutual self-differentiation of primitive Christian messianism and Rabbinic Judaism in a community of Diaspora Jews.[11] Recently, Adele Reinhartz has forcefully restated Kimelman's objection to the idea that Jews were expelling Christians from synagogues.[12] Still, she agrees that some sort of conflict

[6] The relationship between the Fourth Gospel and the Dead Sea Scrolls is explored in *John and Qumran* (ed. James H. Charlesworth; London: Chapman, 1972).

[7] Martyn, *History and Theology*, 30–59.

[8] Brown, *John I–XII*, lxx–lxxv; Barrett, *Gospel According to St. John*, 79.

[9] Raymond E. Brown, "Johannine Ecclesiology: The Community's Origins," *Int* 31 (1977): 379–93.

[10] Raymond E. Brown, *The Community of the Beloved Disciple* (New York: Paulist, 1979).

[11] See Meeks, "Man from Heaven" and "Am I a Jew?," 163–86; Pancaro, *Law*; Oscar Cullmann, *Der johanneische Kreis: Sein Platz im Spätjudentum, in der Jüngerschaft und im Urchristentum: Zum Ursprung des Johannesevangeliums* (Tübingen: Mohr Siebeck, 1975); D. Moody Smith, "Johannine Christianity: Some Reflections on Its Character and Delineation," *NTS* 21 (1975): 222–48; Meeks, "Breaking Away: Three New Testament Pictures of Christianity's Separation from the Jewish Communities," in *"To See Ourselves As Others See Us": Christians, Jews, "Others" in Late Antiquity* (ed. Jacob Neusner and Ernest S. Frerichs; Scholars Press Studies in the Humanities 8; Chico, Calif.: Scholars Press, 1985), 93–115; Alan Segal, *Rebecca's Children: Judaism and Christianity in the Roman World* (Cambridge, Mass.: Harvard University Press, 1986), 156–58; Klaus Wengst, *Bedrängte Gemeinde und verherrlichter Christus: Ein versuch über das Johannesevangelium* (Munich: Kaiser, 1990); Ashton, *Understanding the Fourth Gospel*; Sjef van Tilborg, *Reading John in Ephesus* (NovTSup 83; Leiden: Brill, 1996); Ringe, *Wisdom's Friends*, 10–28.

[12] Reinhartz, *Befriending the Beloved Disciple*, 39–50; Kimelman, "*Birkat Ha-Minim*," 226–44, 391–403.

over Jewish belief in Jesus is indicated.[13] The exact provenance of the Gospel remains a mystery, as do the identities of its author (or authors), redactor (or redactors), and primary source, the so-called "Beloved Disciple" (John 13:23; 19:26; 20:2; 21:7, 20–25).[14]

This reconstruction provides a plausible historical context for the use of Scripture by the Gospel's implied author and audience. They understand Greek and are conversant with a Greek Bible, as might be expected of a first-century community of Jews living outside of Palestine. At the very least, members of such a community would have heard Gen. 29:1–20 and Jer. 33:10–11 read on the Sabbath. The tradition of reading the Song of Songs during Passover may also date back to the first century.[15] Moreover, the Gospel's biblical citations indicate that some community members engaged in close study of the Scripture texts, perhaps in some sort of group.[16] At least one of these may have known the Bible in Hebrew, an accomplishment that would not have been unusual either for an immigrant from Palestine or for a Hellenistic Jew who had been trained there. The Johannine community could certainly have produced both the Evangelist who alluded to biblical texts about marriage and an audience prepared to recognize those allusions.

---

[13] Reinhartz, *Befriending the Beloved Disciple*, 48–53.

[14] Candidates for the place of composition include Alexandria (William H. Brownlee, "Whence the Gospel According to John?" in *John and Qumran*, 189–91), Syria (Wengst, *Bedrängte Gemeinde*, 160–79), and Ephesus (Tilborg, *Reading John in Ephesus*). For reconstructions of stages in the Gospel's composition, see Brown, *John I–XII*, xxxiv–xxxix; Ashton, *Understanding the Fourth Gospel*, 162–66. Charlesworth reviews proposals concerning the identity of the Beloved Disciple and presents evidence linking that character to Thomas (*The Beloved Disciple: Whose Witness Validates the Gospel of John?* [Valley Forge: Trinity, 1995], 127–287). Since there is as yet no consensus about the identity of the Gospel's original author or authors, I will continue to refer to that entity as "John."

[15] See Lundbom, "Between Text and Sermon," 172; Waal, "John and the OT," 34. The fact that John alludes to the Song of Songs, probably read during Passover, in the context of his passion narrative lends support to Guilding's theory that John cites Israel's Scriptures according to a Jewish lectionary. The theory is difficult to prove, since a first-century lectionary must be reconstructed (see Guilding, *Jewish Worship*, 6–44). Even if it is correct, however, it does not undermine the idea that John alludes to certain texts because of their messianic significance. The lectionary would simply have dictated his choices regarding placement of the allusions in the narrative.

[16] For a reconstruction of this enterprise, see R. Alan Culpepper, *The Johannine School: An Examination of the Johannine School Hypothesis Based on the Investigation of the Nature of Ancient Schools* (SBLDS 26; Missoula: Scholars Press, 1975). Charlesworth relates Culpepper's construct to the well-known School of Thomas. He suggests that either the School of Thomas evolved from Johannine traditions or that Thomas traditions shaped both the Fourth Gospel and writings attributed to Thomas (*Beloved Disciple*, 360–89).

This community could also have produced an author and audience who appreciated the allusions' messianic significance. They certainly believed that Jesus was the Messiah; indeed, beliefs about Jesus may have led to the rift between the Johannine community and their Jewish compatriots.[17] It probably also led to the reinterpretation of their Jewish traditions, a process that Luke Timothy Johnson describes as "the reshaping of the symbols of Judaism in the light of the experience of a crucified and raised Messiah."[18] They would certainly have searched their Scriptures for messianic prophecies about Jesus, using exegetical techniques popular in the first century. It is not at all unlikely that the Johannine community, as reconstructed by modern scholars, would have understood Jer. 33:10–11, Gen. 29:1–20, Song 1:12, and Song 3:1–4 as messianic prophecies because of shared vocabulary with Ps. 45.

This community could also have produced an author and audience who understood the Samaritan woman and Mary Magdalene as examples of the people of God. The anonymous bride of John 3:29 and Mary of Bethany in John 12:1–8 should be excluded from consideration as exemplary characters. The bride does not do enough to exemplify anything. Mary of Bethany does only a little more. Her extravagance towards Jesus has caused some commentators to regard her as an example or a representative of devoted believers.[19] John's anointing story, however, does not so much emphasize Mary's devotion as foreshadow Jesus' death. Since the narrative minimizes Mary's faith, one can hardly stress her possible representative value or exemplary role.[20]

The case is somewhat different for the Samaritan woman and Mary Magdalene, whose characters are more developed. The obstacles they face, the persistence they demonstrate, and the insights they gain can be related to a familiar convention whereby Israel's trials and triumphs are portrayed through stories about individual Jews. Daniel 1–6, for instance, is not simply the tale of young Jews in the courts of Gentile

---

[17] For reconstructions of their debate as reflected in the Fourth Gospel, see Martyn, *History and Theology*, 45–142; Marinus de Jonge, "Jewish Expectations about the 'Messiah' According to the Fourth Gospel," *NTS* 19 (1972–73): 246–70; Segal, *Rebecca's Children*, 156–58; Ashton, *Understanding the Fourth Gospel*, 137–51.

[18] Luke Timothy Johnson, *The Writings of the New Testament: An Interpretation* (rev. edn; Minneapolis: Fortress, 1999), 16; cf. 145–49.

[19] See, e.g., Hoskyns, *Fourth Gospel*, 487; Tasker, *Gospel According to St. John*, 144; Culpepper, *Anatomy*, 141–42.

[20] John Rena argues that John's female characters represent various issues or groups within the Johannine community. According to Rena, Mary of Bethany represents a prophet who foretells Jesus' burial ("Women in the Gospel of John," *EgT* 17 [1986], 142). There is very little evidence to support this contention, however.

rulers. It epitomizes the experiences of all faithful Jews whose religious practices are proscribed by Gentile overlords. Like Daniel and his friends, they must keep the dietary laws, worship only Israel's God, and observe the hours of prayer, even in the face of persecution. God will surely reward them for their faithfulness, just as God rewarded Daniel.[21]

Three other stories use women to exemplify the experiences of their Jewish audiences. Esther's loyalty to her uncle Mordecai, her vulnerability to the threats of the royal official Haman, and her seduction of King Ahasuerus reflect the experiences of many Diaspora Jews, who must appease their volatile Gentile overlords while remaining faithful to their heritage.[22] Jewish freedom fighters are paradigmatically portrayed by Judith, who uses her sexual wiles to outwit a Gentile general.[23] Susanna's story mirrors the experiences of Jews threatened by Hellenization. God rewards her purity by protecting her from violation by corrupt elders.[24]

As a group of Diaspora Jews, John's community may well have been used to identifying with characters like Daniel, Esther, Judith, and Susanna. Indeed, John's author seems to have adopted the convention whereby the challenges faced by his audience are met by the characters in his story.[25] For instance, the situation of the man born blind in John 9 may resemble that of Jewish messianists in the late first century. Like them, he is enlightened by Jesus, examined (along with his parents) by the Pharisees, and estranged from the synagogue.[26] In John 11, Martha and Mary of Bethany suffer as do believers whose comrades die before Jesus' prophesied return. They speak for all bereaved Christians when they lament, "Lord, if you had been here, my brother would not have died" (vv. 21, 32).[27]

In the same way, the questions raised by the woman at the well exemplify issues faced by Samaritan believers.[28] They, too, have turned

---

[21] Hartman, *Daniel*, 61.

[22] White, "Esther," 166–73.

[23] Levine, "Sacrifice and Salvation," 18–23.

[24] Levine, "'Hemmed in on Every Side.'"

[25] See also Fehribach, *Women in the Life of the Bridegroom*, 71 n. 83, 176–77.

[26] See Martyn, *History and Theology*, 26–40; Koester, *Symbolism*, 64. Evidence that believers experienced this kind of treatment can be found in John 5:1–18; Mark 13:9; Luke 4:14–30; Acts 13:13–52.

[27] See also Collins, *Representative Figures*, 46; Culpepper, *Anatomy*, 140; Alois Stimpfle, *Blinde Sehen: Die Eschatologie im traditionsgeschichtliche Prozess des Johannesevangeliums* (BZNW 57; Berlin: de Gruyter, 1990), 247–72; Koester, *Symbolism*, 65–67.

[28] The thesis that John's Gospel reflects Samaritan inclusion in the Johannine community is advanced by John W. Bowman ("Samaritan Studies," *BJRL* 40 [1958], 298–308;

from their ancestral worship to serve Jesus, the source of eternal life. Likewise, those who struggled to maintain faith in an absent Jesus might have found comfort in the reassurances given to Mary Magdalene.[29] They, too, must recall that Jesus is now with the Father. These women, and other characters like them, seem to have served as examples for the Gospel's audience. John's community probably related to the interrogation of the man born blind, the grief of Martha and Mary of Bethany, the religious issues confronting the Samaritan woman, and the abandonment felt by Mary Magdalene – just as Diaspora Jews might have aspired to the courage of Daniel, the loyalty of Esther, the cunning of Judith, and the purity of Susanna.

The Samaritan woman and Mary Magdalene may even have served as more than examples for the Fourth Gospel's author and audience. There are some indications that they, along with the anonymous bride of John 3:29 and Mary of Bethany in John 12:1–8, may also have symbolized believers in some way. The Johannine community may well have been aware of a second familiar convention – one that uses marriage imagery to illustrate the relationship between Christ and the church. This convention appears in various New Testament writings. For example, Paul reminds the Corinthian congregation, "I feel a divine jealousy for you, for I promised you in marriage to one husband, to present you as a chaste virgin to Christ" (2 Cor. 11:2). The author of Ephesians instructs married couples that the unity of husband and wife reflects the mystery of Christ and the church (Eph. 5:21–33). The author of Revelation depicts the ultimate salvation of the church as a marriage between the Lamb (that is, Christ) and his bride (Rev. 19:5–9; 21:2, 9). It was not unusual for first-century believers to imagine themselves as the bride of Christ.[30]

The Samaritan Problem: Studies in the Relationships of Samaritanism, Judaism, and Early Christianity [trans. Alfred M. Johnson, Jr.; PTMS 4; Pittsburgh: Pickwick, 1975], 57–69) and Edwin D. Freed ("Samaritan Influence in the Gospel of John," *CBQ* 30 [1968]: 580–87). The idea that Johannine theology was influenced by Samaritan beliefs is further developed by Purvis ("The Fourth Gospel and the Samaritans") and questioned by Margaret Pamment ("Is There Convincing Evidence of Samaritan Influence on the Fourth Gospel?" *ZNW* 73 [1982]: 221–30). Whether or not they exercised theological influence, Samaritans were almost certainly included in (or evangelized by) the Johannine community, as indicated by John 4:4–42.

[29] See also Feuillet, "Recherche du Christ," 97; Collins, "Representative Figures," 124; de Boer, *Johannine Perspectives*, 129; Koester, *Symbolism*, 70; cf. Rena, "Women in the Gospel of John," 145.

[30] For a thorough discussion of the marriage metaphor in these and other passages, see Richard Batey, *New Testament Nuptial Imagery* (Leiden: Brill, 1971). See also Claude Chavasse, *The Bride of Christ: An Enquiry into the Nuptial Element in Early Christianity* (London: Faber & Faber, 1940), 49–98; I. A. Muirhead, "The Bride of Christ," *SJT* 5 (1952): 175–87; Ernest Best, *One Body in Christ* (London: SPCK, 1955), 169–83; Alan

If John's original author and audience had been familiar with this symbolic convention, they would have had no difficulty in understanding the bride in John 3:29 as a representative of believers. More specifically, the Messiah's bride in this context would have represented those going to Jesus for baptism, mentioned in John 3:26.[31] Her role is then undertaken in succession by the Samaritan woman, Mary of Bethany, and Mary Magdalene. The Fourth Evangelist and his audience may well have understood these female characters as representatives of the people of God, in terms of the symbolic convention employed in 2 Cor. 11:2, Eph. 5:21–33, and Rev. 19:5–9; 21:2, 9.

If the Johannine community favored a symbolic interpretation of the brides in the evoked marriage texts, then it is even more likely that they regarded John's female characters as representative figures. Was this because first-century audiences discerned any symbolism in Jer. 33:10–11; Gen. 29:1–20; or the Song of Songs? There is no evidence for a symbolic interpretation of the bride in Jer. 33:11. In addition, there is very little indication that Rachel was understood to represent the people of God. Since Rachel was the grandmother of Ephraim and Manasseh, one might expect that she would come to symbolize Israel in popular imagination.[32] Nevertheless, actual evidence for a symbolic understanding of Rachel is scant. To my knowledge, nothing in the Targums or rabbinic literature suggests that Rachel is more than the wife of Jacob and mother of Joseph and Benjamin. The only place in Scripture where Rachel is clearly used as a figure of speech is in Jer. 31:15, quoted in Matt. 2:18:

> A voice was heard in Ramah,
>   wailing and loud lamentation,
> Rachel weeping for her children;
>   she refused to be consoled,
>   because they are no more.

Richardson, *Introduction to the Theology of the New Testament* (London: SCM Press, 1958), 256–58; Claude Welch, *The Reality of the Church* (New York: Scribner, 1958), 131–38; Paul S. Minear, *Images of the Church in the New Testament* (Philadelphia: Westminster, 1960), 54–56.

[31] So Plummer (*Gospel According to S. John*, 102), Zander ("Précurseur," 105), Boismard ("Ami de l'époux," 291), Sanders (*Commentary*, 134), Feuillet ("Symbolisme de la colombe," 539–40), and Schneiders (*Revelatory Text*, 187; *Written That You May Believe*, 35).

[32] Indeed, Joel W. Rosenberg suggests that the rivalry between Rachel and Leah in Gen. 29–30 reflects the historical conflict between Israel and Judah ("Genesis," in *The HarperCollins Study Bible* [ed. Wayne A. Meeks; New York: HarperCollins, 1993], 38).

Here, even as she expresses Israel's grief, she retains her primary role as their mother.

In this context, it should be noted that part of the Samaritan woman's significance for John's original audience can probably be found in her maternal role. The importance of John's allusion to Gen. 29 lies in the implicit comparison between those who believe in Jesus and God's chosen people. Christian beginnings are just like Israel's beginnings; their spiritual ancestors (Jesus and the Samaritan woman) are just like Israel's biological ancestors (Jacob and Rachel). They seem to have understood their experience of Jesus as the founder of their faith community in terms of their biblical tradition about Jacob as the patriarch of Israel. The Samaritan woman, whose encounter with Jesus and ensuing witness elicits belief among her people, becomes a sort of spiritual mother.

The situation is somewhat different with the Song of Songs. There is plenty of evidence that ancient exegetes regarded the Song's bride as a symbol of the people of God. To be sure, most of this evidence postdates the first century. For Origen (third century), the Song describes the relationship between Christ and believers, both individually and corporately.[33] According to *Song of Songs Rabbah* (sixth century) and the *Song of Songs Targum* (seventh century), it relates God's encounter with Israel at Mount Sinai.[34]

What little evidence there is for first-century readings of the Song of Songs does not conclusively demonstrate that allegorical interpretation of the Song of Songs was an early innovation. It does, however, support the possibility. Especially suggestive are these allusions from the late first-century apocalypse *4 Ezra*: "From all the flowers of the world you have chosen for yourself one lily, . . . and from all the birds that have been created you have named for yourself one dove" (*4 Ezra* 5:24, 26).[35] The "lily" of v. 24 apparently alludes to Song 2:1–2:

> I am a rose of Sharon,
>   a lily of the valleys.

---

[33] See Origen, *Comm. Cant.*

[34] See Jacob Neusner, *Song of Songs Rabbah: An Analytical Translation* (2 vols; BJS 197–98; Atlanta: Scholars Press, 1989) and Isaac Jerusalmi, *The Song of Songs in the Targumic Tradition* (Cincinnati: Ladino Books, 1993). For a discussion on the relationship between Christian and Rabbinic interpretation of the Song of Songs, see Ephraim E. Urbach, "The Homiletical Interpretation of the Sages and the Expositions of Origen on Canticles, and the Jewish-Christian Disputation," in *Studies in Aggadah and Folk-Literature* (ed. Joseph Heinemann and Dov Noy; ScrHier 22; Jerusalem: Magnes, 1971), 247–75.

[35] Trans. Bruce M. Metzger, *OTP* I:533.

> As a lily among brambles,
>   so is my love among maidens.

Similarly, the "dove" of v. 25 echoes Song 2:14:

> O my dove, in the clefts of the rock,
>   in the covert of the cliff,
> let me see your face,
>   let me hear your voice;
> for your voice is sweet,
>   and your face is lovely.

It seems that at least this first-century writer understood that the "lily" of Song 2:1–2 and the "dove" of Song 2:14 represent the people of Israel, chosen by God from all the nations.[36]

Other clues indicate that the Song of Songs was studied and appreciated in the first century, probably for its symbolic significance. Fragments of the Song were discovered at Qumran (4QCant[a-c]; 6QCant), along with a piece of a possible commentary (4QCommCant). There is also evidence that the canonicity of the Song of Songs was contested. The debate persisted into the second century, eliciting the famous dictum of R. Akiba as preserved in *m. Yad.* 3.5: "The entire age is not so worthy as the day on which the Song of Songs was given to Israel. For all the scriptures are holy, but the Song of Songs is the holiest of all."[37] It is difficult to imagine that the Pharisees and sectarians who accepted its canonicity interpreted it literally. They most likely considered it symbolic of the relationship between God and Israel.[38]

If Johannine exegetes interpreted the Song in light of Ps. 45 as a messianic prophecy, then it symbolized the relationship between God and God's people in a slightly different way. For them, the Song was about the Messiah, Jesus, and the community of believers. They appropriated Israel's Scriptures not only to describe Jesus but also to illustrate their experience of Jesus. In so doing, they affirmed their identity as the people of God – in this case, by identifying with the Song's bride.

Thus two symbolic conventions – one that uses marriage to illustrate the relationship between Christ and the church, and another that regards

---

[36] Pope, *Song of Songs*, 92.

[37] Trans. Jacob Neusner, in *Israel's Love Affair with God: Song of Songs* (Bible of Judaism Library; Valley Forge: Trinity, 1993), 3.

[38] Symbolic interpretation of erotic poetry is not at all improbable. That the Qumran covenanters practiced it is evident from 11QPs[a] 21:11–17, a version of Sir. 51:13–19 that describes a young man's discovery of wisdom in terms of sexual intercourse.

the Song as an allegory concerning God and Israel – suggest that John's female characters might have represented the people of God for the Gospel's original author and audience. It should be noted, however, that the Gospel narrative does not place equal emphasis on each woman's symbolic function. The bride of John 3:29 plays only a minor part. John the Baptist's saying does not stress the identity of the bride. It is more concerned with the identity of the bridegroom. For the Johannine community, the bridegroom whose voice is heard in Judea is the Messiah prophesied in Jer. 33:10–11. He was introduced at Cana (2:1–11), and he will increase in Samaria (4:4–42).

The Samaritan woman is given a more significant role. There is every indication that she exemplifies Samaritan believers. She is identified as a Samaritan (vv. 7, 9); she refers to her ancestor Jacob (v. 12); she is designated with the plural pronouns ὑμεῖς and ἡμεῖς (vv. 12, 20–22); she has had five husbands and now lives with a sixth man (v. 18). John's original author and audience, observing conventions by which women and brides symbolize the people of God, may even have understood her as a representative figure. Like Samaritan believers, she forsakes her ancestral religions and joins herself to Jesus, the Messiah who offers eternal life.[39] Like Rachel, she becomes the mother of a family of faith.[40]

Mary of Bethany plays the part of the Song's bride, whose nard perfumes the king on the couch (Song 1:12 in John 12:3). If the symbolic value of the Song's bride is transferred to Mary of Bethany, then she, too, can be understood as a representative of the people of God.[41] The narrative minimizes her representative role, however. More important than the bride with the nard is the bridegroom perfumed by the nard.

[39] See also Bligh, "Jesus in Samaria," 337; Marsh, *Saint John*, 209; Jaubert, *Approches*, 61; Boismard and Lamouille, *Évangile de Jean*, 137; Culpepper, *Anatomy*, 137; Girard, "Jésus en Samarie," 303; Schneiders, *Revelatory Text*, 188–91; Koester, *Symbolism*, 49; Fehribach, *Women in the Life of the Bridegroom*, 58–61, 69. One of the ancestral traditions forsaken by the Samaritan believers seems to have been the expectation of an eschatological prophet. Samaritans did not look for a Davidic Messiah. Indeed, they and their ancestors had been officially distancing themselves from Judeans and their Davidic leaders since the secession under Jeroboam I in 922 BCE (1 Kings 12). Instead of a Davidic Messiah, they expected a prophet like Moses as foretold in Deut. 18:18 (see Ferdinand Dexinger, *Der Taheb: Ein "messianischer" Heilsbringer der Samaritaner* [Salzburg: Müller, 1986] and "Samaritan Eschatology," in *The Samaritans* [ed. Alan D. Crown; Tübingen: Mohr Siebeck, 1989], 272–76). In light of this, it seems incongruous that John's Samaritan woman expects the "Messiah" (John 4:25, 29).

[40] See also Carmichael, "Marriage and the Samaritan Woman," 333; Cahill, "Narrative Art," 47; Fehribach, *Women in the Life of the Bridegroom*, 56–58.

[41] See also Cambe, "Influence du Cantique," 25; Fehribach, *Women in the Life of the Bridegroom*, 93.

John 12:3 serves mainly to fulfill the messianic prophecy in Song 1:12. The king on the couch is surrounded by the fragrance of nard – nard that foreshadows his death and burial.

The Fourth Gospel places more emphasis on the role of Mary Magdalene (20:1, 11–18). She exemplifies the disciples who seek Jesus and recognize him (cf. 1:35–39; 6:16–21; 21:1–8). She fulfills prophecies in Jesus' Farewell Discourse about disciples who weep and mourn before they see Jesus again (16:20–22) and about disciples who remain in the world while Jesus ascends to the Father (13:33, 38; 17:11). For John's original author and audience, her exemplary role may be reinforced by a representative one. They might have recognized her as the conventional woman who represents the people of God or as the bride who symbolizes the faithful community. They might even have transferred to her the representative value of the Song's bride.[42] Indeed, it has been argued that John's community would have perceived their own experience of Jesus' absence in the frantic search of Mary Magdalene. She certainly resembles Jesus' first disciples, whose faith provided an example for that community. Like them – and like the Song's bride – she looks for the Messiah and finally recognizes him.

Hearing the echoes in the twenty-first century

Throughout this study, I have acknowledged that several members of John's modern audience have perceived at least some of his allusions to marriage texts. Perhaps another interpreter has drawn their attention to the echoes. Perhaps they have sensed the reverberations on their own. In either case, it is not surprising that biblical scholars would recognize instances of correspondence with Israel's Scriptures. They possess the necessary prerequisites: they are familiar with Israel's Scriptures and they are able to compare the Fourth Gospel with its evoked texts in Greek.

Contemporary Christians who are not biblical scholars may have more difficulty hearing the echoes. This does not necessarily result from ignorance of Greek. Many translations retain instances of verbal correspondence. In the NRSV, for example, both John 3:29 and Jer. 33:11 feature a "bride," a "bridegroom," and the bridegroom's "voice." John 4:4–42 and Gen. 29:1–20 each mention "Jacob," a woman's "coming" to a "well," and the woman's "father." John 12:3 and Song 1:12 both contain the words "nard" and "fragrance," and John 20:11–18

---

[42] See also Cambe, "Influence du Cantique," 25; Feuillet, "Recherche du Christ," 97.

and Song 3:1–4 both use the verb "seek." In addition, John's allusions to marriage texts are clearly marked by circumstantial correspondence, apparent in a comparison between the Fourth Gospel and the MT in any translation.

The biggest hindrance for contemporary Christian audiences is not their ignorance of Greek but rather their ignorance of Israel's Scriptures, the Christian Old Testament. An audience will not recognize an evoked text unless that audience is thoroughly familiar with that text. Sadly, most twenty-first-century Christians are not as well acquainted with Israel's Scriptures as were their first-century counterparts. Furthermore, John's evoked marriage texts are not among the best-known passages. Congregations that use the standard three-year lectionary never hear any of them read on Sundays. In addition, only one of them is a popular Sunday school lesson. For this reason, some churchgoers might recall that Jacob met Rachel at a well. Few, however, would know of Jeremiah's bridegroom prophecies. Still fewer would be able to recall anything from the Song of Songs, with the possible exception of passages that are set to music or read at weddings (e.g., Song 2:4, 10–13; 8:6–7), along with memorable lines such as, "Your neck is like the tower of David" (Song 4:4). Only Christians who have taken the trouble to study these books closely, either in school or on their own, might hear their echoes.[43]

This kind of deafness has an easy cure: when one of the allusive texts is read during worship, the evoked text can be read as well.[44] Listeners might catch John's echoes if a reading of the evoked text has tuned their ears to the appropriate frequencies. This cure offers only a partial solution to the problem, however, since hearing does not necessarily lead to comprehension. Even if contemporary audiences are able to discern the echoes, they might not appreciate how those echoes enhance John's portrayal of the bridegroom-Messiah and the people of God. For one thing, Jer. 33:10–11, Gen. 29:1–20, and the Song of

---

[43] Jewish congregations might be slightly more familiar with John's evoked texts – especially Jer. 33:10–11, which is usually recited at weddings.

[44] In the three-year lectionary, John 3:23–30 is an alternate lesson for the Third Sunday of Advent in Year B. On that occasion, a reading of Jer. 33:10–16 might be substituted for the assigned Old Testament lesson (Isa. 65:17–25). On the Third Sunday of Lent in Year A, Gen. 29:1–20 could be read along with John 4:5–42. On Monday in Holy Week, Years A and B, the reading of John 12:1–11 could be accompanied by a selection that includes Song 1:12, such as Song 1:12; 2:1–4. Finally, on Easter Sunday, Year A, John 20:1–18 could be read together with Song 3:1–4. This can also be done when John 20:1–18 is read in Years A and B on the Tuesday of Easter Week. John 20:1–18 and Song 3:1–4 are in fact read together on the feast of St Mary Magdalene.

Songs are not generally recognized as messianic prophecies. What is more, the term "Messiah" retains little of the meaning that it had for John's original audience. "Messiah" or "Christ" has become just another designation for Jesus or a synonym for "Savior." Many do not even know that the word "Christ" means "Anointed One." For most Christians today, "Messiah" is a less meaningful concept than "Son of God," "Redeemer," or "Lord." Therefore, a connection between Jesus' role as a bridegroom and his messianic identity loses much of its significance.

It is somewhat difficult to impart contemporary relevance to the term "Messiah." Even those Christians who understand its significance for John's original audience lack the beliefs that made Jesus' messianic identity important for that audience. This especially hinders contemporary understanding of John the Baptist's bridegroom saying and Mary of Bethany's anointing scene. How can Christians appreciate John 3:22–30 as a fulfillment of messianic prophecy when they do not persistently hope that God will restore David's dynasty? How can they understand the irony of John 12:1–8 unless they realize that the Messiah was not expected to die?

Fortunately, one aspect of the concept has not been robbed of its cultural significance: the royal element. Everyone is familiar with the idea of a king. Even Americans, who have no monarch and who supposedly eschew the notion of hereditary titles, know all about kings from histories, fiction, film, television, and news reports (sensationalistic or otherwise) about royalty in other countries. Moreover, the idea that Jesus is a king enjoys popular currency in the church. The belief that Jesus, who now reigns with God in heaven, will someday come back to earth and establish an everlasting kingdom inspires Christian art, iconography, and hymnody to this day. Congregations that frequently celebrate Christ's kingship might at the very least be able to appreciate the image of Jesus as a king who dies as presented in John's allusion to Song 1:12.[45]

For many Christians, it is more difficult to comprehend the messianic significance of the echoes than it is to perceive a connection between

---

[45] The royal significance of John's allusions to Jer. 33:10–11 and Song 1:12 can be enhanced for Sunday congregations by the choice of psalms and hymns. In Advent, the reading of John 3:23–30 could be preceded by a recitation of Ps. 45:6–14 and the singing of the Advent hymn "Wake, Awake." This would reinforce the image of a royal wedding banquet. On Monday in Holy Week, reading Song 1:12 and 2:1–4, reciting Ps. 45:1–9, and singing "Cross of Jesus, Cross of Sorrow" might enable worshipers to visualize the Jesus of John 12:1–11 as a king.

the bride – as mentioned by John the Baptist and played by the Samaritan woman, Mary of Bethany, and Mary Magdalene – and the people of God. This is because of popular conventions in which the church is symbolized by a woman.[46] Mary the mother of Jesus frequently represents the church, especially in Roman Catholic tradition.[47] In addition, the convention reflected in 2 Cor. 11:2; Eph. 5:21–33; and Rev. 19:5–9; 21:2, 9 continues to influence the Christian imagination. Wedding guests often hear that marriage signifies the mystery of the union between Christ and the church (a clear allusion to Eph. 5:31–32), and worshipers sing hymns like "The Church's One Foundation," which begins:

> The Church's one foundation is Jesus Christ her Lord;
> She is his new creation by water and the word:
> From heaven he came and sought her to be his holy bride;
> With his own blood he bought her, and for her life he died.[48]

Unfortunately, John's portrayal of female characters as brides renders the echoes discordant for many contemporary listeners, especially those accustomed to another popular interpretation of these characters' significance. This interpretation dates from 1966, when Ernst Käsemann proposed that the Fourth Gospel flouts late first-century praxis by reflecting an earlier experience of "Spirit-effected emancipation of women."[49] Since then, a broad consensus has emerged among scholars that John depicts women as independent disciples and apostolic

---

[46] These conventions probably account for the widespread recognition among scholars that the bride of John 3:29, the Samaritan woman, Mary of Bethany, and Mary Magdalene represent the people of God. Such scholars include Loisy (*Quatrième Évangile*, 672), Colson ("Noces du Christ," 134–35), Cambe ("Influence du Cantique," 25), Feuillet, ("Recherche du Christ," 97), Schneiders ("Resurrection Narrative," I:338; *Revelatory Text*, 189, 191; "Easter Jesus," 161; *Written That You May Believe*, 35), Jaubert ("Symbolique du puits," 73), Stockton ("Fourth Gospel and the Woman," 143–44), Baril (*Feminine Face*, 97), and Fehribach (*Women in the Life of the Bridegroom*, 58–61, 85, 161). Erich Przywara offers a reflection on John's "*analogia fidei*" with marriage imagery as the main interpretive lens. The Cana story, John the Baptist's bridegroom saying, the well encounter, and the anointing at Bethany – as well as Gen. 2–3 and the Song of Songs – reach their fulfillment when the sinner Mary Magdalene and the risen Jesus celebrate their spiritual nuptials in the garden (*Christentum gemäss Johannes* [Evangelium; Nuremberg: Glock & Lutz, 1954], 66–67, 87, 97–98, 189, 298–303).

[47] See, e.g., La Potterie, *Mary*, xxiii–xl.

[48] Lyrics by Samuel John Stone (1839–1900).

[49] Ernst Käsemann, *The Testament of Jesus: A Study of the Gospel of John in the Light of Chapter 17* (trans. Gerhard Krodel; Philadelphia: Fortress, 1968), 31; trans. of *Jesu letzter Wille nach Johannes 17* (Tübingen: Mohr Siebeck, 1966).

witnesses.[50] The suggestion that the Samaritan woman, Mary of Bethany, and Mary Magdalene are instead portrayed as the Messiah's brides is out of harmony with this consensus, if not downright offensive to those who agree with it.[51] It even contradicts the "reformed patriarchy" discerned by Ben Witherington III.[52]

[50] See René Laurentin, "Le sens de la femme dans le Nouveau Testament," *Bulletin de la Société française d'études mariales* 30–31 (1973–74), 125–26; Raymond E. Brown, "Roles of Women in the Fourth Gospel," *TS* 36 (1975): 688–99; Sandra M. Schneiders, "Women in the Fourth Gospel and the Role of Women in the Contemporary Church," *BTB* 12 (1982): 35–45; Elisabeth Schüssler Fiorenza, *In Memory of Her: A Feminist Theological Reconstruction of Christian Origins* (New York: Crossroad, 1983), 323–34; Adela Yarbro Collins, "New Testament Perspectives: The Gospel of John," *JSOT* 22 (1982): 47–53; Stephen E. Dollar, "The Significance of Women in the Fourth Gospel" (Th.D. diss., New Orleans Baptist Theological Seminary, 1983); John R. Schmitz, "Women in John's Gospel," *Emmanuel* 90 (1984): 191–96; Jane Kopas, "Jesus and Women: John's Gospel," *ThTo* 41 (1984): 201–5; Hans-Josef Klauck, "Gemeinde oder Amt: Erfahrungen mit der Kirche in den johanneischen Schriften," *BZ* 29 (1985): 193–220; S. J. Nortjé, "The Role of Women in the Fourth Gospel," *NeoT* 20 (1986): 21–28; Rena, "Women in the Gospel of John," 131–47; Turid Karlsen Seim, "Roles of Women in the Gospel of John," in *Aspects on the Johannine Literature* (ed. Lars Hartmann and Birger Olsson; ConBNT 18; Stockholm: Almkvist & Wiksell, 1987), 56–73; Karen Heidebrecht Thiessan, "Jesus and Women in the Gospel of John," *Direction* 19 (1990): 56–64; Martinus C. de Boer, "John 4:27: Women (and Men) in the Gospel and Community of John," in *Women in the Biblical World* (ed. George J. Brooke; Studies in Women and Religion 31; Lewiston, N.Y.: Mellen, 1992), 208–30; O'Day, "John"; Andrea Link, "Botschafterinnen des Messias: Die Frauen des vierten Evangeliums im Spiegel johanneischer Redactionsgeschichte," in *Theologie im Werden. Studien zu theologischen Konzeptionen im Neuen Testament* (ed. Josef Hainz; Paderborn: Schöningh, 1992), 247–78; Scott, *Sophia and the Johannine Jesus*, 174–240; Robert Kysar, *John: The Maverick Gospel*, (rev. edn; Louisville: Westminster John Knox, 1993), 147–54; Mary-Elsie C. Fletcher, "The Role of Women in the Book of John," *EvJ* 12 (1994): 41–48; Reinhartz, "The Gospel of John"; Ingrid Rosa Kitzberger, "Mary of Bethany and Mary of Magdala: Two Female Characters in the Johannine Passion Narrative: A Feminist, Narrative-Critical Reader Response," *NTS* 41 (1995): 564–86; Lee, "Partnership in Easter Faith," 40, 46; Maccini, *Her Testimony Is True*; Conway, *Men and Women*; Ringe, *Wisdom's Friends*, 16–18; D'Angelo, "(Re)Presentations of Women," 131–37, 145; Margaret Beirne, *Women and Men in the Fourth Gospel: A Genuine Discipleship of Equals* (JSNTSup 242; Sheffield: Sheffield Academic Press, 2003).

[51] Possible exceptions include Kopas ("Jesus and Women") and Nortjé ("Role of Women"), who emphasize that John's female characters are not only honored and assertive but also vulnerable and receptive. A different mediating position is taken by Sjef van Tilborg, who points out that although John's women enjoy a relative measure of independence, they are still excluded from the inner circle of male disciples ("The Women in John: On Gender and Gender Bending," in *Families and Family Relations As Represented in Early Judaism and Early Christianity: Texts and Fictions* [ed. Jan Willem van Henten and Athalya Brenner; Leiden: Deo, 2000], 192–212). In her *Befriending the Beloved Disciple* (120–24), Reinhartz also adopts this stance. More thoroughgoing dissent comes from Alison Jasper ("Interpretive Approaches to John 20:1–18: Mary at the Tomb of Jesus," *ST* 47 [1993]: 107–18). She views Mary Magdalene not as the valiant *apostola apostolorum* but as a tragic figure who is at first bereft; then confused, abandoned, misled, spurned, and used.

[52] Ben Witherington III, *Women in the Earliest Churches* (SNTSMS 59; Cambridge: Cambridge University Press, 1988), 174–82.

Fehribach recognizes several aspects of the offense inherent in the Fourth Gospel's marriage imagery. First, it reflects the androcentric tendency to portray women only as they relate to men rather than as human beings in their own right.[53] This tendency prevails in stories created by men for men (a category that includes virtually all ancient stories preserved in writing). The main characters of such stories are usually men, while women are most often portrayed as their wives, mistresses, mothers, sisters, and aunts. Second, once John's female characters have fulfilled their function in relation to the central male character, they are inevitably marginalized. The Samaritan woman, Mary of Bethany, and Mary Magdalene fade from the scene, and their stories end with a proclamation about, or by, Jesus. More important than the women is the bridegroom whose life they adorn.[54] Third, John draws on several components of a patriarchal world-view, including the convention by which the love relationship between a male deity and his people is represented by the marriage of a man and a woman.[55]

Because Fehribach finds her own literary-historical interpretation of John's marriage imagery morally repugnant, she advocates reading the Gospel in ways that offer a more acceptable perspective on its female characters. For example, she outlines a reader-response approach to John 4:4–42 that affirms the Samaritan woman, a female member of a minority group, for her refusal to give the drink demanded by Jesus, a male member of the dominant majority. This approach would applaud the woman's willingness to accept Jesus as a prophet, her courage to engage in a theological discussion with him, her intelligent articulation of her people's traditions, her consenting to meet Jesus on the equal terms he proposes, and her ability to lead other members of her minority group into a similar egalitarian relationship with him. This approach would also acknowledge that, since it is the Samaritan people who minimize the importance of the woman's testimony (John 4:42), Jesus himself does not necessarily support her marginalization.[56]

My own literary analysis of John's allusions to marriage texts leads to different conclusions. While I agree with Fehribach that John's female characters are portrayed only as they relate to Jesus and then sidelined, I disagree that this demeans women in any way. John does not practice gender discrimination in this regard. Like female characters, male characters are also used to enhance the character of Jesus and then sidelined. John the Baptist, Nathanael, Nicodemus, the royal

---

[53] Fehribach, *Women in the Life of the Bridegroom*, 172.
[54] Ibid., 172–74.   [55] Ibid., 174.   [56] Ibid., 183.

official, the man born blind, Lazarus, Thomas, Peter – each fulfills his role as witness, seeker, foil, suppliant, or disciple, and then yields to a pronouncement by Jesus. The only secondary character not sidelined is the Beloved Disciple, whose testimony ends the Gospel. Still, even the Beloved Disciple plays a stock role: that of faithful follower and reliable witness.

Fehribach acknowledges this position, but then argues that, since various men continue to reappear in the story, they are not marginalized.[57] I would contend that multiple appearances do not necessarily establish a character as more central to the story. Furthermore, male characters do not consistently appear more often than their female counterparts. Most of John's female characters grace the narrative more than once. Martha and Mary of Bethany are mentioned in two scenes, as is the mother of Jesus. In contrast, some male characters never get an encore. They include the royal official of John 4:46–54 and the man born blind in John 9. All of John's secondary characters – whether male or female; whether they make one or more appearances – are important only as they develop the central character, Jesus.[58]

More difficult to contradict is the criticism that John relies on a patriarchal convention that uses the metaphor of marriage to illustrate the relationship between God and God's people. This may well have been the case – for the Gospel's original author. The implied author, however, betrays no knowledge of such a convention. He simply alludes to biblical texts about marriage, casting certain female characters in the role of the bride. In theory, then, a literary interpretation of the Fourth Gospel would not involve patriarchal conventions that demean women.

Nevertheless, the fact remains that the Samaritan woman, Mary of Bethany, and Mary Magdalene assume a role in relationship to Jesus dictated wholly by their gender.[59] For some contemporary Christians, this alone may constitute an offense so great as to preclude any appreciation of John's allusions to marriage texts. Fehribach, for instance, follows the lead of Elisabeth Schüssler Fiorenza, who believes that

---

[57] Ibid., 79.

[58] See also Culpepper, *Anatomy*, 145.

[59] According to Fehribach, so do the mother of Jesus and Mary's sister Martha (*Women in the Life of the Bridegroom*, 23–43, 102–11). I would agree that the mother of Jesus performs a typical female function: that of a mother. I am less sure about Martha. Her most important role is that of the sister of Lazarus. To be sure, this constitutes another typical female role – that is, a role in relation to Lazarus. She approaches Jesus, however, as a loyal follower and nothing else.

anything oppressive in the biblical text comes from its human authors and does not constitute the word of God.[60] Fehribach seeks to acknowledge the patriarchy inherent in the marriage imagery used by John's original author, mourn it, and move beyond it to interpretations never imagined by that author.[61]

I would like to suggest another option. There is a way to appreciate John's marriage imagery without reinforcing oppressive gender roles. This approach is modeled by Gail O'Day in a discussion of John's Father-language for God. In her article for the *Woman's Bible Commentary*, O'Day points out that John calls God "Father" more than one hundred times.[62] She also acknowledges that the patriarchy frequently inherent in Father-language for God makes such language abhorrent to many women. She notes, however, that John uses "Father" as a metaphor, not a synonym, for God. As a metaphor, the term "Father" indicates ways in which God is like a father. For O'Day, the primary way is that God welcomes believers into a new family (John 1:12–13; 3:3–10; 8:31–47; 14:1–3, 18–24; 16:20–24; 19:25–27; 20:17). "John speaks of God as Father not in order to reinforce patriarchy," she concludes, "but in order to evoke a new world in which intimate relations with God and one another are possible."[63]

Although I might quibble with O'Day's assessment of the main purpose of John's Father metaphor, I salute her strategy.[64] When the text itself offers an opportunity to develop a persuasive, egalitarian interpretation for an androcentric metaphor, that opportunity should be seized. John's Gospel offers such an opportunity with regard to its use of marriage as a metaphor for the relationship between Jesus and believers. The aspects of marriage exploited in John's metaphor are aspects that most people should be able to appreciate.

This is not necessarily true of other New Testament books that use marriage to illustrate the relationship between God and God's people.

---

[60] Elisabeth Schüssler Fiorenza, *Bread Not Stone* (Boston: Beacon, 1984), 140.

[61] Fehribach, *Women in the Life of the Bridegroom*, 179–80.

[62] Donald Juel and Patrick Keifert put the number at 118 ("'I Believe in God': A Johannine Perspective," *HBT* 12 [1990], 43). The difficulty of an exact count involves issues like whether to include both references to "Father" that occur in the same phrase.

[63] O'Day, "John," 304. Marianne Meye Thompson makes a similar argument (*The Promise of the Father: Jesus and God in the New Testament* [Louisville: Westminster John Knox, 2000], 133–54). According to Thompson, John designates God as "Father" in order to emphasize God's life-giving power (John 5:26; 6:57).

[64] Whereas I agree that John's use of the term "Father" has some bearing on his family motif, I suspect that it originated as a reflection of Father-Son language in messianic prophecy (e.g., 2 Sam. 7:14; Pss. 2:7; 89:26). Cf. Juel, *Messianic Exegesis*, 81.

Ephesians 5:21–33, for example, compares the relationship between a husband and wife to the relationship between Christ and the church. "The husband is the head of the wife just as Christ is the head of the church," so that "just as the church is subject to Christ, so also wives ought to be, in everything, to their husbands" (vv. 23–24). The aspect of first-century marriage exploited in this metaphor is male dominance. To be sure, a less objectionable aspect is emphasized in the following instructions for husbands: that of a husband's love for his wife (vv. 25–30). For many, however, this fails to mitigate the offense occasioned by the advocacy of wifely submission on the grounds that the church is subject to Christ.[65]

In contrast, John's echoes of marriage texts do not emphasize gender roles. Therefore, his use of the marriage metaphor presents no such difficulties. Indeed, some of his allusions to marriage texts do not even evoke marriage as a metaphor.[66] In the stories about Mary of Bethany and Mary Magdalene, the allusions function chiefly to establish a connection with the Song of Songs. John 12:3 fulfills the prophecy in Song 1:12: the reclining king is perfumed with nard. John 20:1–18 uses the prophecy in Song 3:1–4 to enhance the ironies of Mary Magdalene's search: she cannot find Jesus because she is looking in the wrong place, and when she does find him, she cannot hold him because he is in the process of departing. For John, the Song is about Jesus, prepared for burial, then risen and ascending to the Father. As the prophecies are fulfilled, Mary of Bethany and Mary Magdalene simply assume the role of the Song's bride. No attention is paid to how the metaphor of marriage illustrates their relationship with Jesus.

The marriage metaphor is more important in John's allusions to Jer. 33:10–11 and Gen. 29:1–20. As we have seen, the primary function of the allusion in John 3:22–30 is to evoke Jeremiah's messianic prophecy: the bridegroom's voice is heard in the Judean countryside by a rejoicing John the Baptist. It also invokes an aspect of the marriage metaphor. That aspect, however, is not used to describe the relationship between Jesus and "the bride." Although John asserts that Jesus "has the bride," she is never described and her role is never delineated. Instead, the metaphor is used to describe the rejoicing of John the Baptist. The allusion to Jer. 33:10–11 in John 3:22–30 emphasizes the aspect of joy. A wedding is a cause for celebration, and this "wedding" is

---

[65] See, e.g., Schüssler Fiorenza, *Bread Not Stone*, 65–92.

[66] Similarly, many of John's referents to God as "Father" do not involve family imagery (e.g., 2:16; 5:17–47).

no exception. When John the Baptist hears the voice of Jesus, the bridegroom-Messiah, his joy is made complete – just as the voices of joy and gladness accompany the voice of the bridegroom in Jeremiah's prophecy, and just as the church still celebrates the advent of the Messiah.

Likewise, the allusion to Jacob's betrothal narrative in John 4:4–42 does not stress the gender roles of bride and bridegroom. The conversation between Jesus and the Samaritan woman concerns wells and worship, not honor and obedience. The aspect of the marriage metaphor emphasized in John 4 is procreation. Jesus and the Samaritan woman resemble a married couple only in that they generate a family of sorts. Just as Jacob's meeting Rachel at a well leads to betrothal and birth, so Jesus' meeting the woman at a well leads to belief. The citizens of Sychar become the children of God, as do all who receive the testimony about Jesus and join the family of faith.

For most contemporary Christians, John's echoes of marriage texts are hard to hear. Even if churchgoers could hear, few would be able to make sense of them. Others would find them discordant and would deliberately choose to ignore them. Those of us who strive to listen and understand, however, can discern the harmonies that resonate when John's story is heard in concert with Israel's Scriptures – harmonies that enhance themes of rejoicing and procreation, symbols of water and nard, motifs of seeking and finding. Most importantly, we can perceive the nuances of the Gospel's portrayal of Jesus. For John, Jesus is the bridegroom-Messiah whose voice is heard in Judea, the Messiah greater than Jacob who offers eternal life, the king perfumed in preparation for his burial, the risen Messiah who cannot be located in his tomb, and the ascending Messiah who cannot be held. John has searched biblical texts about marriage, and has discovered that they testify to Jesus.

7

CONCLUSION

I have attempted to identify and account for echoes of biblical texts about marriage in the Fourth Gospel. First, I used Hays' criteria to discern and interpret four evoked texts. Two of them emerge at the beginning of John's narrative. John the Baptist's bridegroom saying in John 3:22–30 alludes to Jer. 33:10–11. When Jesus baptizes at Aenon near Salim, the bridegroom's voice is heard with rejoicing in the Judean countryside. Next, the story about Jesus and the Samaritan woman in John 4:4–42 is reminiscent of the story about Jacob and Rachel in Gen. 29:1–20. John uses the similarities to promote his own thematic agenda. The travelling stranger offers the water of eternal life to an apostate Samaritan. He then reveals his identity: he is the Messiah. The woman's ensuing report to her people becomes the testimony that leads to their belief.

The other two texts are evoked at the end of John's story. Song of Songs 1:12 is echoed when Mary of Bethany perfumes the reclining Jesus with nard in John 12:1–8. This allusion adds an ironic twist to the episode, as Mary's nard is not meant for the king's pleasure but rather for his burial. Finally, Mary Magdalene's search in John 20:1–18 follows the format of Song 3:1–4. Like other disciples, Mary looks for Jesus in the darkness of her own ignorance. She seeks a corpse, but then suddenly meets and eventually recognizes the risen and ascending Lord.

These allusions can be accounted for by Juel's concept of messianic exegesis. Messianic exegesis begins with an acknowledged messianic text – in this case, Ps. 45. The Song of Songs can be interpreted in light of Ps. 45 on the basis of shared vocabulary. Both are love songs about a handsome king, fragrant with myrrh and aloes, and a beautiful bride who is led to him in a joyful procession. Jeremiah 33:11 also describes the joyful procession of a bride and bridegroom. Genesis 29:1–20 can then be linked to the Song of Songs, whose protagonist is a shepherd with a well who loves a beautiful daughter. Jeremiah 33:10–11,

Gen. 29:1–20, and the Song of Songs can be understood as messianic prophecies because they share vocabulary with Ps. 45.

It is generally accepted that the Johannine community evolved among Diaspora Jews. The late first century found them struggling to define themselves with respect to a Jewish establishment that rejected their claims about Jesus. It is certainly plausible that they might have interpreted Jer. 33:10–11, Gen. 29:1–20, and the Song of Songs as messianic prophecies in light of Ps. 45, and then used those texts to illustrate episodes in the life of Jesus. It is also possible that they viewed John's female characters – especially the Samaritan woman and Mary Magdalene – as representatives of the people of God.

Contemporary Christian communities might be less likely to hear John's echoes of marriage texts or to recognize their messianic significance. Even if they do hear, they may take offense at John's use of marriage imagery to illustrate the relationship between God, imagined as male, and God's people. Nevertheless, there is a way to appreciate John's marriage metaphor without reinforcing oppressive gender roles. John's allusions do not emphasize male dominance or female allure. Instead, they highlight celebration and procreation, aspects of the marriage metaphor that do not involve gender inequality. The image of a wedding celebration illustrates the church's joy at Jesus' advent, while the image of procreation describes how the church's testimony attracts new believers.

There is much more that can be said about both the marriage metaphor in general and messianic exegesis based on Ps. 45 in particular. For example, one might investigate the extent of this exegetical tradition. The theme of marriage certainly emerges in early Christian literature associated with the Fourth Gospel and the Johannine epistles. This literature includes the story of the woman caught in adultery, found in English Bibles at John 7:53–8:11. The episode is missing from the earliest and most reliable manuscripts of the Fourth Gospel (such as $\mathfrak{p}^{66}$, $\mathfrak{p}^{75}$, ℵ, B, and apparently A).[1] It might be worth investigating whether those who inserted it at the beginning of John 8 – perhaps during the Novatian controversy of 251 – thought that the story of an unfaithful woman would extend John's use of marriage as a metaphor for the relationship between the Messiah and the people of God.

Literature associated with the Fourth Gospel also includes the Book of Revelation and the *Odes of Solomon*. Arguments that Revelation is

---

[1] For a discussion of the textual evidence for this pericope, see Metzger, *Textual Commentary*, 219–22.

somehow related to the Fourth Gospel could be further developed if it were possible to demonstrate a link between the Apocalypse's bride and bridegroom (Rev. 19:5–9; 21:2, 9; 22:17) and the Gospel's marriage motif.[2] Similarly, a proposed connection between John and the *Odes of Solomon* could be further explored in terms of the Ode's references to "the Beloved" (*Odes Sol.* 3:5, 7; 7:1; 8:21) and "the Beloved and his bride" (*Odes Sol.* 38:11).[3] It is entirely possible that these designations were influenced in some way by messianic interpretation of Jer. 33:10–11, the Song of Songs, and Ps. 45 in Johannine tradition.

In addition, it is certainly worth exploring the possible effects of Ps. 45 on New Testament Christology. John is not the only New Testament author who likens Jesus to a bridegroom. Marriage imagery also illustrates Jesus' relationship with his followers in Mark's parable about the feasting bridegroom (Mark 2:18–20), Matthew's stories of the wedding banquet (Matt. 22:1–14) and the foolish bridesmaids (Matt. 25:1–13), and Paul's image of the bride of Christ (2 Cor. 11:2; Eph. 5:21–33). Many scholars argue that this imagery derives from prophecies like Hos. 1–3; Jer. 2:2; and Isa. 61:10.[4] Can these passages be interpreted as messianic prophecies on the basis of shared vocabulary with Ps. 45? A cursory glance suggests that at least Isa. 61:10 can, since it contains the words "rejoice (εὐφραίνω)" (cf. Ps. 45:15; Jer. 33:11), "exalt (גִּיל; ἀγαλλιάω)" (cf. Ps. 45:15; Jer. 33:11); "garment (בֶּגֶד; ἱμάτιον)" (cf. Ps. 45:8), "bride (כַּלָּה; νύμφη)" (cf. Jer. 33:11), and "bridegroom (חָתָן; νυμφίος)" (cf. Jer. 33:11). Perhaps New Testament marriage imagery originated with messianic interpretation of texts like Isa. 61:10, Jer. 33:10–11, and the Song of Songs in light of Ps. 45.

Psalm 45, a song about "the beloved (τοῦ ἀγαπητοῦ)" (LXX Ps. 44:1), should also be considered in relationship to instances in the New Testament where Jesus is called "beloved." Matthew 12:18–21 traces this designation to Isa. 42:1–5:

---

[2] Among those who make such arguments are Schüssler Fiorenza ("The Quest for the Johannine School: The Book of Revelation and the Fourth Gospel," in *The Book of Revelation: Justice and Judgment* [2nd edn.; Minneapolis: Fortress, 1998], 85–113) and Luke Johnson (*Writings*, 579–81).

[3] Trans. James H. Charlesworth, "Odes of Solomon," in *OTP* II:735, 739, 742, 767. Charlesworth and R. Alan Culpepper discuss the connection between the *Odes of Solomon* and the Fourth Gospel in their article "The Odes of Solomon and the Gospel of John," *CBQ* 35 (1973): 298–322.

[4] See, e.g., Chavasse, *Bride of Christ*, 19–48; Muirhead, "Bride of Christ," 176–77; Batey, *Nuptial Imagery*, 3–8.

Here is my servant, whom I have chosen,
  my beloved (ὁ ἀγαπητός μου), with whom my soul is well
  pleased.

In statements reminiscent of Isa. 42:1–5, Jesus is also called "the Beloved (ὁ ἀγαπητός)" in Mark 1:11 and 9:6 (cf. Matt. 3:17; 17:5; Luke 3:22). The term appears again in Eph. 1:6, this time as a title. Juel suggests that the first believers recognized Isa. 42:1–5 as a messianic prophecy because of verbal links with texts that describe the Messiah as God's servant (Ps. 89:39; Zech. 3:8).[5] Psalm 45 may also have belonged to the web of associated texts that led to messianic interpretation of Isa. 42:1–5. Perhaps "the Beloved" is a christological title that ultimately reflects the influence of Ps. 45.

Finally, Reim's proposal that John's high Christology may be based on an interpretation of Ps. 45:6 deserves some attention.[6] It is certainly possible that the statement in John 1:1, "The Word was with God, and the Word was God," is partly the result of theological reflection on Ps. 45:6, "Your throne, O God, endures forever and ever." This verse, taken literally, deifies the anointed king. It could have helped to inspire the first Christians' belief that Christ, the Son of God, partakes in God's divine nature. Perhaps Ps. 45:6, quoted in Heb. 1:8, also influences the high Christology of Heb. 1:3: "He is the reflection of God's glory and the exact imprint of God's very being, and he sustains all things by his powerful word." Juel suggests that Ps. 89 played a central role as the first believers came to terms with the crucifixion of the Messiah, and that Ps. 110 became an important key for understanding Jesus' enthronement at God's right hand.[7] Surely Ps. 45 might have performed an equally important function as they strove to comprehend Christ's relationship to God.

---

[5] Juel, *Messianic Exegesis*, 131.
[6] Reim, "Jesus As God."
[7] Juel, *Messianic Exegesis*, 107–17, 135–50.

BIBLIOGRAPHY

Adam, A. K. M. *Making Sense of New Testament Theology: "Modern" Problems and Prospects.* StABH 11. Macon, Ga.: Mercer University Press, 1995.

Alter, Robert. *The Art of Biblical Narrative.* New York: Basic Books, 1981.

Ashton, John. *Understanding the Fourth Gospel.* Oxford: Clarendon, 1991.

Attridge, Harold W. " 'Don't Be Touching Me': Recent Feminist Scholarship on Mary Magdalene." Pages 140–66 in vol. II of *A Feminist Companion to John.* Edited by Amy-Jill Levine. 2 vols. London: Sheffield Academic Press, 2003.

Baril, Gilberte. *The Feminine Face of the People of God: Biblical Symbols of the Church as Bride and Mother.* Translated by Florestine Audette. Collegeville, Minn.: Liturgical Press, 1990.

Barrett, C. K. *The Gospel According to St. John.* London: SPCK, 1955.

"The Old Testament in the Fourth Gospel." *JTS* 48 (1947): 155–69.

Batey, Richard A. *New Testament Nuptial Imagery.* Leiden: Brill, 1971.

Bauer, Walter. *Das Johannes-Evangelium.* 3rd edn. HNT 6. Tübingen: Mohr Siebeck, 1933.

Bauer, Walter, Frederick W. Danker, W. F. Arndt, and F. W. Gingrich. *A Greek–English Lexicon of the New Testament and Other Early Christian Literature.* Revised and edited by Frederick W. Danker. 3rd edn. Chicago: University of Chicago Press, 1999.

Beirne, Margaret. *Women and Men in the Fourth Gospel: A Genuine Discipleship of Equals.* JSNTSup 242. Sheffield: Sheffield Academic Press, 2003.

Ben-Porat, Ziva. "The Poetics of Literary Allusion." *PTL: A Journal for Descriptive Poetics and Theory of Literature* 1 (1976): 105–28.

Berenson Maclean, Jennifer K. "The Divine Trickster: A Tale of Two Weddings in John." Pages 48–77 in vol. I of *A Feminist Companion to John.* Edited by Amy-Jill Levine. London: Sheffield Academic Press, 2003.

Bernard, John H. *A Critical and Exegetical Commentary on the Gospel According to St. John.* Edited by A. H. McNeile. ICC. 2 vols. Edinburgh: T&T Clark, 1928.

Best, Ernest. *One Body in Christ.* London: SPCK, 1955.

Betz, Otto. " 'To Worship God in Spirit and in Truth': Reflections on John 4, 20–26." Translated by Nora Quigley. Pages 53–72 in *Standing Before God: Studies on Prayer in Scriptures and in Tradition.* Edited by Asher Finkel and Lawrence Frizzell. New York: Ktav, 1981.

Beutler, Johannes. "The Use of 'Scripture' in the Gospel of John." Pages 147–62 in *Exploring the Gospel of John*. Edited by R. Alan Culpepper and C. Clifton Black. Louisville: Westminster John Knox, 1996.

Biblia Hebraica Stuttgartensia. Edited by Albrecht Alt et al. 4th ed. Stuttgart: Deutsche Bibelgesellschaft, 1990.

Black, C. Clifton. "Rhetorical Criticism and the New Testament." Pages 256–77 in *Hearing the New Testament: Strategies for Interpretation*. Edited by Joel B. Green. Grand Rapids: Eerdmans, 1995.

Blass, Friedrich and Albert Debrunner. *A Greek Grammar of the New Testament and Other Early Christian Literature*. Translated and edited by Robert W. Funk. Chicago: University of Chicago Press, 1961.

Bligh, John. "Jesus in Samaria." *HeyJ* 3 (1962): 329–46.

Bloch, Renée. "Midrash." Translated by Mary Howard Callaway. Pages 29–50 in *Approaches to Ancient Judaism: Theory and Practice*. Edited by William S. Green. BJS 1. Missoula, Mont.: Scholars Press, 1978.

Bode, Edward L. *The First Easter Morning: The Gospel Accounts of the Women's Visit to the Tomb of Jesus*. AnBib 45. Rome: Biblical Institute, 1970.

Boer, Martinus C. de. *Johannine Perspectives on the Death of Jesus*. CBET 17. Kampen: Pharos, 1996.

———. "John 4:27: Women (and Men) in the Gospel and Community of John." Pages 208–30 in *Women in the Biblical Tradition*. Edited by George J. Brooke. Studies in Women and Religion 31. Lewiston, N.Y.: Mellen, 1992.

Boismard, Marie-Émile. "Aenon près de Salem: Jean III.23." *RB* 80 (1973): 218–29.

———. "L'ami de l'époux (Jo., III, 29)." Pages 289–95 in *A la rencontre de Dieu*. Paris: Mappus, 1961.

Boismard, Marie-Émile and Arnaud Lamouille. *L'Évangile de Jean*. Vol. III in *Synopse des quatre évangiles en français*. Paris: Cerf, 1979.

Bonneau, Normand R. "The Woman at the Well, John 4 and Genesis 24." *TBT* 67 (1973): 1252–59.

Booth, Wayne C. *The Rhetoric of Fiction*. Chicago: University of Chicago Press, 1961.

Borgen, Peder. "John and the Synoptics." Pages 408–37 in *The Interrelations of the Gospels*. Edited by David L. Dungan. BETL 95. Louvain: Louvain University Press, 1990.

Bowman, John W. *The Samaritan Problem: Studies in the Relationships of Samaritanism, Judaism, and Early Christianity*. Translated by Alfred M. Johnson, Jr. PTMS 4. Pittsburgh: Pickwick, 1975.

———. "Samaritan Studies." *BJRL* 40 (1958): 298–327.

Braun, François-Marie. *Jean le théologien 2: Les grandes traditions d'Israël et l'accord des écritures selon le quatrième évangile*. Ebib. Paris: Gabalda, 1964.

———. *Jean le théologien 3.1: Sa théologie: Le mystère de Jésus-Christ*. Ebib. Paris: Gabalda, 1966.

Brawley, Robert L. *Text to Text Pours Forth Speech: Voices of Scripture in Luke-Acts*. Indiana Studies in Biblical Literature 18. Bloomington: Indiana University Press, 1995.

Brown, Raymond E. *The Community of the Beloved Disciple*. New York: Paulist, 1979.

The Gospel According to John I–XII. AB 29. Garden City: Doubleday, 1966.

The Gospel According to John XIII–XXI. AB 29a. Garden City: Doubleday, 1970.

"Johannine Ecclesiology: The Community's Origins." *Int* 31 (1977): 379–93.

"Roles of Women in the Fourth Gospel." *TS* 36 (1975): 688–99.

Brownlee, William H. "Whence the Gospel According to John?" Pages 166–94 in *John and Qumran*. Edited by James H. Charlesworth. London: Chapman, 1972.

Bruce, F. F. *The Epistle to the Hebrews*. Rev. edn. NICNT. Grand Rapids: Eerdmans, 1990.

Bultmann, Rudolf. *The Gospel of John: A Commentary*. Translated by George R. Beasley-Murray. Philadelphia: Westminster, 1971.

Burge, Gary M. *The Anointed Community: The Holy Spirit in Johannine Tradition*. Grand Rapids: Eerdmans, 1987.

Cahill, P. Joseph. "Narrative Art in John IV." *Religious Studies Bulletin* 2 (1982): 41–48.

Cambe, Michel. "L'influence du Cantique des Cantiques sur le Nouveau Testament." *RThom* 62 (1962): 5–26.

Carmichael, Calum M. "Marriage and the Samaritan Woman." *NTS* 26 (1980): 332–46.

Carson, D. A. "John and the Johannine Epistles." Pages 245–64 in *It Is Written: Scripture Citing Scripture*. Edited by D. A. Carson and H. G. M. Williamson. Cambridge: Cambridge University Press, 1988.

Charlesworth, James H. *The Beloved Disciple: Whose Witness Validates the Gospel of John?* Valley Forge: Trinity, 1995.

"From Messianology to Christology: Problems and Prospects." Pages 3–35 in *The Messiah: Developments in Earliest Judaism and Christianity*. Edited by James H. Charlesworth. Minneapolis: Fortress, 1992.

"Messianology in the Biblical Pseudepigrapha." Pages 21–52 in *Qumran-Messianism: Studies on the Messianic Expectations in the Dead Sea Scrolls*. Edited by James H. Charlesworth, Hermann Lichtenberger, and Gerbern S. Oegema. Tübingen: Mohr Siebeck, 1998.

"Odes of Solomon." Pages 725–71 in vol. II of *The Old Testament Pseudepigrapha*. Edited by James H. Charlesworth. Garden City: Doubleday, 1985.

Charlesworth, James H., ed. *John and Qumran*. London: Chapman, 1972.

Charlesworth, James H. and R. Alan Culpepper. "The Odes of Solomon and the Gospel of John." *CBQ* 35 (1973): 293–322.

Chatman, Seymour. *Story and Discourse: Narrative Structure in Fiction and Film*. Ithaca, N.Y.: Cornell University Press, 1978.

Chavasse, Claude. *The Bride of Christ: An Enquiry into the Nuptial Element in Early Christianity*. London: Faber & Faber, 1940.

Collins, Adele Yarbro. "New Testament Perspectives: The Gospel of John." *JSOT* 22 (1982): 47–53.

Collins, Raymond F. "Cana (John 2:1–12): The First of His Signs or the Key to His Signs?" Pages 158–82 in *These Things Have Been Written: Studies on the Fourth Gospel*. Louvain Theological and Pastoral Monographs 2. Louvain: Peeters, 1990. Repr. from *ITQ* 47 (1980): 79–95.

"Discipleship in John's Gospel." Pages 46–55 in *These Things Have Been Written: Studies on the Fourth Gospel*. Louvain Theological and Pastoral

Monographs 2. Louvain: Peeters, 1990. Repr. from *Emmanuel* 91 (1985): 248–55.

"The Representative Figures of the Fourth Gospel." *DRev* 94 (1976): 26–46, 118–32. Repr. as pages 1–45 in *These Things Have Been Written: Studies in the Fourth Gospel*. Louvain Theological and Pastoral Monographs 2. Louvain: Peeters, 1990.

Colson, Joseph. "Les noces du Christ (Nouveau Testament)." Pages 86–165 in *Un roi fit des noces à son fils*. C. Wiener and Joseph Colson. Bruges: Desclée de Brouwer, 1961.

Conway, Colleen M. *Men and Women in the Fourth Gospel: Gender and Johannine Characterization*. SBLDS 167. Atlanta: Society of Biblical Literature, 1999.

Cook, Joan E. "Wells, Women, and Faith." *Proceedings, Eastern Great Lakes and Midwest Biblical Societies* 17 (1997): 11–18.

Couchoud, Paul-Louis. "Notes de critique verbale sur St. Marc et St. Matthieu." *JTS* 34 (1933): 113–38.

Culley, Robert C. *Studies in the Structure of Hebrew Narrative*. Philadelphia: Fortress, 1976.

Cullmann, Oscar. *Der johanneische Kreis: Sein Platz im Spätjudentum, in der Jüngerschaft Jesu und im Urchristentum: Zum Ursprung des Johannes-evangeliums*. Tübingen: Mohr Siebeck, 1975.

"Samaria and the Origins of the Christian Church: Who Are the ἄλλοι of John 4.38?" Pages 185–92 in *The Early Church*. Edited by A. J. B. Higgins. London: SCM Press, 1956.

Culpepper, R. Alan. *Anatomy of the Fourth Gospel: A Study in Literary Design*. Philadelphia: Fortress, 1983.

The Johannine School: An Examination of the Johannine School Hypothesis Based on the Investigation of the Nature of Ancient Schools. SBLDS 26. Missoula: Scholars Press, 1975.

Dagonet, Philippe. *Selon Saint Jean: Une femme de Samarie*. Paris: Cerf, 1979.

Dahl, Nils A. "The Johannine Church and History." Pages 124–42 in *Current Issues in New Testament Interpretation*. Edited by William Klassen and Graydon F. Snyder. New York: Harper, 1962.

Daise, Michael A. " 'Rivers of Living Water' as New Creation and New Exodus: A Traditio-Historical Vantage Point for the Exegetical Problems and Theology of John 7:37–39." Ph.D. diss., Princeton Theological Seminary, 2000.

D'Angelo, Mary Rose. "A Critical Note: John 20:17 and Apocalypse of Moses 31." *JTS* 41 (1990): 529–36.

"(Re)Presentations of Women in the Gospels: John and Mark." Pages 129–49 in *Women and Christian Origins*. Edited by Ross Shepard Kraemer and Mary Rose D'Angelo. New York: Oxford University Press, 1999.

Derrett, J. Duncan M. "Miriam and the Resurrection (John 20:16)." *DRev* 111 (1993): 174–88.

"The Samaritan Woman's Pitcher." *DRev* 102 (1984): 252–61.

Dexinger, Ferdinand. "Samaritan Eschatology." Pages 266–92 in *The Samaritans*. Edited by Alan D. Crown. Tübingen: Mohr Siebeck, 1989.

Der Taheb: Ein "messianischer" Heilsbringer der Samaritaner. Salzburg: Müller, 1986.

Dijkema, F. "Zu Psalm 45." *ZAW* 27 (1907): 26–32.

Dodd, C. H. *According to the Scriptures: The Substructure of New Testament Theology*. London: Nisbet, 1952.

———. *Historical Tradition in the Fourth Gospel*. Cambridge: Cambridge University Press, 1965.

———. *The Interpretation of the Fourth Gospel*. Cambridge: Cambridge University Press, 1953.

Dollar, Stephen E. "The Significance of Women in the Fourth Gospel." Th.D. diss., New Orleans Baptist Theological Seminary, 1983.

Donahue, John R. "The Changing Shape of New Testament Theology." *HBT* 11 (1989): 1–30.

Duke, Paul D. *Irony in the Fourth Gospel*. Atlanta: John Knox, 1985.

Eslinger, Lyle. "The Wooing of the Woman at the Well: Jesus, the Reader, and Reader-Response Criticism." *Literature and Theology* 1/1 (1987): 167–83. Repr. as pages 165–82 in *The Gospel of John as Literature*. Edited by Mark W. G. Stibbe. Leiden: Brill, 1993.

Evans, Craig A. *Noncanonical Writings and New Testament Interpretation*. Peabody, Mass.: Hendrickson, 1992.

Feenstra, Ronald J. "Hills Flowing with Wine: A Meditation on John 2:1–11." *Reformed Journal* 38, no. 4 (April 1988): 9–10.

Fehribach, Adeline. *The Women in the Life of the Bridegroom: A Feminist Historical-Literary Analysis of the Female Characters in the Fourth Gospel*. Collegeville, Minn.: Liturgical Press, 1998.

Feuillet, André. "Le Cantique des cantiques et l'Apocalypse." *RSR* 49 (1961): 321–53.

———. *Jesus and His Mother: The Role of the Virgin Mary in Salvation History and the Place of Woman in the Church*. Translated by L. Maluf. Still River, Mass.: St. Bede's, 1974.

———. *Le Mystère de l'amour divin dans la théologie johannique. Ebib*. Paris: Gabalda, 1972.

———. "La recherche du Christ dans la nouvelle alliance d'après la christophanie de Jo 20,11–18: Comparaison avec Cant. 3,1–4 et l'épisode des pèlerins d'Emmaüs." Pages 93–112 in Vol. I of *L'homme devant Dieu*. 3 vols. Théologie 56–58. Paris: Aubier, 1963.

———. "Le symbolisme de la colombe dans les récits évangéliques du Baptême." *RSR* 46 (1958): 524–44.

———. "The Time of the Church in St. John." Pages 149–68 in *Johannine Studies*. Translated by Thomas E. Crane. Staten Island: Alba House, 1965.

Fletcher, Mary-Elsie. "The Role of Women in the Book of John." *EvJ* 12 (1994): 41–48.

Freed, Edwin D. *Old Testament Quotations in the Gospel of John*. SNT 11. Leiden: Brill, 1965.

———. "Samaritan Influence in the Gospel of John." *CBQ* 30 (1968): 580–87.

Friedrich, Gerhard. *Wer ist Jesus? Die Verkündigung des Vierten Evangelisten, dargestellt an Joh 4,4–42*. Stuttgart: Calwer, 1967.

Girard, Marc. "Jésus en Samarie (Jean 4,1–42): Analyse des structures stylistiques et du procès de symbolisation." *EgT* 17 (1986): 275–310.

Goodspeed, Edgar J., ed. *Die ältesten Apologeten: Texte mit kurzen Einleitungen*. Göttingen: Vanderhoeck & Ruprecht, 1914.

Grassi, Carolyn M. and Joseph A. Grassi. *Mary Magdalene and the Women in Jesus' Life*. Kansas City, Mo.: Sheed & Ward, 1986.

Grothe, Jonathan. "Seventh Sunday after Pentecost: John 4:5–15." *Concordia Journal* 11 (1985): 108–10.

Guilding, Aileen. *The Fourth Gospel and Jewish Worship: A Study of the Relation of St. John's Gospel to the Ancient Jewish Lectionary System*. Oxford: Oxford University Press, 1960.

Guthrie, Donald. *The Letter to the Hebrews: An Introduction and Commentary*. TNTC. Grand Rapids: Eerdmans, 1983.

Hanson, Anthony Tyrrell. *The New Testament Interpretation of Scripture*. London: SPCK, 1980.

The Prophetic Gospel: A Study of John and the Old Testament. Edinburgh: T&T Clark, 1991.

Harris, Wendell V. "Allusion." Pages 10–14 in *Dictionary of Concepts in Literary Criticism and Theory*. New York: Greenwood, 1992.

"Symbol." Pages 398–405 in *Dictionary of Concepts in Literary Criticism and Theory*. New York: Greenwood, 1992.

Hartman, Louis F. *The Book of Daniel*. AB 23. Garden City: Doubleday, 1978.

Hays, Richard B. *Echoes of Scripture in the Letters of Paul*. New Haven: Yale University Press, 1989.

Hengel, Martin. "The Interpretation of the Wine Miracle at Cana: John 2:1–11." Translated by Gerhard Schmidt. Pages 83–112 in *The Glory of Christ in the New Testament: Studies in Christology*. Edited by L. D. Hurst and N. T. Wright. Oxford: Clarendon, 1987.

"Die Schriftauslegung des 4. Evangeliums auf dem Hintergrund der urchristlichen Exegese." *Jahrbuch zur biblische Theologie* 4 (1989): 249–88.

Hippolytus. Εἰς τὸ ᾆσμα. in *Exegetische und Homiletische Schriften*. Edited and translated by G. Nathanael Bonwetsch and Hans Achelis. GCS, Hippolytus I, Part I. Leipzig: Hinrichs, 1897.

Hollander, John. *The Figure of Echo: A Mode of Allusion in Milton and After*. Berkeley: University of California Press, 1981.

Hoskyns, E. C. *The Fourth Gospel*. Edited by Francis Noel Davey. London: Faber & Faber, 1940.

Hurst, L. D. "The Christology of Hebrews 1 and 2." Pages 151–64 in *The Glory of Christ in the New Testament: Studies in Christology*. Edited by L. D. Hurst and N. T. Wright. Oxford: Clarendon, 1987.

Jasper, Alison. "Interpretive Approaches to John 20:1–18: Mary at the Tomb of Jesus." *ST* 47 (1993): 107–18.

Jaubert, Annie. *Approches de l'Évangile de Jean*. Paris: Seuil, 1976.

"La symbolique des femmes dans les traditions religieuses: Une reconsidération de l'Évangile de Jean." *RUO* 50 (1980): 114–21.

"La symbolique du puits de Jacob: Jean 4,12." Pages 63–73 in Vol. I of *L'homme devant Dieu*. 3 vols. Théologie 56–58. Paris: Aubier, 1963.

Jeremias, Joachim. *Jesus als Weltvollender*. BFCT 33, no. 4. Gütersloh: Bertelsmann, 1930.

Jerusalmi, Isaac, trans. and ed. *The Song of Songs in the Targumic Tradition*. Cincinnati: Ladino Books, 1993.

John of the Cross. *Dark Night of the Soul*. Translated and edited by E. Allison Peers. 3 vols. 3rd rev. edn. New York: Doubleday, 1990.

Johnson, Elisabeth A. "Barrenness, Birth, and Biblical Allusions in Luke 1–2." Ph.D. diss., Princeton Theological Seminary, 2000.

Johnson, Luke Timothy. *The Writings of the New Testament: An Interpretation*. Rev. edn. Minneapolis: Fortress, 1999.

Jones, Larry Paul. *The Symbol of Water in the Gospel of John*. JSNTSup 145. Sheffield: Sheffield Academic Press, 1997.

Jonge, Marinus de. "Jewish Expectations about the 'Messiah' According to the Fourth Gospel." *NTS* 19 (1972–73): 246–70.

  The Testaments of the Twelve Patriarchs: A Critical Edition of the Greek Text. Leiden: Brill, 1978.

Joüon, P. *Le Cantique des cantiques*. Paris: Beauchesne, 1909.

Juel, Donald. *Messianic Exegesis: Christological Interpretation of the Old Testament in Earliest Christianity*. Philadelphia: Fortress, 1988.

Juel, Donald and Patrick Keifert. "'I Believe in God': A Johannine Perspective." *HBT* 12 (1990): 39–60.

Karlsen Seim, Turid. "Roles of Women in the Gospel of John." Pages 56–73 in *Aspects on the Johannine Literature*. Edited by Lars Hartmann and Birger Olsson. ConBNT 18. Stockholm: Almkvist & Wiksell, 1987.

Käsemann, Ernst. *The Testament of Jesus: A Study of the Gospel of John in the Light of Chapter 17*. Translated by Gerhard Krodel. Philadelphia: Fortress, 1968. Translation of *Jesu letzter Wille nach Johannes 17*. Tübingen: Mohr Siebeck, 1966.

Kee, Howard Clark. "Testament of the Twelve Patriarchs." Pages 775–828 in vol. I of *The Old Testament Pseudepigrapha*. Edited by James H. Charlesworth. Garden City: Doubleday, 1983.

Kimelman, Reuven. "*Birkat Ha-Minim* and the Lack of Evidence for an Anti-Christian Jewish Prayer in Late Antiquity." Pages 226–44 in vol. II of *Jewish and Christian Self-Definition*. Edited by E. P. Sanders et al. 2 vols. Philadelphia: Fortress, 1981.

Kittel, Gerhard and Gerhard Friedrich, eds. *Theological Dictionary of the New Testament*. Translated by Geoffrey W. Bromiley. 10 vols. Grand Rapids: Eerdmans, 1964–76.

Kitzberger, Ingrid Rosa. "Mary of Bethany and Mary of Magdala: Two Female Characters in the Johannine Passion Narrative: A Feminist, Narrative-Critical Reader Response." *NTS* 41 (1995): 564–86.

Klauck, Hans-Josef. "Gemeinde oder Amt: Erfahrungen mit der Kirche in den johanneischen Schriften." *BZ* 29 (1985): 193–220.

Klijn, A. F. J. "2 (Syriac Apocalypse of) Baruch." Pages 615–52 in vol. I of *The Old Testament Pseudepigrapha*. Edited by James H. Charlesworth. Garden City: Doubleday, 1983.

Koester, Craig A. "Hearing, Seeing, and Believing in the Gospel of John." *Bib* 70 (1989): 327–48.

  "'The Savior of the World' (John 4:42)." *JBL* 109 (1990): 665–80.

  Symbolism in the Fourth Gospel: Meaning, Mystery, Community. Minneapolis: Fortress, 1995.

Kopas, Jane. "Jesus and Women: John's Gospel." *ThTo* 41 (1984): 201–5.

Krafft, Eva. "Die Personen des Johannesevangeliums." *EvT* 16 (1956): 18–32.

Kysar, Robert. *John: The Maverick Gospel*. Rev. edn. Louisville: Westminster John Knox, 1993.

Lagrange, Marie-Joseph. *L'Évangile selon S. Jean*. 3rd edn. *Ebib*. Paris: Gabalda, 1927.

La Potterie, Ignace de. *Mary in the Mystery of the Covenant*. Translated by Bertrand Buby. New York: Alba, 1992.

Laurentin, René. "Le sens de la femme dans le Nouveau Testament." *Bulletin de la Société française d'études mariales* 30–31 (1973–74): 109–33.

Le Déaut, Roger. "Apropos a Definition of Midrash." Translated by Mary Howard. *Int* 25 (1971): 259–82.

Lee, Dorothy A. "Partnership in Easter Faith: The Role of Mary Magdalene and Thomas in John 20." *JSNT* 58 (1995): 37–49.

Levine, Amy-Jill. " 'Hemmed in on Every Side': Jews and Women in the Book of Susanna." Pages 175–90 in *Reading from This Place*. Edited by Fernando F. Segovia and Mary Ann Tolbert. Minneapolis: Fortress, 1995.

"Sacrifice and Salvation: Otherness and Domestication in the Book of Judith." Pages 17–30 in *No One Spoke Ill of Her: Essays on Judith*. Edited by James C. Vanderkam. Atlanta: Scholars Press, 1992.

Lichtenberger, Hermann. "Messianic Expectations and Messianic Figures in the Second Temple Period." Pages 9–20 in *Qumran-Messianism: Studies on the Messianic Expectations in the Dead Sea Scrolls*. Edited by James H. Charlesworth, Hermann Lichtenberger, and Gerbern S. Oegema. Tübingen: Mohr Siebeck, 1998.

Lightfoot, Robert Henry. *St. John's Gospel: A Commentary*. Edited by C. F. Evans. Oxford: Clarendon, 1956.

Lindars, Barnabas. "The Composition of John xx." *NTS* 7 (1960–61): 142–47.

The Gospel of John. NCB 43. Grand Rapids: Eerdmans, 1972.

New Testament Apologetic: The Doctrinal Significance of the Old Testament Quotations. Philadelphia: Westminster, 1961.

"The Place of the Old Testament in the Formation of New Testament Theology," *NTS* 23 (1976): 59–66.

Link, Andrea. "Botschafterinnen des Messias: Die Frauen des vierten Evangeliums im Spiegel johanneischer Redactionsgeschichte." Pages 247–78 in *Theologie im Werden. Studien zu theologischen Konzeptionen im Neuen Testament*. Edited by Josef Hainz. Paderborn: Schöningh, 1992.

Loisy, Alfred F. *Le quatrième Évangile: Les épîtres dites de Jean*. Paris: Picard, 1903.

Longenecker, Richard N. *Biblical Exegesis in the Apostolic Period*. Grand Rapids: Eerdmans, 1975.

Lorentz, Oswald. *Das althebräische Liebeslied: Untersuchungen zur Stichometrie und Redaktionsgeschichte des Hohenliedes und des 45. Psalms*. AOAT 14/1. Kevelaer: Butzon & Bercker, 1971.

Lundbom, Jack R. "Mary Magdalene and Song of Songs 3:1–4." *Int* 49 (1995): 172–75.

Maccini, Robert Gordon. *Her Testimony Is True: Women As Witnesses According to John*. JSNTSup 125. Sheffield: Sheffield Academic Press, 1996.

MacRae, George W. *Invitation to John: A Commentary on the Gospel of John with Complete Text from the Jerusalem Bible.* Garden City: Doubleday, 1978.

Manns, Frédéric. *L'évangile de Jean à la lumière du judaïsme.* Studium Biblicum Franciscanum 33. Jerusalem: Franciscan, 1991.

"Exégèse rabbinique et exégèse johannique." *RB* 92 (1985): 525–38.

Marsh, John. *Saint John.* Westminster Pelican Commentaries. Philadelphia: Westminster, 1968.

Martyn, J. Louis. *History and Theology in the Fourth Gospel.* Nashville: Abingdon, 1968.

McGehee, Michael. "A Less Theological Reading of John 20:17." *JBL* 105 (1986): 299–302.

McWhirter, Jocelyn. Review of Craig R. Koester, *Symbolism in the Fourth Gospel. Koinonia Journal* 9 (1997): 188–90.

Meeks, Wayne A. "'Am I a Jew?' Johannine Christianity and Judaism." Pages 163–86 in *Christianity, Judaism, and Other Greco-Roman Cults: Part I, New Testament.* Edited by Jacob Neusner. SJLA 12. Leiden: Brill, 1975.

"Breaking Away: Three New Testament Pictures of Christianity's Separation from the Jewish Communities." Pages 93–115 in *"To See Ourselves As Others See Us": Christians, Jews, "Others" in Late Antiquity.* Edited by Jacob Neusner and Ernest S. Frerichs. Scholars Press Studies in the Humanities 8. Chico, Calif.: Scholars Press, 1985.

"The Man from Heaven in Johannine Sectarianism." *JBL* 91 (1972): 44–72.

Mendels, Doron. *The Land of Israel as a Political Concept in Hasmonean Literature.* TSAJ 15. Tübingen: Mohr Siebeck, 1987.

Menken, Maarten J. J. *Old Testament Quotations in the Fourth Gospel: Studies in Textual Form.* CBET 15. Kampen: Pharos, 1996.

Meshorer, Ya'akov. *Jewish Coins of the Second Temple Period.* Tel Aviv: Am Hassefer, 1967.

Metzger, Bruce M. "4 Ezra." Pages 519–59 in vol. I of *The Old Testament Pseudepigrapha.* Edited by James H. Charlesworth. Garden City: Doubleday, 1983.

A Textual Commentary on the Greek New Testament. Stuttgart: United Bible Societies, 1971.

Minear, Paul S. *Images of the Church in the New Testament.* Philadelphia: Westminster, 1960.

"'We Don't Know Where . . .': John 20:2." *Int* 30 (1976): 125–39.

Moloney, Francis J. *The Gospel of John.* SP 4. Collegeville, Minn.: Liturgical Press, 1998.

Morgan, Richard. "Fulfillment in the Fourth Gospel: The Old Testament Foundations." *Int* 11 (1957): 155–65.

Moule, C. F. D. "Fulfillment Words in the New Testament: Use and Abuse." *NTS* 14 (1968): 293–320.

Muirhead, I. A. "The Bride of Christ." *SJT* 5 (1952): 175–87.

Mulder, Johannes S. M. *Studies on Psalm 45.* Oss: Witsiers, 1972.

Neirynck, Frans. "John and the Synoptics." Pages 73–106 in *L'évangile de Jean: Sources, rédaction, théologie.* Edited by Marinus de Jonge. BETL 44. Louvain: Louvain University Press, 1977.

Nestle, Eberhard. "Die fünf Männer des samaritanischen Weibes." *ZNW* 5 (1904): 166–67.

Neusner, Jacob. *Israel's Love Affair with God: Song of Songs*. Bible of Judaism Library. Valley Forge: Trinity, 1993.

Song of Songs Rabbah: An Analytical Translation. 2 vols. BJS 197–98. Atlanta: Scholars Press, 1989.

Neyrey, Jerome H. "Jacob Traditions and the Interpretation of John 4:10–26." *CBQ* 41 (1979): 419–37.

Nicholson, Godfrey C. *Death As Departure: The Johannine Descent-Ascent Schema*. SBLDS 63. Chico, Calif.: Scholars Press, 1983.

Nicklesburg, George W. E. *Resurrection, Immortality, and Eternal Life in Intertestamental Judaism*. HTS 26. Cambridge, Mass.: Harvard University Press, 1972.

Nortjé, S. J. "The Role of Women in the Fourth Gospel." *NeoT* 20 (1986): 21–28.

Novum Testamentum Graece. Edited by Kurt Aland et al. 27th rev. edn. Stuttgart: Deutsche Bibelgesellschaft, 1993.

Obermann, Andreas. *Die christologische Erfüllung der Schrift im Johannesevangelium: Eine Untersuchung zur johanneischen Hermeneutik anhand der Schriftzitate*. WUNT Second Series 83. Tübingen: Mohr Siebeck, 1996.

O'Day, Gail R. "John." Pages 293–304 in *The Women's Bible Commentary*. Edited by Carol A. Newsom and Sharon H. Ringe. Louisville: Westminster John Knox, 1992.

The Word Disclosed: John's Story and Narrative Preaching. St. Louis, Mo.: CBP Press, 1987.

Okure, Teresa. *The Johannine Approach to Mission: A Contextual Study of John 4:1–42*. WUNT 31. Tübingen: Mohr Siebeck, 1988.

"The Significance Today of Jesus' Commission of Mary Magdalene." *International Review of Mission* 81 (1992): 177–88.

Olsson, Birger. *Structure and Meaning in the Fourth Gospel: A Text-Linguistic Analysis of John 2:1–11 and 4:1–42*. Translated by Jean Gray. CB 6. Lund: Gleerup, 1974.

Origen. *Commentary on the Gospel According to John: Books 13–32*. Translated by Ronald E. Heine. FC 89. Washington, D.C.: The Catholic University of America Press, 1993.

Homilies on Genesis and Exodus. Translated by Ronald E. Heine. FC 71. Washington, D.C.: The Catholic University of America Press, 1982.

The Song of Songs: Commentary and Homilies. Translated by R. P. Lawson. ACW 26. Westminster, Md.: Newman, 1957.

Painter, John. *The Quest for the Messiah: The History, Literature, and Theology of the Johannine Community*. Edinburgh: T&T Clark, 1991.

Pamment, Margaret. "Is There Convincing Evidence of Samaritan Influence on the Fourth Gospel?" *ZNW* 73 (1982): 221–30.

Pancaro, Severino. *The Law in the Fourth Gospel: The Torah and the Gospel, Moses and Jesus, Judaism and Christianity According to John. NovTSup* 42. Leiden: Brill, 1975.

Patrologia latina. Edited by J.-P. Migne. 217 vols. Paris, 1844–64.

Perkins, Pheme. *Resurrection: New Testament Witness and Contemporary Reflection*. New York: Doubleday, 1984.

Plummer, Alfred. *The Gospel According to S. John.* CGTSC. Cambridge: Cambridge University Press, 1892.

Pope, Marvin H. *Song of Songs.* AB 7C. Garden City: Doubleday, 1977.

Przywara, Erich. *Christentum gemäss Johannes.* Evangelium. Nuremberg: Glock & Lutz, 1954.

Purvis, James D. "The Fourth Gospel and the Samaritans." *NovT* 17 (1975): 161–98.

Rebell, Walter. *Gemeinde als Gegenwelt: Zur soziologischen und didaktischen Funktion des Johannesevangelium.* Frankfurt: Lang, 1987.

Reim, Günter. "Jesus As God in the Fourth Gospel: The Old Testament Background." *NTS* 30 (1984): 158–60. Repr. as pages 348–51 in *Jochanan: Erweitere Studien zum alttestamentliche Hintergrund des Johannesevangeliums.* Erlangen: Ev-Luth. Mission, 1995.

——. "Paralleltraditionen zum Johannesevangelium aus Justins Werken." Pages 487–534 in *Jochanan: Erweitere Studien zum alttestamentliche Hintergrund des Johannesevangeliums.* Erlangen: Ev-Luth. Mission, 1995.

——. *Studien zum alttestamentlichen Hintergrund des Johannesevangeliums.* SNTSMS 22. Cambridge: Cambridge University Press, 1974.

——. *Zugänge zum Evangelium des Johannes.* Erlangen: Ev.-Luth. Mission, 1994.

Reinhartz, Adele. *Befriending the Beloved Disciple: A Jewish Reading of the Gospel of John.* New York: Continuum, 2001.

——. "The Gospel of John." Pages 561–600 in vol. II of *Searching the Scriptures: A Feminist Commentary.* Edited by Elisabeth Schüssler Fiorenza et al. New York: Crossroad, 1994.

Rena, John. "Women in the Gospel of John." *EgT* 17 (1986): 131–47.

Richardson, Alan. *Introduction to the Theology of the New Testament.* London: SCM Press, 1958.

Ridderbos, Herman N. *The Gospel According to John: A Theological Commentary.* Translated by John Vriend. Grand Rapids: Eerdmans, 1997.

Riffaterre, Michel. *Semiotics of Poetry.* Advances in Semiotics. Bloomington: Indiana University Press, 1978.

Ringe, Sharon H. *Wisdom's Friends: Community and Christology in the Fourth Gospel.* Louisville: Westminster John Knox, 1999.

Robert, André and Raymond Tournay. *Le Cantique des Cantiques. Ebib.* Paris: Gabalda, 1963.

Rosenberg, Joel W. "Genesis." Pages 3–76 in *The HarperCollins Study Bible.* Edited by Wayne A. Meeks. New York: HarperCollins, 1993.

Sanders, J. N. *A Commentary on the Gospel According to St John.* Edited by B. A. Mastin. BNTC. London: Black, 1968.

Schaff, Philip, ed. *The Nicene and Post-Nicene Fathers,* Series 1. 1886–1889. 14 vols. Repr. Peabody, Mass.: Hendrickson, 1994.

Schlatter, Adolf. *Der Evangelist Johannes.* Stuttgart: Calwer, 1948.

Schmitz, John R. "Women in John's Gospel." *Emmanuel* 90 (1984): 191–96.

Schnackenburg, Rudolf. *The Gospel According to St. John.* Translated by Kevin Smyth et al. 3 vols. Herder's Theological Commentary on the New Testament. New York: Herder & Herder, 1968–75.

Schneiders, Sandra M. "The Johannine Resurrection Narrative: An Exegetical and Theological Study of John 20 as a Synthesis of Johannine Spirituality." 2 vols. D.S.T. diss., Pontificia Universitas Gregoriana, 1975.

"John 20:11–18: The Encounter of the Easter Jesus with Mary Magdalene: A Transformative Feminist Reading." Pages 155–68 in vol. I of *"What is John?" Readers and Readings of the Fourth Gospel*. Edited by Fernando F. Segovia. 2 vols. SBLSymS 3. Atlanta: Scholars Press, 1996.

The Revelatory Text: Interpreting the New Testament as Sacred Scripture. 2nd edn. Collegeville, Minn.: Liturgical Press, 1999.

"Women in the Fourth Gospel and the Role of Women in the Contemporary Church." *BTB* 12 (1982): 35–45.

Written That You May Believe: Encountering Jesus in the Fourth Gospel. New York: Crossroad, 1999.

Schuchard, Bruce G. *Scripture within Scripture: The interrelationship of Form and Function in the Explicit Old Testament Citations in the Gospel of John*. SBLDS 133. Atlanta: Scholars Press, 1992.

Schüssler Fiorenza, Elisabeth. *Bread Not Stone*. Boston: Beacon, 1984.

In Memory of Her: A Feminist Theological Reconstruction of Christian Origins. New York: Crossroad, 1983.

"The Quest for the Johannine School: The Book of Revelation and the Fourth Gospel." Pages 85–113 in *The Book of Revelation: Justice and Judgment*. 2nd edn. Minneapolis: Fortress, 1998.

Scott, Martin. *Sophia and the Johannine Jesus*. JSNTSup 71. Sheffield: JSOT Press, 1992.

Segal, Alan F. *Rebecca's Children: Judaism and Christianity in the Roman World*. Cambridge, Mass.: Harvard University Press, 1986.

Senior, Donald. *The Passion of Jesus in the Gospel of John*. The Passion Series 4. Collegeville: Liturgical Press, 1991.

Septuaginta. Edited by Alfred Rahlfs. Stuttgart: Deutsche Bibelgesellschaft, 1979.

Smith, Dwight Moody. "Johannine Christianity: Some Reflections on Its Character and Delineation." *NTS* 21 (1975): 222–48.

John among the Gospels: The Relationship in Twentieth-Century Research. Minneapolis: Fortress, 1992.

"The Use of the Old Testament in the New." Pages 3–65 in *The Use of the Old Testament in the New and Other Essays*. Edited by J. M. Efird. Durham, N.C.: Duke University Press, 1972.

Smitmans, Adolf. *Das Weinwunder von Kana: Die Auslegung von Jo 2,1–11 bei den Vätern und heute*. BGBE 6. Tübingen: Mohr Siebeck, 1966.

Staley, Jeffrey Lloyd. *The Print's First Kiss: A Rhetorical Investigation of the Implied Reader in the Fourth Gospel*. SBLDS 82. Atlanta: Scholars Press, 1988.

Stibbe, Mark W. G. *John*. Sheffield: JSOT Press, 1993.

Stimpfle, Alois. *Blinde Sehen: Die Eschatologie im traditionsgeschichtliche Prozess des Johannesevangeliums*. BZNW 57. Berlin: De Gruyter, 1990.

Stockton, Eugene D. "The Fourth Gospel and the Woman." Pages 132–44 in *Essays in Faith and Culture*. Edited by Neil Brown. Faith and Culture 3. Catholic Institute of Sydney, 1979.

Stone, Michael. "The Question of the Messiah in 4 Ezra." Pages 209–24 in *Judaisms and Their Messiahs*. Edited by Jacob Neusner, William S. Green, and Ernest Frerichs. Cambridge: Cambridge University Press, 1984.

Strauss, David Friedrich. *The Life of Jesus Critically Examined*. Edited by Peter C. Hodgson. Translated by George Eliot. Philadelphia: Fortress, 1972.

Tasker, Randolph V. G. *The Gospel According to St. John: An Introduction and Commentary*. TNTC. London: Tyndale, 1960.

Tenney, Merrill C. "The Old Testament and the Fourth Gospel." *BSac* 120 (1963): 300–308.

Terrien, Samuel. *Till the Heart Sings: A Biblical Theology of Manhood and Womanhood*. Philadelphia: Fortress, 1985.

Thiessan, Karen Heidebrecht. "Jesus and Women in the Gospel of John." *Direction* 19 (1990): 56–64.

Thompson, Marianne Meye. *The Promise of the Father: Jesus and God in the New Testament*. Louisville: Westminster John Knox, 2000.

Tilborg, Sjef van. *Reading John in Ephesus*. NovTSup 83. Leiden: Brill, 1996.

"The Women in John: On Gender and Gender Bending." Pages 192–212 in *Families and Family Relations As Represented in Early Judaism and Early Christianity: Texts and Fictions*. Edited by Jan Willem van Henten and Athalya Brenner. Leiden: Deo, 2000.

Tolbert, Mary Ann. "Defining the Problem: The Bible and Feminist Hermeneutics." *Semeia* 28 (1983): 113–26.

Tournay, Raymond. "Les affinités du Ps. xlv avec le Cantique des Cantiques et leur interprétation messianique." Pages 168–212 in *Congress Volume: Bonn, 1962*. VTSup 9. Leiden: Brill, 1963.

Tov, Emanuel. "The Septuagint." Pages 161–88 in *Mikra: Text, Translation, Reading and Interpretation of the Hebrew Bible in Ancient Judaism and Early Christianity*. Edited by Martin Jan Mulder. CRINT, sec. 2, vol. I. Philadelphia: Fortress, 1988.

Trudinger, Paul. "Of Women, Wells, Waterpots and Wine! Reflections on Johannine Themes (John 2:1–11 and 4:1–42)," *St. Mark's Review* 151 (1992): 10–16.

Urbach, Ephraim E. "The Homiletical Interpretation of the Sages and the Expositions of Origen on Canticles, and the Jewish-Christian Disputation." Pages 47–75 in *Studies in Aggadah and Folk-Literature*. Edited by Joseph Heinemann and Dov Noy. ScrHier 22. Jerusalem: Magnes, 1971.

Waal, C. van der. "The Gospel According to John and the Old Testament." *NeoT* 6 (1972): 28–47.

Wead, David W. *The Literary Devices in John's Gospel*. Theologischen Dissertationen 4. Basel: Reinhart, 1970.

Webster, Jane S. "Transcending Alterity: Strange Woman to Samaritan Woman." Pages 126–42 in vol. I of *A Feminist Companion to John*. Edited by Amy-Jill Levine. 2 vols. London: Sheffield Academic Press, 2003.

Welch, Claude. *The Reality of the Church*. New York: Scribner, 1958.

Wengst, Klaus. *Bedrängte Gemeinde und verherrlichter Christus: Ein versuch über das Johannesevangelium*. Munich: Kaiser, 1990.

Westcott, B. F. *The Gospel According to St. John*. London: Murray, 1892.

White, Sidnie Ann. "Esther: A Feminine Model for Jewish Diaspora." Pages 161–77 in *Gender and Difference in Ancient Israel*. Edited by Peggy L. Day. Minneapolis: Fortress, 1989.

Winandy, Jacques. "Le Cantique des cantiques et le Nouveau Testament." *RB* 71 (1964): 161–90.

Le Cantique des cantiques: Poème d'amour mué en écrit de sagesse. BVC 16. Tournai, Belgium: Castermann, 1960.

Winsor, Ann Roberts. *A King Is Bound in the Tresses: Allusions to the Song of Songs in the Fourth Gospel.* Studies in Biblical Literature 6. New York: Lang, 1999.

Witherington, Ben III. *Women in the Earliest Churches.* SNTSMS 59. Cambridge: Cambridge University Press, 1988.

Wright, Robert B. "Psalms of Solomon." Pages 639–70 in vol. II of *The Old Testament Pseudepigrapha.* Edited by James H. Charlesworth. Garden City: Doubleday, 1985.

Zander, Léon. "Le Précurseur selon le P. Boulgakof." *Dieu vivant* 7 (1949): 89–115.

Ziegler, Joseph, ed. *Jeremias, Baruch, Threni, Epistula Jeremiae.* Vetus Testamentum graecum auctoritate Academiae Scientarium Gottingensis editum 15. Göttingen: Vandenhoeck & Ruprecht, 1957.

Zimmermann, Mirjam, and Ruben Zimmermann. "Der Freund des Bräutigams (Joh 3,29): Deflorations- oder Christuszeuge?" *ZNW* 90 (1999): 123–30.

SCRIPTURE INDEX

INDEX OF ANCIENT COMMENTATORS

INDEX OF MODERN COMMENTATORS